اركان
الإسلام والإيمان

THE PILLARS OF
ISLAM & IMAN

First Edition   الطبعة الأولى

Supervised by:

ABDUL MALIK MUJAHID

Published by:

Dar-us-Salam Publications   دار السلام للنشر
P.O. Box 22743, Riyadh 11416   ص.ب. ٢٢٧٤٣ – الرياض ١١٤١٦
Tel: 4033962 Fax: 4021659   ت: ٤٠٣٣٩٦٢ فاكس ٤٠٢١٦٥٩
Kingdom of Saudi Arabia   المملكة العربية السعودية

Branches in other Countries:

Dar-us-Salam Publications
P.O. Box: 737651, Corona
Elmhurst Queen
NY11373, USA
Tel: (718) 699-5366

Dar-us-Salam Publications
10107, Westview 308
Houston,Tx 77043, USA
Tel: (713) 935-9206
Fax: (713) 722-0431

Dar-us-Salam Publications
50, Lower Mall Road
Near M.A.O. College
Lahore, Pakistan
Tel & Fax: (042) 7354072

Dar-us-Salam Publications
Rahman Market
Ghazni Street, Urdu Bazar
Lahore, Pakistan.
Tel: (042) 7120054

أَرْكَانُ الإِسْلامِ وَالإِيمَانِ

THE PILLARS OF ISLAM & IMAN

وَمَا يَجِبُ أَنْ يَعْرِفَهُ كُلُّ مُسْلِمٍ عَنْ دِينِهِ

and what every Muslim must know about his religion

Written by:

محمد بن جميل زينو

Muhammad bin Jamil Zeno
Teacher at Dar-ul-Hadith Al-Khairiyah
Makkah Al-Mukarramah

Translated by:
**Research & Compilation Department
Dar-us-Salam Publications**

دار السلام للنشر

Dar-us-Salam Publications
Riyadh-Saudi Arabia

In the Name of Allah, the Most
Beneficent, the Most Merciful

TABLE OF CONTENTS

5

The Book of *Salât* (prayer)

6

Publishers Note

Sheikh Muhammad bin Jamil Zeno is originally from Syria, but since a long time he has been a teacher in the Dar-ul-Hadith Al-Khairiyah, Makkah Al-Mukarramah. Besides being a great scholar, he is also the author and compiler of many books. He holds the honour to have a place in the rank of those authors of present time whose works have been widely accepted.

The original text of this book is in the Arabic language. The distinctive feature of this book is its simplicity. While writing, Sheikh Muhammad bin Jamil Zeno has his direct concern with the common people. To prove any point, first of all he presents the verses of the Noble Qur'ân, then he puts all the related authentic *Ahadith* before the readers; afterwards, if he finds it necessary, cites a few instances from the early scholars and jurisprudents.

Because of his simple style, his books gained popularity in the Islamic world. He uses authentic sources while writing the books, that is why his books are appreciated by the scholars. Generally in the Islamic world, and specially in the Arab world, the authenticity of a book is judged by its author's name, and his name has acquired such position.

In this book, Sheikh Muhammad bin Jamil Zeno has discussed the fundamental constituents of Islam - *Salat, Saum, Hajj* and *Zakat* etc. in a lucid and impressive manner. The discussion regarding Faith and Belief in the first part is an added value to the book. A number of editions and innumerable copies of this book in Arabic have been published and printed up till now.

Dar-us-Salam Publications has the honour of translating the different books of Sheikh Muhammad bin Jamil Zeno in various languages. We have earlier published this book in Urdu also. The translations of his other books are in the printing stages, and will be available to the readers in the near future.

We must thank Brother Majad Al-Ghamlas, Manager, Maktaba Dar-ul-Khair, Jeddah, by whose help and cooperation, we are able to present this book. Our thanks are also to the members of Dar-us-Salam Publications who worked enthusiastically to produce this book in the present form.

May Allah benefit the readers by the sincer efforts made by all of us - *Amin!*

Abdul-Malik Mujahid
General Manager
Dar-us-Salam Publications

INTRODUCTION

Verily all praise is for Allah, we praise Him, seek His help, and seek His forgiveness. We seek refuge with Allah from the evil of ourselves and our deeds. Whomsoever Allah guides, no one can misguide him; and whomsoever He leads astray, none can guide him.

I bear witness that none has the right to be worshipped but Allah. He is Alone without any partner, and I bear witness that Muhammad is His servant and Messenger.

This book covers the following subjects: *Taharah* (purification), *Salât* (prayers), *Zakât* (obligatory charity), *Saum* (fasting during the month of Ramadan), *Hajj* and *Umrah* (the greater and lesser pilgrimages), as well as *Aqîdah* (creed), the life of Prophet Muhammad صلى الله عليه وسلم, *Hadîth* studies, general advice, and other important topics.

I have chosen the name of my book "Pillars of Islam & Iman (faith)" since it covers many of these valuable topics, while adding to it considerable supplementary materials related to acts of worship, especially *Tahârah* (purification), *Salât* (prayer), marriage, *Hijâb* (veiling), social & business transactions, interest, rulings concerning lost and found properties, the exemplary life of the Prophet صلى الله عليه وسلم, Prophetic traditions, and various other instructions and important matters which every Muslim male and female must know.

I ask Allah to make it beneficial to the Muslims and to make it solely for His sake, and to reward all those who participated in the printing and distribution of this book or its translation, and to enable all to serve Islam, and to call the Muslims back to it in a way that pleases Allah and His Messenger, in order that the Muslims might realize the victory He promised them when He said:

> "...and (as for) the believers it was incumbent upon Us to help (them)" (V. 30: 43).

Muhammad bin Jamil Zeno

13

THANKS & ACKNOWLEDGMENT

I thank my fellow teachers, students, and others who participated in the production of all my books to the required standard. I request everyone to send to me the comments on it, if he has any, in compliance with the statement of the Prophet صلى ٱلله عليه وسلم:

$$\text{«اَلدِّينُ النَّصِيحَةُ»}$$

"The religion is sincere advice." (*Muslim*)

I also thank the author of *Fiqh-us-Sunnah* which I've used as a reference for *Fiqh* (Islamic jurisprudence) rulings, as I have indicated wherever I quoted him.

I ask Allah to place this work in the scales of our good deeds and Allah is the Granter of success.

Muhammad bin Jamil Zeno

TAUHID (ISLÂMIC MONOTHEISM), AND THE FACTORS WHICH NULLIFY FAITH & ISLÂM

* The Pillars of Islam
* The Pillars of *Imân* (Faith)
* The meanings of Islam, *Imân* and *Ihsân*
* The meaning of *La ilaha illa-Allah*
* The meaning of *Muhammadur Rasûlullah*
* Where is Allah? Allah is above the heavens
* Belief in *Qadar* (Divine Preordainment), the good of it and the bad of it
* Some benefits of belief in Divine Preordainment
* Do not use fate as an excuse
* Factors which nullify *Imân* and Islam

15

THE PILLARS OF ISLAM

The Messenger of Allah ﷺ stated that Islam is based on five [things]:

شَهَادَةِ أَنْ لاَ إِلَه إِلاَّ الله وَأَنَّ مُحَمَّداً رَسُولُ الله وَإِقَام الصَّلاَةِ
وَإِيتَاءِ الزَّكَاةِ وَحَجُّ الْبَيْتِ ﴿مَنِ اسْتَطَاعَ إِلَيْهِ سَبِيلاً﴾ وَصَوْمِ رَمَضَانِ .

1. The *Shahadah* (testimony): *La ilaha illa-Allah, Muhammadur Rasulullah* (None has the right to be worshipped but Allah, and Muhammad is the Messenger of Allah).

2. *Iqâmat-as-Salât* (to offer the compulsory congregational prayers dutifully and perfectly).

3. To pay *Zakât* (*Zakât* is mandatory charity. When a Muslim owns 85 grams of gold or its equivalent in cash, 2.5% must be paid after possessing this quantity for a year. *Zakât* is also due on other forms of property, the details of which will be discussed later).

4. *Hajj* (the greater pilgrimage to the House of Allah in Makkah) for whoever is able to do so.

5. To observe *Saum* (fasting during the month of Ramadan): [With the intention to abstain from the start of dawn until sunset from food, drink and everything else which breaks (invalidates) the fast].

(Agreed upon)[1]

---

[1] Through out the book henceforth, a *Hadîth* related by Bukhâri and Muslim both will be called agreed upon.

THE PILLARS OF *IMAN* (FAITH)

To believe in:

1. Allah [in His Existence, His Oneness in His Attributes, His deserving to be worshipped and supplicated and His right to legislate].

2. His angels [beings created from light for obeying Allah's Orders].

3. His Books [the Torah, the Gospel of Jesus, the Psalms of David and the Qur'ân which is the best of them].

4. His Messengers [the first of them was Noah and the last of them was Muhammad صلى الله عليه وسلم, being the Seal of the Prophets].

5. The Last Day [the day of resurrection for the reckoning of the people according to their deeds, and their appropriate compensation (award or punishment)].

6. And to believe in *Qadar* (Divine Preordainment) [that all which occurs of good and evil is by Divine decree, accompanied by the employment of means to achieve desired results with satisfaction of what happens of good or bad, the sweet and the bitter, because it occurs by Allah's Decree].

THE MEANINGS OF ISLAM, *IMAN* AND *IHSAN*

Umar رضي الله عنه narrated:

«بَيْنَمَا نَحْنُ جُلُوسٌ عِنْدَ رَسُولِ اللهِ ـ ﷺ ـ ذَاتَ يَوْمٍ إِذْ طَلَعَ عَلَيْنَا رَجُلٌ شَدِيدُ بَيَاضِ الثِّيَابِ شَدِيدُ سَوَادِ الشَّعَرِ لَا يُرَى عَلَيْهِ أَثَرُ السَّفَرِ وَلَا يَعْرِفُهُ مِنَّا أَحَدٌ، حَتَّى جَلَسَ إِلَى النَّبِيِّ ـ ﷺ ـ فَأَسْنَدَ رُكْبَتَيْهِ إِلَى رُكْبَتَيْهِ وَوَضَعَ كَفَّيْهِ عَلَى فَخِذَيْهِ، وَقَالَ: يَامُحَمَّدُ أَخْبِرْنِي عَنِ الْإِسْلَامِ؟ فَقَالَ رَسُولُ اللهِ ـ ﷺ ـ: «الْإِسْلَامُ أَنْ تَشْهَدَ أَنْ لَا إِلَهَ إِلَّا اللهُ، وَأَنَّ مُحَمَّداً رَسُولُ اللهِ وَتُقِيمَ الصَّلَاةَ، وَتُؤْتِيَ الزَّكَاةَ، وَتَصُومَ رَمَضَانَ، وَتَحُجَّ الْبَيْتَ إِنِ اسْتَطَعْتَ إِلَيْهِ سَبِيلاً ـ قَالَ صَدَقْتَ ـ فَعَجِبْنَا لَهُ يَسْأَلُهُ وَيُصَدِّقُهُ.

قَالَ: فَأَخْبِرْنِي عَنِ الْإِيمَانِ، قَالَ: أَنْ تُؤْمِنَ بِاللهِ وَمَلَائِكَتِهِ وَكُتُبِهِ وَرُسُلِهِ وَالْيَوْمِ الْآخِرِ وَتُؤْمِنَ بِالْقَدَرِ خَيْرِهِ وَشَرِّهِ ـ قَالَ صَدَقْتَ. قَالَ فَأَخْبِرْنِي عَنِ الْإِحْسَانِ ـ قَالَ أَنْ تَعْبُدَ اللهَ كَأَنَّكَ تَرَاهُ فَإِنْ لَمْ تَكُنْ تَرَاهُ فَإِنَّهُ يَرَاكَ. قَالَ: فَأَخْبِرْنِي عَنِ السَّاعَةِ ـ قَالَ مَا الْمَسْئُولُ عَنْهَا بِأَعْلَمَ مِنَ السَّائِلِ.

قَالَ: فَأَخْبِرْنِي عَنْ أَمَارَاتِهَا قَالَ: أَنْ تَلِدَ الْأَمَةُ رَبَّتَهَا وَأَنْ تَرَى الْحُفَاةَ الْعُرَاةَ الْعَالَةَ رِعَاءَ الشَّاءِ يَتَطَاوَلُونَ فِي الْبُنْيَانِ». ثُمَّ انْطَلَقَ فَلَبِثْتُ مَلِيًّا ثُمَّ قَالَ لِي: «يَاعُمَرُ أَتَدْرِي مَنِ السَّائِلُ؟» قُلْتُ اللهُ وَرَسُولُهُ أَعْلَمُ. قَالَ: «فَإِنَّهُ جِبْرِيلُ أَتَاكُمْ يُعَلِّمُكُمْ دِينَكُمْ».

18

One day while we were sitting with Allâh's Messenger صلى الله عليه وسلم a man suddenly appeared before us, wearing a very white dress and having very black hair, without any signs of journey upon him, and none of us knew him. He approached until he sat before the Prophet صلى الله عليه وسلم with his knees touching the Prophet's knees and he placed his hands on his thighs and said, "O Muhammad inform me about Islâm."Allâh's Messenger صلى الله عليه وسلم said, "Islâm is to bear witness that none has the right to be worshipped but Allah, and that Muhammad is the Messenger of Allah, to offer the *Salât*, pay *Zakât*, fast during the month of Ramadan and to make *Hajj* (the pilgrimage to Makkah) if you are able and have the means to make the journey." The man said, "You spoke the truth." We were surprised at his asking and confirming at the same time. He said, "Inform me about *Imân.*" The Prophet صلى الله عليه وسلم said, "*Imân* is to believe in Allah, His angels, His Books and Messengers, the Last Day and to believe in the Divine Preordainment of all that is good and evil." He again said, "You spoke the truth." He said, "Inform me about *Ihsân.*" He صلى الله عليه وسلم said: "*Ihsân* (perfection) is to worship Allah as if you see Him; if you can't see Him, surely He sees you." He said, "Inform me about the Hour (Doomsday)." He صلى الله عليه وسلم said, "The one asked has no more knowledge of it than the questioner." He said, "Inform me about its signs." He said, "(Its signs are) the slave-girl will give birth to her mistress and you will see the barefooted, naked, impoverished sheepherders competing with each other in tall buildings." Then the stranger left. The Prophet صلى الله عليه وسلم remained seated for quite a while, then he asked me, "O 'Umar, do you know who the questioner was?" I said, "Allah and His Messenger know best." He said, "That was Jibrael, he came to teach you your religion." (*Muslim*)

THE MEANING OF *LA ILAHA ILLA-ALLAH*

"None has the right to be worshipped but Allah," in it (i.e. the Testimony) is the negation of worship to other than Allah and its affirmation with regard to Allah alone.

1. Allah عز وجل said:

$$﴿ فَٱعۡلَمۡ أَنَّهُۥ لَآ إِلَٰهَ إِلَّا ٱللَّهُ ﴾$$

"So know (O Muhammad صلى الله عليه وسلم) that *La ilâha illa-Allah* (none has the right to be worshipped but Allah)..." (V.47:19)

2. The Prophet صلى الله عليه وسلم said:

«مَنْ قَالَ لَا إِلَهَ إِلَّا الله مُخْلِصاً دَخَلَ الْجَنَّةَ» . [رواه البزار

وصححه الألباني في صحيح الجامع].

"Whoever says *La ilaha illa-Allah* sincerely will enter Paradise." (Reported by Bazzar and declared authentic by Al-Albani in *Sahih Al-Jami'*).

The sincere person is the one who understands, acts according to its requirements, invites others to it, and gives it precedence over all other issues, because it is the concise formula of *Tauhîd* (Islâmic Monotheism) for which human beings and jinns were created.

3. Allâh's Messenger صلى الله عليه وسلم said to his uncle Abû Tâlib when he was on his death bed:

«يَا عَمِّ قُلْ لَا أَلَـه إِلَّا الله ، كَلِمَةً أُحَاجُّ لَكَ بِهَا عِنْدَ الله ، وَأَبَـى أَنْ يَقُـولَ لَا إِلَـه إِلَّا الله» . [رواه البخاري ومسلم].

"O uncle, say *La ilaha illa-Allah*, a statement by which I can plead on your behalf before Allah." But his uncle refused to say *La ilaha illa-Allah*. (*Bukhâri* and *Muslim*).

4. The Messenger ﷺ preached in Makkah for 13 years inviting the idol-worshippers, saying:

"Testify that none has the right to be worshipped but Allah"

But their response as reported in the Qur'ân was :

﴿ وَعَجِبُوٓا أَن جَآءَهُم مُّنذِرٌ مِّنْهُمْ وَقَالَ ٱلْكَٰفِرُونَ هَٰذَا سَٰحِرٌ كَذَّابٌ ○ أَجَعَلَ ٱلْأَلِهَةَ إِلَٰهًا وَٰحِدًا إِنَّ هَٰذَا لَشَىْءٌ عُجَابٌ ○ وَٱنطَلَقَ ٱلْمَلَأُ مِنْهُمْ أَنِ ٱمْشُوا۟ وَٱصْبِرُوا۟ عَلَىٰٓ ءَالِهَتِكُمْ إِنَّ هَٰذَا لَشَىْءٌ يُرَادُ ○ مَا سَمِعْنَا بِهَٰذَا فِى ٱلْمِلَّةِ ٱلْءَاخِرَةِ إِنْ هَٰذَآ إِلَّا ٱخْتِلَٰقٌ ﴾

"And they (Arab pagans) wonder that a warner (Prophet Muhammad ﷺ) has come to them from among themselves! And the disbelievers say: 'This (Prophet Muhammad ﷺ) is a sorcerer, a liar. Has he made the *âlihâ* (gods) (all) into One *Ilâh* (God — Allah). Verily, this is a curious thing!' And the leaders among them went about (saying): 'Go on, and remain constant to your *âlihâ* (gods)! Verily, this is a thing designed (against you)! We have not heard (the like) of this among the people of these later days. This is nothing but an invention!'" (V. 38: 4-7)

The Arabs understood its meaning that one who said it (with conviction), would not call upon (invoke, pray, supplicate etc.) anyone other than Allah. So they abstained from it and refused to say it. Allah عز وجل said:

﴿ إِنَّهُمْ كَانُوٓا۟ إِذَا قِيلَ لَهُمْ لَآ إِلَٰهَ إِلَّا ٱللَّهُ يَسْتَكْبِرُونَ ○ وَيَقُولُونَ أَئِنَّا لَتَارِكُوٓا۟ ءَالِهَتِنَا لِشَاعِرٍ مَّجْنُونٍ ○ بَلْ جَآءَ بِٱلْحَقِّ وَصَدَّقَ ٱلْمُرْسَلِينَ ﴾

"Truly, when it was said to them: '*Lâ ilaha illa-Allah* (none has the right to be worshipped but Allah)' they puffed themselves up with pride (i.e. denied it). And (they) said: 'Are we going to abandon our *âlihâ* (gods) for the sake of a mad poet?' Nay! he (Muhammad ﷺ) has come with the truth (i.e. Allah's religion — Islamic

21

Monotheism and this Qur'ân) and he confirms the Messengers (before him who brought Allah's religion - Islamic Monotheism)." (V. 37: 35-37)

And the Prophet ﷺ said:

«مَنْ قَالَ لاَ إِلهَ إِلاَّ اللهُ ، وَكَفَرَ بِمَا يُعْبَدُ مِنْ دُونِ اللهِ ، حَرُمَ مَالُهُ وَدَمُهُ وَحِسَابُهُ عَلَى اللهِ عَزَّ وَجَلَّ» . [رواه مسلم].

"Whoever says *La ilaha illa-Allah* and rejects whatever is worshipped besides Allah, his property and blood becomes sacrosanct and his reckoning is [only] with Allah the Mighty and Exalted." (*Muslim*)

This *Hadîth* teaches us that the verbal declaration of the testimony of Faith requires the rejection of all worship directed to other than Allah, such as supplication to the dead, etc.

Indeed, it is strange that some Muslims say *La ilaha illa-Allah* with their tongues and contradict its meaning with their deeds and their supplication to other than Allah.

5. *La ilaha illa-Allah* is the foundation of *Tauhîd* (Islâmic Monotheism) and Islam. It is a complete system of life, through which, all forms of worship (of Allah) are realized. That happens when a Muslim submits himself to Allah, and calls upon Him alone, and refers all issues (of right and wrong) to His Law, to the exclusion of all other systems of law.

6. The scholar Ibn Rajab said: "The word *Ilâh* (i.e. God) means the One Who is obeyed and not defied, out of ones sense of awe and reverence, love, fear, and hope, placing ones trust in Him, asking Him and supplicating Him alone. And all of these are invalid except for Allah [alone]. So, whoever directs any of these matters (which are the rights of Allah) to a created being, has detracted from the sincerity of his statement *La ilaha illa-Allah*. And he has worshipped that created being to the extent

22

he directed those matters toward it.

7. The Prophet ﷺ said:

«لَقِّنُوا مَوْتَاكُمْ لاَ إِلَهَ إِلاَّ اللهُ فَإِنَّهُ مَنْ كَانَ آخِرُ كَلاَمِهِ لاَ إِلَه إِلاَّ اللهُ دَخَلَ الْجَنَّةَ يَوْماً مِنَ الدَّهْرِ وَإِنْ أَصَابَهُ قَبْلَ ذَلِكَ مَا أَصَابَهُ» . [رواه ابن حبان في صحيحه وصححه الألباني في صحيحه الجامع].

"Urge those of you who are on their deathbeds to say *La ilaha illa-Allah;* for verily, whoever's last words are *La ilaha illa-Allah,* will eventually enter Paradise even if he has to go through (before that) whatever (punishment) he has to go through." (Reported by Ibn Hibban in his *Sahih* and declared authentic by Al-Albani in *Sahih-ul-Jami*').

"Urging" as mentioned in the *Hadîth* is not the mere repetition of the *Shahadah* — "*La ilaha illa-Allah"* in the presence of the dying person, as some people have understood of it, rather it is to instruct him to say it. The proof for that is the *Hadîth* narrated by Anas bin Malik رضي الله عنه :

«أَنَّ رَسُولَ اللهِ ـ ﷺ ـ عَادَ رَجُلاً مِنَ الأَنْصَارِ، فَقَالَ: يَاخَالُ، قُلْ : لاَ إِله إِلاَّ اللهِ ، فَقَالَ : أَخَالٌ أَمْ عَمٌّ؟ فَقَالَ : بَلْ خَالٌ ، فَقَالَ : فَخَيرٌ لِي أَنْ أَقُولَ : لاَ إِلَهَ إِلاَّ اللهُ فَقَالَ النَّبِيُّ ـ ﷺ ـ نَعَمْ» . [أخرجه الإمام أحمد ٣/١٥٢ بإسناد صحيح على شرط مسلم»

«انظر أحكام الجنائز للألباني ص١١].

Allah's Messenger ﷺ visited a (dying) man of the *Ansâr* and said to him, "Uncle, say *La ilaha illa-Allah.*" The *Ansâri* asked, "Do you consider me a maternal uncle or paternal uncle?" The Prophet ﷺ said, "A maternal uncle". The man said, "Then it is better for me to

23

say *La ilaha illa-Allah.*" The Prophet صلى الله عليه وسلم said, "Yes." [Reported by Ahmad– 3/152 with authentic chain of narrators according to the criteria of Imam Muslim. See *Ahkâm-ul-Janâiz* (funeral rulings) by Albani p.11]

8. The word *La ilaha illa-Allah* will benefit the one who says it if he conforms to its meaning in his life, and doesn't nullify it by associating partners with Allah, such as supplicating to the dead or calling upon the living who are absent. This can be compared to *Wudû* (i.e. ablution which puts one into a state of purity) which is nullified by urination, defecation, ... etc.

The Prophet صلى الله عليه وسلم said:

«مَنْ قَالَ لَا إِلَه إِلَّا الله أَنْجَتْهُ يَوْماً مِنْ دَهْره يُصِيبُه قَبْلَ ذَلِكَ مَاأَصَابَهُ». [رواه البيهقي، وصححه الألباني في الأحاديث الصحيحة رقم ١٩٣٢].

"Whoever says *La ilaha illa-Allah,* it will be his salvation someday, no matter what befalls him before that." (Reported by Baihaqi, declared authentic by Albani in *Ahâdith Sahiha* –No. 1932).

THE MEANING OF
MUHAMMADUR RASULULLAH
[Muhammad is the Messenger of Allah]

This statement encodes the belief that Muhammad صلى الله عليه وسلم was sent as a Messenger by Allah. So, we believe in what he reported as truth, we obey him in whatever he commanded, we abstain from whatever he prohibited, and we worship Allah in the manner he prescribed.

1. Abul-Hasan Ali An-Nadwi says in his book *An-Nubuwwah*:

"The first concern of all the Prophets in every age and in every environment was to correct the belief of people regarding Allah عز وجل , to correct the relationship between the servant and his Lord, to call towards the dedication of religion purely to Allah, and to single out Allah as the only object of worship, [believing with certainty] that He is the Sole Dispenser of benefit and harm, the only One Who has the right to be worshipped, supplicated, and resorted to, and in Whose Name [Alone] animals may be sacrificed. Their campaigns were concentrated and directed against paganism during their own eras, which was exemplified in the worship of idols (in human and animal forms), and 'saints' and other human beings (considered to be holy or to have a divine power) from among the living and the dead."

2. Allah addressed His Messenger صلى الله عليه وسلم in the Qur'ân:

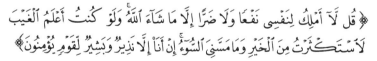

"Say (O Muhammad صلى الله عليه وسلم): I possess no power of benefit or hurt to myself except as Allah wills. If I had the knowledge of the *Ghaib* (unseen), I should have secured

25

for myself an abundance of wealth, and no evil should have touched me. I am but a warner, and a bringer of glad tidings unto people who believe."(V. 7: 188)

And the Prophet صلى الله عليه وسلم said:

«لَا تُطْرُوني كَمَا أَطْرَتِ النَّصَارَى ابْنَ مَرْيَمَ، فَإِنَّمَا أَنَا عَبْدٌ فَقُولُوا عَبْدُ اللهِ وَرَسُولُهُ» . [رواه البخاري].

"Do not exaggerate in praising me as the Christians did to (Jesus) the son of Mary, for I am only a servant, so say [he is] the servant of Allah and His Messenger." (*Bukhâri*)

The exaggeration referred to in the *Hadîth* is excessive praise, so we may not supplicate him instead of Allah, as the Christians did with Jesus, the son of Mary, falling thereby into the worship of Jesus along with Allah. Instead, he صلى الله عليه وسلم instructed us to call to him as "Muhammad, the servant of Allah and His Messenger."

As for his praise [the kind of] which is mentioned in the Qur'ân and *Sunnah*, it is his due right.

3. True love of the Prophet صلى الله عليه وسلم lies in obedience to him, by supplicating Allah alone, and not supplicating anyone else, even a Prophet or a saint.

The Prophet صلى الله عليه وسلم said:

«إِذَا سَأَلْتَ فَاسْأَلِ اللهَ وَإِذَا اسْتَعَنْتَ فَاسْتَعِنْ باللهِ» . [رواه الترمذي وقال حسن صحيح].

"When you ask, ask from Allah, and when you seek help, seek the help of Allah." (Reported by Tirmidhi as good and authentic *Hadîth*)

When something happened that caused him concern or grief,

26

the Prophet صلى الله عليه وسلم used to say:

«يَاحَيُّ يَاقَيُّومُ بِرَحْمَتِكَ اسْتَغِيثُ». [رواه الترمذي وقال حسن صحيح].

"O Everliving and Everlasting (Allah), in Your Mercy I seek help." (Reported by Tirmidhi as *Hasan*).

May Allah have mercy on the poet who said about true love :

If your love was true you would have obeyed him. Verily the lover is to the beloved obedient."

And among the signs of true love for him (صلى الله عليه وسلم) is to love the call to *Tauhîd* (Islâmic Monotheism) by which he commenced his mission, and also to love those who call for *Tauhîd* and dislike *Shirk* (associating partners to Allah) and all those who call people towards it.

WHERE IS ALLAH?
ALLAH IS ABOVE THE HEAVENS

Mu'awiyah bin Al-Hakam As-Salmi رضي الله عنه said:

« . . . وَكَانَتْ لِي جَارِيَةٌ تَرْعَى غَنَماً لِي قِبَلَ (أُحُدٍ والـجَوَّانِيَّةِ) فَاطَّلَعْتُ ذَاتَ يَوْمٍ فَإِذَا بِالذِّئْبِ قَدْ ذَهَبَ بِشَاةٍ مِنْ غَنَمِهَا، وَأَنَا رَجُلٌ مِنْ بَنِي آدَمَ آسَفُ كَمَا يَأْسَفُونَ لَكِنِّي صَكَكْتُهَا صَكَّةً، فَأَتَيْتُ رَسُولَ الله ـ ﷺ ـ فَعَظَّمَ ذَلِكَ عَلَيَّ، قُلْتُ يَارَسُولَ الله، أَفَلَا أُعْتِقُهَا؟ قَالَ: ائْتِنِي بِهَا، فَقَالَ لَهَا: أَيْنَ الله؟ قَالَتْ فِي السَّمَاءِ، قَالَ مَنْ أَنَا؟ قَالَتْ: أَنْتَ رَسُولُ الله، قَالَ: أَعْتِقْهَا فَإِنَّهَا مُؤْمِنَةٌ ». [رواه مسلم وأبوداود].

I had a slave-girl who used to herd sheep for me. One day I discovered that a wolf had killed one of her sheep, and I'm a man from the children of Adam, I get upset like they get upset, and I slapped her in the face. Then I went to the Prophet صلى الله عليه وسلم who impressed upon me the seriousness of my act. I said, "O Messenger of Allah, should I not set her free?" He said, "Bring her to me." He asked her, "Where is Allah?" She said, "He is above the heavens." He said, "Who am I?" She said, "You are the Messenger of Allah." He said, "Free her, for she is a believer." (*Muslim* and *Abû Dâwûd*)

Among the benefits to be derived from this *Hadîth* are:

1. The Companions of the Prophet صلى الله عليه وسلم used to refer to him their problems, even a small one, to know what is the Law of Allah regarding it.

2. All issues for judgement should be referred to Allah and His Messenger, acting upon the Statement of Allah تعالى :

﴿ فَلَا وَرَبِّكَ لَا يُؤْمِنُونَ حَتَّىٰ يُحَكِّمُوكَ فِيمَا شَجَرَ بَيْنَهُمْ ثُمَّ لَا يَجِدُوا فِىٓ أَنفُسِهِمْ حَرَجًا مِّمَّا قَضَيْتَ وَيُسَلِّمُوا تَسْلِيمًا ﴾

"But no, by your Lord, they can have no Faith, until they make you (صلى الله عليه وسلم) a judge in all disputes between them, and find in themselves no resistance against your decisions, and accept (them) with full submission." (V.4: 65)

3. The Prophet صلى الله عليه وسلم reproached the Companion for slapping the slave-girl and considered it a serious matter.

4. Belief is a condition for freeing a slave; since the Prophet صلى الله عليه وسلم tested her, and after learning she was a believer, he ordered her to be set free; and if she had been a disbeliever, he wouldn't have ordered for her freedom.

5. The necessity of asking about *Tauhîd* (Islâmic Monotheism); and part of it is the belief that Allah is above His Throne, and knowledge of that is mandatory.

6. The legitimacy of asking "Where is Allah?"; in fact it is *Sunnah*, since the Prophet صلى الله عليه وسلم asked it.

7. The legitimacy of replying that Allah is above the heavens, since the Prophet صلى الله عليه وسلم affirmed the reply of the slave-girl and it also goes along with the Statement of Allah in the Qur'ân:

﴿ ءَأَمِنتُم مَّن فِى ٱلسَّمَآءِ أَن يَخْسِفَ بِكُمُ ٱلْأَرْضَ ﴾

"Do you feel secure that He, Who is over the heaven (Allah), will not cause the earth to sink with you?" (V. 67: 16)

Ibn Abbas رضي الله عنهما said that the One referred to in the verse by the word 'Who' is Allah.

[Note: The literal translation of *'fis-sama'* is 'in heavens', the scholars explained it according to the Arabic language to have the meaning of (above) as it is not possible for Allah to be surrounded by His creation, and sometimes the word *'Fi'* is used in the meaning of *'Ala'* (on) as stated in the verse:

$$﴿ وَلَأُصَلِّبَنَّكُمْ فِى جُذُوعِ ٱلنَّخْلِ ﴾$$

"I will surely crucify you on the trunks of palm-trees". (20:71)

The other interpretation is based on the variant meanings of the word (السَّماء) , *Samâ'* in Arabic refers to that which is elevated. It is used to refer to the ceiling of a house, to the sky, to the heavens and to elevation and transcendence. So the phrase could be translated: 'in transcendence'].

8. The correctness of Belief includes the testimony that Muhammad صلى الله عليه وسلم is the Messenger of Allah.

9. The belief that Allah is above the heaven is an indicator of the soundness of one's Belief, and it is mandatory on every believer.

10. The refutation of the erroneous belief that Allah is in every place by His Self. The truth is that Allah is with us by His Knowledge not by His Self.

11. The fact that the Prophet صلى الله عليه وسلم ordered to bring the slave-girl in order to test her, shows that he did not possess the knowledge of the unseen [except what Allah informed him] which in this case is the belief of the slave-girl. This refutes the claim of many *Sufi* that he had a complete knowledge of the unseen.

BELIEF IN *QADAR* (DIVINE PREORDAINMENT) THE GOOD OF IT AND THE BAD OF IT

This is the sixth pillar of *Iman* (Faith). Imam Nawawi explained it like this in his collection of 40 *Ahadîth*:

Verily Allah decreed all matters before its existence, and Allah knows exactly when and where every thing will occur, and every thing occurs according to His Decree.

Belief in the Divine Preordainment has several facets:

1 *Divine Preordainment regarding knowledge:*

Allah's Knowledge of everything, means to believe that Allah knows previously what His slaves will do of good and evil, obedience and disobedience—before their creation; who from among them will be destined for Paradise and who will be destined for the Hell-fire, and He prepared for them reward and punishment according to their deeds even before their creation. All of that is recorded and accounted for with Him, and all His slave's deeds unfold and occur in accord with what He already knew and recorded. (This passage was quoted from *Jami' Al-Ulûm wal-Hikam* by Ibn Rajab, p. 24).

2. *Divine Preordainment regarding the Preserved Tablet:*

What is recorded in *Al-Lauh Al-Mahfûz* (the Preserved Tablet). Ibn Kathîr in his commentary of the Qur'ân quotes Abdur-Rahman bin Salman: There is nothing which Allah decreed, including the Qur'ân and whatever was before it or after it, but was recorded in the Preserved Tablet.[1]

3. *Divine Preordainment regarding the womb:*

It is mentioned in *Hadîth*:

«ثُمَّ يُرْسِلُ إِلَيْهِ المَلَكَ فَيَنْفَخُ فِيهِ الرُّوحَ، وَيُؤْمَرُ بِكَتْبِ أَرْبَعِ

---

[1] Volume 4, page 497.

كَلِمَاتٍ : يَكْتُبُ رِزْقَــهُ وَأَجَلَهُ وَعَمَلَهُ وَشَقِيٌّ أَوْ سَعِيدٌ» . [رواه

البخاري ومسلم] .

"Then an angel is sent to blow the soul into the fetus, and is ordered to record four matters: its sustenance, life span, deeds and whether he will be unlucky or lucky (i.e. whether he/she will dwell in Paradise or Hell-fire)". (Agreed upon)

4. *Divine Preordainment of how and when:*

The Divine Preordainment of how and when everything will occur: Allah created all that is good and bad, and decreed exactly when they would occur to the slave. (As is mentioned in Nawawi's commentary on his collection of 40 *Ahadîth*).

<hr>

32

SOME BENEFITS OF BELIEF IN DIVINE PREORDAINMENT

1. Contentment, firmness in Faith, and the hope of compensation. Allah عز وجل said:

$$ ﴿ مَآ أَصَابَ مِن مُّصِيبَةٍ إِلَّا بِإِذِنِ ٱللَّهِ ﴾ $$

"No calamity befalls, but with the Leave [i.e. Decision and *Qadar* (Divine Preordainments)] of Allah..." (V. 64:11)

Ibn Abbas رضي الله عنهما said: His Leave or Permission means His Command and Decree.

And Allah عز وجل said:

$$ ﴿ وَمَن يُؤْمِنۢ بِٱللَّهِ يَهْدِ قَلْبَهُۥ ﴾ $$

"...And whosoever believes in Allah, He guides his heart [to the true Faith with certainty, i.e. what has befallen him was already written for him by Allah from the *Qadar* (Divine Preordainments)]..." (V. 64:11)

Ibn Kathir said in his commentary: "It means that when a person who is beset by misfortune and knows that it occurred by the Order and Decree of Allah, remains patient, seeking thereby reward, in submission to Allah's Decree. Allah guides his heart, and compensates him for his material loss. Ibn Abbas رضي الله عنهما said: Allah guides his heart to conviction in Faith; he knows what occurred to him was unavoidable, and what did not occur, could not have occurred. Alqamah said : It refers to a man beset by a calamity and he knows it is from Allah.

2. The expiation of sins. The Prophet صلى الله عليه وسلم said :

«مَا يُصِيبُ الْمُؤْمِنَ مِنْ وَصَبٍ وَلَا نَصَبٍ، وَلَا سَقَمٍ ، وَلَا حَزَنٍ، حَتَّى الْهَمَّ يَهُمُّهُ إِلَّا كَفَّرَ اللهُ بِهِ سَيِّئَاتِهِ». [متفق عليه].

"A believer is not beset by any hardship or fatigue or illness or grief or even a worry except that Allah will expiate thereby his sins." (Agreed upon).

3. Great reward. Allah عز وجل said:

﴿ وَبَشِّرِ الصَّابِرِينَ ٠ الَّذِينَ إِذَآ أَصَابَتْهُم مُّصِيبَةٌ قَالُوٓا إِنَّا لِلَّهِ وَإِنَّآ إِلَيْهِ رَاجِعُونَ ٠ أُوْلَٰٓئِكَ عَلَيْهِمْ صَلَوَٰتٌ مِّن رَّبِّهِمْ وَرَحْمَةٌ وَأُوْلَٰٓئِكَ هُمُ ٱلْمُهْتَدُونَ ﴾

"...and give glad tidings to the patient ones. Who, when afflicted with calamity, say: 'Truly! To Allah we belong and truly, to Him we shall return'. They are those on whom are the *Salawât* (i.e. blessings etc.) (i.e. who are blessed and will be forgiven) from their Lord, and (they are those who) receive His Mercy, and it is they who are the guided ones." (V. 2 : 155-157)

4. Self-contentment. The Prophet صلى الله عليه وسلم said:

« . . وَارْضَ بِمَا قَسَمَهُ اللهُ لَكَ تَكُنْ أَغْنَىٰ النَّاسِ » . [رواه أحمد والترمذي وحسنه محقق جامع الأصول].

"If you are satisfied with what Allah has apportioned for you, you will be the wealthiest of people." (*Ahmad* and *Tirmidhi*)

He صلى الله عليه وسلم also said:

«لَيْسَ الْغِنَىٰ عَنْ كَثْرَةِ الْعَرْضِ ، وَلكِنَّ الْغِنَىٰ غِنَىٰ النَّفْسِ » . [متفق عليه].

"To be well off is not through possessing lots of transitory goods rather true well-being comes from a contented soul." (Agreed upon)

34

We see that many who possess massive wealth are not satisfied with what they have, they are disturbed, their souls are impoverished; whereas one whose material possessions are few yet is content with what Allah apportioned for him after his efforts, he is a satisfied soul.

5. Lack of happiness and grief. Allah عز وجل said:

﴿ مَآ أَصَابَ مِن مُّصِيبَةٍ فِى ٱلْأَرْضِ وَلَا فِىٓ أَنفُسِكُمْ إِلَّا فِى كِتَـٰبٍ مِّن قَبْلِ أَن نَّبْرَأَهَآ إِنَّ ذَٰلِكَ عَلَى ٱللَّهِ يَسِيرٌ ٠ لِّكَيْلَا تَأْسَوْا۟ عَلَىٰ مَا فَاتَكُمْ وَلَا تَفْرَحُوا۟ بِمَآ ءَاتَىٰكُمْ وَٱللَّهُ لَا يُحِبُّ كُلَّ مُخْتَالٍ فَخُورٍ ﴾

"No calamity befalls on the earth or in yourselves but is inscribed in the Book of Decrees (*Al-Lauh Al-Mahfûz*), before We bring it into existence. Verily, that is easy for Allah. In order that you may not be sad over matters that you fail to get, nor rejoice because of that which has been given to you. And Allah likes not prideful boasters." (V. 57 : 22, 23)

Ibn Kathîr said: Don't act haughty towards people because of what Allah has blessed you with, because it didn't come to you through your effort, but by the Decree of Allah and so don't take the blessings of Allah arrogantly and wantonly and He is your Sustainer.

Ikramah said: There is none who does not get happy or sad. Hence make your happiness gratitude, and your grief patience. (See *Tafsîr Ibn Kathîr* : 4/314.)

6. Courage and boldness. The person who believes in *Qadar* becomes bold, and is not in awe of anyone except Allah, because he knows his life span is preordained and whatever he misses could not have occurred to him and what happened to him could not have been avoided, and that victory comes with patience, and that after every affliction there is relaxation and along with hardship comes ease.

7. No fear of the harm of human beings. The Prophet ﷺ said:

«وَاعْلَمْ أَنَّ الْأُمَّةَ لَوِ اجْتَمَعَت عَلَى أَنْ يَنْفَعُوكَ بِشَيْءٍ لَمْ يَنْفَعُوكَ إِلَّا بِشَيْءٍ قَدَ كَتَبَهُ اللهُ لَكَ، وَإِنِ اجْتَمَعُوا عَلَى أَنْ يَضُرُّوكَ بِشَيْءٍ لَمْ يَضُرُّوكَ إِلَّا بِشَيْءٍ قَدْ كَتَبَهُ اللهُ عَلَيْكَ، رُفِعَتِ الْأَقْلَامُ وَجَفَّتِ الصُّحُفُ». [رواه الترمذي وقال حديث حسن صحيح].

"And know that if the whole world were to join hands in order to benefit you with something, they couldn't benefit you except by what Allah already wrote for you. And if they join together to harm you, they wouldn't be able to harm you except that Allah has ordained for you. The pens are lifted and the ink has dried on the pages (of the Preserved Tablet)." (*Tirmidhi*)

8. No fear of death. The following is the import of the couplets attributed to Ali رضي الله عنه:

"Which of my two days will I flee from death? The day it was not decreed or the day it was decreed?

The day it was not decreed, I fear it not and from what is written, even the cautious will not escape."

9. No remorse for what has missed. The Prophet ﷺ also said:

«الْـمُؤْمِنُ الْقَوِيُّ خَيْرٌ وَأَحَبُّ إِلَى اللهِ مِنَ الْـمُؤْمِنِ الضَّعِيفِ، وَفِي كُلِّ خَيْرٌ، احْرِصْ عَلَـى مَايَنْفَعُكَ وَاسْتَعِنْ بِاللهِ وَلَا تَعْجَزْ، فَإِنْ أَصَابَكَ شَيْءٌ فَلَا تَقُلْ لَوْ أَنِّي فَعَلْتُ كَذَا وَكَذَا لَكَانَ كَذَا وَكَذَا، وَلَكِنْ قُلْ قَدَّرَ اللهِ وَمَاشَاءَ اللهُ فَعَلَ، فَإِنَّ لَوْ تَفْتَحُ عَمَلَ الشَّيْطَانِ». [متفق عليه].

36

"The strong believer is better and more beloved to Allah than the weak believer, though both are good; work hard for that which is beneficial for you and seek Allah's help, and do not give up. If you are stricken by misfortune do not say: 'If only I had done differently...', rather say: 'That is what Allah decreed, He does as He wills.' 'If only' opens the door to Satan's works." (Agreed upon)

10. Good is in what Allah has decided. We can understand this by an example: If a believer's hand is wounded, he should praise Allah that it wasn't fractured; but if it got fractured, he should praise Allah that it wasn't cut off, or that he didn't fracture his back, which is more serious. Once, a businessman was waiting for a plane to close an important business deal. When the *Adhân* was called for *Salât*, he went for *Salât* (prayer). When he came back, the plane had already departed, so he sat down, sad about missing it. Shortly after that the news came that the plane had caught fire in mid-air. He prostrated in gratitude to Allah for his safety as a result of being delayed by *Salât* and he remembered Allah's Statement:

$$\text{﴿ وَعَسَىٰٓ أَن تَكْرَهُواْ شَيْـًٔا وَهُوَ خَيْرٌ لَّكُمْ وَعَسَىٰٓ أَن تُحِبُّواْ شَيْـًٔا وَهُوَ شَرٌّ لَّكُمْ وَٱللَّهُ يَعْلَمُ وَأَنتُمْ لَا تَعْلَمُونَ ﴾}$$

"...and it may be that you dislike a thing which is good for you, and that you like a thing which is bad for you. Allah knows but you do not know." (V. 2 : 216).

DO NOT USE FATE AS AN EXCUSE

A Muslim must have the belief that all that is good and bad exists by Allah's Decree, Knowledge and Will. But at the same time every person's actions of good and evil, happen by his own choice. The observation of Allah's Commands and Prohibitions are mandatory on believers and it is not lawful to disobey Allah and then say: "That's what Allah decreed for me." Allah sent His Prophets and revealed to them His Books to make clear the path of happiness and of misery, and blessed the human being with faculty and the ability to think. He made known to mankind the difference between guidance and error. Allah عز وجل said:

$$ ﴿ إِنَّا هَدَيْنَٰهُ ٱلسَّبِيلَ إِمَّا شَاكِرًا وَإِمَّا كَفُورًا ﴾ $$

"Verily, We showed him the way, whether he be grateful or ungrateful." (V. 76 :3).

So if a person abandoned *Salât* or drank liquor, he deserves the penalty for his transgression against Allah's Order and Prohibition and he must repent and regret for it. He will not get off by using *Qadar* as an excuse.

FACTORS WHICH NULLIFY *IMÂN* AND ISLÂM

There are things which nullify *Imân* (Faith) i.e. Belief, just as there are things which nullify *Wudû*, if a person does any single one of them, he loses his state of ritual purity. The same is true with Belief. The nullifiers of Belief can be classified into four categories:

First category: Denial of the *Rubb's*[1] existence or deprecating and calumniating Him.

Second category: Denial of Allah's right to be worshipped or worshipping anything or anyone along with Him.

Third category: Denial of any of Allah's Names or Attributes established in the Qur'ân and *Sunnah* or deprecation of them.

Fourth category: Denial of the role of Muhammad صلى الله عليه وسلم as the Messenger of Allah, or deprecation of His Message.

---

[1] *Rubb* means the One Who is the Creator, the Sustainer, the Lord, etc. in Whose Hand is the disposal of all affairs.

1. Denial of the existence of *Rubb* nullifies *Imân*

This first category encompasses several types:

1. Pure atheism; such as the belief of communists who deny that the universe has a creator and say: "There is no god, and life is a purely material phenomenon." They attribute the creation and all actions to pure chance, or "nature" but forget the One Who created even the "chance" and the "nature," as Allah said:

$$﴿ ٱللَّهُ خَٰلِقُ كُلِّ شَىْءٍ وَهُوَ عَلَىٰ كُلِّ شَىْءٍ وَكِيلٌ ﴾$$

"Allah is the Creator of all things, and He is the *Wakîl* (Trustee, Disposer of affairs, Guardian, etc.) over all things." (V. 39: 62)

This category of disbeliever is more hardened in their apostasy than the polytheist Arabs of post-Islamic period, and even Satan himself, as those polytheist Arabs did admit the existence of their creator as the Qur'ân states about them saying:

$$﴿ وَلَئِن سَأَلْتَهُم مَّنْ خَلَقَهُمْ لَيَقُولُنَّ ٱللَّهُ ﴾$$

"And if you ask them who created them, they will surely say: 'Allah...'" (V.43:87)

and the Quran mentions statement of Satan:

$$﴿ قَالَ أَنَا۠ خَيْرٌ مِّنْهُ خَلَقْتَنِى مِن نَّارٍ وَخَلَقْتَهُ مِن طِينٍ ﴾$$

"(*Iblîs*) said: I am better than he, You created me from fire, and You created him from clay." (V.38:76)

It is an act of disbelief for a Muslim to say "nature created something or that it came into being by chance".

2. Or if a person claims to be the *Rubb*; as Pharaoh claimed saying:

$$\text{﴿ فَقَالَ أَنَا رَبُّكُمُ الأَعْلَى ﴾}$$

"I am your lord, most high", (V.79:24).

3. Or to claim that there are great saints [called *"Qutb"* in *Sufi* terminology, which literally means axes (of creation)] who have control over what happens in the universe, even if this claim is accompanied with the admissions that Allah, the Soverign Lord exists. People who have this belief are in a worse condition than the idol worshippers before Islâm, who used to admit that Allah is the Sole Controller of the affairs of the universe, as is indicated by Allah's Statement:

$$\text{﴿ قُلْ مَن يَرْزُقُكُم مِّنَ ٱلسَّمَآءِ وَٱلأَرْضِ أَمَّن يَمْلِكُ ٱلسَّمْعَ وَٱلأَبْصَٰرَ وَمَن يُخْرِجُ ٱلْحَىَّ مِنَ ٱلْمَيِّتِ وَيُخْرِجُ ٱلْمَيِّتَ مِنَ ٱلْحَىِّ وَمَن يُدَبِّرُ ٱلأَمْرَ فَسَيَقُولُونَ ٱللَّهُ فَقُلْ أَفَلَا تَتَّقُونَ ﴾}$$

"Say: 'Who provides for you from the sky and from the earth? Or who owns hearing and sight? And who brings out the living from the dead and brings out the dead from the living? And who disposes the affairs?' They will say: 'Allah.' Say: 'Will you not then be afraid of Allah's punishment (for setting up rivals in worship with Allah)?'" (V.10:31)

4. Or the statements of some *Sufis* that Allah pervades in His creation, or became incarnate in it. The *Sufi*, Ibn Arabi, who is buried in Damascus, said:

"The Lord is a slave, and the slave is a Lord. I only wish I knew, which one is the *Mukallaf*".

[*Mukallaf* is a basic term of *Shariah* terminology, it refers to the essential role of the adult, sane human being : That he or she is charged by Allah with a series of duties and responsibilities, orders and prohibitions, and he will be questioned, on the basis of how well he discharged his responsibilities].

40

And the transgressor of the Sufism has stated:

"And the dog and the pig is nothing other than our deity, nor is Allah other than a monk in a church."

And Hallaj (a *Sufi* of Baghdad) stated: "I am He (i.e. *Rubb*) and He is I" on the basis of his statement, which he would not retract; the scholars agreed that he should be executed as an apostate. High Exalted is Allah above what such people say.

2. *Shirk* (polytheism) in Worship nullifies *Imân*

This second category includes denial of Allah as the object of worship or ascribing partner along with Allah. It too has various manifestations:

1. Those who worship the sun, the moon and the stars and trees and Satan or any other created being, and abandon the worship of Allah, Who created all these things which have no power to benefit nor to harm. Allah عز وجل said:

﴿ وَمِنْ ءَايَٰتِهِ ٱلَّيۡلُ وَٱلنَّهَارُ وَٱلشَّمۡسُ وَٱلۡقَمَرُۚ لَا تَسۡجُدُواْ لِلشَّمۡسِ وَلَا لِلۡقَمَرِ وَٱسۡجُدُواْ لِلَّهِ ٱلَّذِى خَلَقَهُنَّ إِن كُنتُمۡ إِيَّاهُ تَعۡبُدُونَ ﴾

"And from among His Signs are the night and the day, and the sun and the moon. Prostrate not to the sun nor to the moon, but prostrate to Allah Who created them, if you (really) worship Him." (V. 41:37)

2. Those who worship Allah, and worship along with Him some of His creation, such as saints, as embodied in idols, grave-worship, etc. The Arab idol worshippers before Islam were of this category, as they used to call upon Allah only in times of hardship and pressing need, and would worship others in times of ease. As the Qur'ân described them :

﴿ فَإِذَا رَكِبُواْ فِى ٱلۡفُلۡكِ دَعَوُاْ ٱللَّهَ مُخۡلِصِينَ لَهُ ٱلدِّينَ فَلَمَّا نَجَّىٰهُمۡ إِلَى ٱلۡبَرِّ إِذَا هُمۡ يُشۡرِكُونَ ﴾

"And when they embark on a ship, they invoke Allah, making their Faith pure for Him only, but when He brings them safely to land, behold, they give a share of their worship to others." (V. 29:65)

They are characterized as *Al-Mushrikûn*, (i.e. those who associate and attribute partner with Allah), even though they made supplication to Allah Alone when they were afraid of drowning at sea, because they didn't stay like that, instead they called upon others after He saved them.

3. Since Allah was displeased with the idol worshipping Arabs before Islam, rather than, He branded them *Kafir* (i.e. the disbelievers), and ordered His Prophet to fight them, because they called upon others besides Allah at the time of ease, and He didn't accept their whole-heartedness when they called upon Him alone in hardship, and He labelled them *Mushrikîn*. What can we say about certain Muslims today, who resort to dead saints at the time of ease as well as at the time of hardship? And they ask of them what only Allah has the power to bestow, like curing the sick, and granting sustenance and guidance etc., and they forget the Creator of those saints, whereas He is the only One Who cures, the Sustainer, and the Guide. And those dead people have no power at all and cannot even hear those who are calling upon them, as Allah عز وجل stated:

﴿ وَٱلَّذِينَ تَدْعُونَ مِن دُونِهِۦ مَا يَمْلِكُونَ مِن قِطْمِيرٍ ٠ إِن تَدْعُوهُمْ لَا يَسْمَعُوا دُعَآءَكُمْ وَلَوْ سَمِعُوا مَا ٱسْتَجَابُوا لَكُمْ وَيَوْمَ ٱلْقِيَٰمَةِ يَكْفُرُونَ بِشِرْكِكُمْ وَلَا يُنَبِّئُكَ مِثْلُ خَبِيرٍ ﴾

"...And those, whom you invoke or call upon instead of Him, own not even a *Qitmîr* (the thin membrane over the date-stone). If you invoke (or call upon) them, they hear not your call, and if (in case) they were to hear, they could not grant it (your request) to you. And on the Day of Resurrection, they will disown your worshipping them. And none can inform you (O Muhammad صلى الله عليه وسلم) like Him Who is the All-Knower (of each and every thing)." (V. 35: 13,14)

This verse is explicit to the effect that the dead cannot hear those who call upon them, and explicit in stating that their supplication is major *Shirk*.

Some of them might say : we don't believe that these saints and righteous people have the power to benefit or harm, we only take them as intermediaries who will intercede with Allah on our behalf, and through them we get closer to Allah. Our reply to them is that the idolaters before Islam used to hold a similar belief, as is mentioned in the Qur'ân:

﴿ وَيَعْبُدُونَ مِن دُونِ ٱللَّهِ مَا لَا يَضُرُّهُمْ وَلَا يَنفَعُهُمْ وَيَقُولُونَ هَٰٓؤُلَآءِ شُفَعَٰٓؤُنَا عِندَ ٱللَّهِ قُلْ أَتُنَبِّـُٔونَ ٱللَّهَ بِمَا لَا يَعْلَمُ فِى ٱلسَّمَٰوَٰتِ وَلَا فِى ٱلْأَرْضِ سُبْحَٰنَهُۥ وَتَعَٰلَىٰ عَمَّا يُشْرِكُونَ ﴾

"And they worship besides Allah things that hurt them not, nor profit them, and they say: 'These are our intercessors with Allah.' Say: 'Do you inform Allah of that which He knows not in the heavens and on the earth?' Glorified and Exalted is He above all that which they associate as partners with Him!" (V. 10:18)

This verse is explicit in proving that whoever worships and supplicates other than Allah, he is a *Mushrik* even if he believes that those other beings cannot benefit nor harm, but only sees them as intercessors.

Allah said about the idolaters:

﴿ وَٱلَّذِينَ ٱتَّخَذُوا۟ مِن دُونِهِۦٓ أَوْلِيَآءَ مَا نَعْبُدُهُمْ إِلَّا لِيُقَرِّبُونَآ إِلَى ٱللَّهِ زُلْفَىٰٓ إِنَّ ٱللَّهَ يَحْكُمُ بَيْنَهُمْ فِى مَا هُمْ فِيهِ يَخْتَلِفُونَ إِنَّ ٱللَّهَ لَا يَهْدِى مَنْ هُوَ كَٰذِبٌ كَفَّارٌ ﴾

"...And those who take *'Auliya'* (protectors and helpers) besides Him (say): 'We worship them only that they may bring us near to Allah.' Verily, Allah will judge between them concerning that wherein they differ. Truly, Allah guides not him who is a liar, and a disbeliever." (V. 39 : 3)

This verse is explicit in proving the disbelief of those who call upon other than Allah with the intention of getting thereby closer to Allah.

The Prophet صلى الله عليه وسلم said:

«لأَنَّ الـدُّعَاءَ هُوَ العِبَادَةُ» . [رواه الترمزي] .

"Because supplication is worship" (*Tirmidhi*).

4. Among the nullifiers of Belief is to rule by other than what Allah has revealed; if it is accompanied by the belief that Allah's Laws are inappropriate or less appropriate, or that man made laws which contradict them are equally appropriate; Allah said:

﴿ إِنِ ٱلْحُكْمُ إِلَّا لِلَّهِ أَمَرَ أَلَّا تَعْبُدُوٓا۟ إِلَّآ إِيَّاهُ ذَٰلِكَ ٱلدِّينُ ٱلْقَيِّمُ وَلَـٰكِنَّ أَكْثَرَ ٱلنَّاسِ لَا يَعْلَمُونَ ﴾

"...The command (or the judgement) is for none but Allah. He has commanded that you worship none but Him (i.e. His Monotheism), that is the (true) straight religion, but most men know not." (V. 12: 40)

And Allah said:

﴿ وَمَن لَّمْ يَحْكُم بِمَآ أَنزَلَ ٱللَّهُ فَأُو۟لَـٰٓئِكَ هُمُ ٱلْكَـٰفِرُونَ ﴾

"...And whosoever does not judge by what Allah has revealed, such are the *Kâfirûn* (i.e. disbelievers — of a lesser degree as they do not act on Allah's Laws)." (V. 5: 44)

In case the ruler is applying the law other than what Allah

has revealed, while believing that the revealed Law is the only Legitimate Law, but he contradicted it on the basis of personal whim and inclination or because of what he considers to be external pressure beyond his control, then he is unjust and tyrannical or corrupt, but he did not cross the line of disbelief, this is according to the statement of Ibn Abbas رضي الله عنهما who said:

"Whoever repudiates what Allah has revealed, then he surely disbelieved, while one who accepted it (while acting in contradiction to it), he is unjust and corrupt."

This is the interpretation of the verse chosen by the great exegete Ibn Jarir At-Tabari, and 'Ata said with regard to the second state:

"A level of disbelief below the level which takes one out of Islam."

As for those who suspended the Laws of Allah and replaced them with man-made laws which oppose them, believing in the validity of their man-made laws, they have disbelieved and gone out of Islam, by the consensus of the scholars.

5. Among the nullifiers of Belief is displeasure with Allah's Legislation, or the opinion that it is too confining and strict or that it imposes undue hardship. Allah said:

﴿ فَلَا وَرَبِّكَ لَا يُؤْمِنُونَ حَتَّى يُحَكِّمُوكَ فِيمَا شَجَرَ بَيْنَهُمْ ثُمَّ لَا يَجِدُوا فِي أَنفُسِهِمْ حَرَجًا مِّمَّا قَضَيْتَ وَيُسَلِّمُوا تَسْلِيمًا ﴾

"But no, by your Lord, they can have no Faith, until they make you (صلى الله عليه وسلم) judge in all disputes between them, and find in themselves no resistance against your decisions, and accept (them) with full submission." (V. 4: 65)

Or to dislike the order which is revealed, as Allah عز وجل said:

45

$$\{ \text{وَٱلَّذِينَ كَفَرُواْ فَتَعْسًا لَّهُمْ وَأَضَلَّ أَعْمَٰلَهُمْ ۝ ذَٰلِكَ بِأَنَّهُمْ كَرِهُواْ مَآ أَنزَلَ ٱللَّهُ فَأَحْبَطَ أَعْمَٰلَهُمْ} \}$$

"But those who disbelieve (in the Oneness of Allah — Islamic Monotheism), for them is destruction, and (Allah) will make their deeds vain. That is because they hate that which Allah has sent down (this Qur'ân and Islamic laws, etc.), so He has made their deeds fruitless." (V. 47: 8, 9)

3. *Shirk* in Allah's Attributes nullifies *Imân*

This third category includes denial of some or all of Allah's Attributes or His Names or their deprecation.

1. It nullifies Belief when a believer denies the Names of Allah or His Attributes which are established by the texts of the Qur'ân and the authentic *Sunnah*; for example, to deny that Allah's Knowledge is total, or His Power, or His Life or His Hearing or Sight or Speech or Mercy, or His Establishment over His Throne or His Transcendence above it, or His Descent to the lowest heaven or that He has a Hand or an Eye, or other than that of the Attributes which befit His Splendour and which do not resemble the attributes of anything in creation. Allah said:

$$\{ \text{لَيْسَ كَمِثْلِهِۦ شَىْءٌ ۖ وَهُوَ ٱلسَّمِيعُ ٱلْبَصِيرُ} \}$$

"...There is nothing like unto Him, and He is the All-Hearer, the All-Seer." (V. 42: 11)

In this verse Allah denied His Resemblance to His creatures, and attributed to Himself the faculties of hearing and sight; and all His other Attributes must be understood in the same way.

2. It is an error and misguidance to interpret some of His affirmed Attributes, and to divert the meanings of the words

used to describe them from their primary meaning in the Arabic language to obscure meanings, like the interpretation of the word *Istawa* which means ascension and establishment above something, to mean *Istila* which means to take power. Imam Bukhari in his *Sahih* transmitted the authentic interpretation of *Istawa* from Mujahid and Abul-Aliyah, two of the prominent scholars among the *Tabi'în*, the successors of the *Sahâba*. The diversionary interpretation of Allah's Attributes leads to their denial. As the interpretation of *Istawa* meaning to take power is, in fact, a denial of one of Allah's Attributes, which is Allah's Elevation above His Throne, which is established in numerous places in the Qur'ân and *Sunnah*. Allah عز وجل said:

$$﴿ ٱلرَّحْمَٰنُ عَلَى ٱلْعَرْشِ ٱسْتَوَىٰ ﴾$$

"The Most Beneficent (Allah) *Istawa* (rose over) the (mighty) Throne (in a manner that suits His Majesty)." (V. 20:5)

And Allah عز وجل said:

$$﴿ ءَأَمِنتُم مَّن فِي ٱلسَّمَآءِ أَن يَخْسِفَ بِكُمُ ٱلْأَرْضَ ﴾$$

Do you feel secure that He, Who is over the heaven (Allah), will not cause the earth to sink with you..." (V. 67:16)

And the Prophet صلى الله عليه وسلم said:

«إنَّ اللهَ كَتَبَ كِتَاباً. . فَهُوَ عِنْدَهُ فَوْقَ الْـعَرْشِ». [متفق عليه].

"Allah recorded a Book which is with Him above the Throne." (Agreed upon).

This type of interpretation of the Divine Attributes is a form of distortion as Sheikh Muhammad Amin Shinqeeti states in his book "منهج و دراسات في الأسماء والصفات - Studies in the (Divine) Names and Attributes" on page 26:

47

"To sum up the issue, I would like to make two points. First the interpreter should consider Allah's Statement to the Jews:

$$﴿ وَقُولُواْ حِطَّةٌ ﴾$$

"...say *Hittatun*..." (V. 2:58)

Hittatun (حطة) means repentance, they added a letter "N- ن" in it and said "*Hintatun*" (حنطة meaning wheat), Allah called this addition a change. Allah said in *Surah Al-Baqarah:*

$$﴿ فَبَدَّلَ ٱلَّذِينَ ظَلَمُواْ قَوْلاً غَيْرَ ٱلَّذِى قِيلَ لَهُمْ فَأَنزَلْنَا عَلَى ٱلَّذِينَ ظَلَمُواْ رِجْزاً مِّنَ ٱلسَّمَآءِ بِمَا كَانُواْ يَفْسُقُونَ ﴾$$

"But those who did wrong changed the word from that which had been told to them for another, so We sent upon the wrong-doers *Rijzan* (a punishment) from the heaven because of their rebelling against Allah's obedience." (*T. At-Tabari*, Vol. I, P. 305). (V. 2:59)

Likewise are those who interpret Allah's Attributes with diversionary interpretation, it was said to them *Istawa* (استوى), so they added an "L-ل" and said *Istawla* (استولى). Consider the resemblance between the "L-ل" they added and the "N-ن" the Jews added (this point was originally mentioned by Ibn Qaiyim)."

3. There are certain Attributes which are exclusive to Allah, like Knowledge of the unseen, which no one in creation possesses. Allah said in His Book:

$$﴿ ۞ وَعِندَهُۥ مَفَاتِحُ ٱلْغَيْبِ لاَ يَعْلَمُهَآ إِلاَّ هُوَ ﴾$$

"And with Him are the keys of the *Ghaib* (all that is hidden), none knows them but He..." (V. 6: 59)

Allah might reveal certain aspects of the unseen to His Messengers through Revelation when He wants; Allah said:

$$﴿ عَـٰلِمُ ٱلۡغَيۡبِ فَلَا يُظۡهِرُ عَلَىٰ غَيۡبِهِۦٓ أَحَدًا ۝ إِلَّا مَنِ ٱرۡتَضَىٰ مِن رَّسُولٍ ﴾$$

"(He Alone) the All-Knower of the *Ghaib* (unseen), and He reveals to none His *Ghaib* (unseen) except to a Messenger (from mankind) whom He has chosen (He informs him of unseen as much as He likes)..." (V. 72: 26, 27)

Among the statements of disbelief and error is the statement of the poet Al-Busairy in *Qasidah Burdah* describing the Prophet صلى الله عليه وسلم :

"Verily, from your generosity is the world and its rival (that is the Hereafter) and a part of your knowledge is the knowledge of the Tablet and the Pen."

This world and the Hereafter are certainly part of the creation of Allah and from His Generosity, not from the generosity or creation of the Messenger, as the poet claimed.

Allah عز وجل said:

$$﴿ وَإِنَّ لَنَا لَلۡأَخِرَةَ وَٱلۡأُولَىٰ ﴾$$

"And truly, unto Us (belong) the last (Hereafter) and the first (this world)." (V. 92: 13)

And Allah's Messenger صلى الله عليه وسلم does not know what is in the Preserved Tablet, nor what the Pen wrote, as the poet claimed, since this is part of the absolute unseen, which no one knows except Allah. As the Qur'ân mentioned :

$$﴿ قُل لَّا يَعۡلَمُ مَن فِي ٱلسَّمَـٰوَٰتِ وَٱلۡأَرۡضِ ٱلۡغَيۡبَ إِلَّا ٱللَّهُ ﴾$$

"Say: None in the heavens and the earth knows the *Ghaib* (unseen) except Allah." (V. 27: 65)

As for the saints, it is only logical that they have less access to knowledge of the absolute unseen as they do not even have access to direct Revelation by which Allah informed His Prophets and Messengers of certain aspects of the unseen, because Revelation does not descend on saints; it is reserved for Prophets and Messengers, so whoever else claims knowledge of the unseen, and whoever believes their claims, has nullified his belief in Islâm. The Prophet صلى الله عليه وسلم said:

$$\text{«مَنْ أَتَى كَاهِناً أَوْ عَرَّافاً فَصَدَّقَهُ بِمَا يَقُولُ فَقَدْ كَفَرَ بِمَا أُنْزِلَ عَلَى مُحَمَّدٍ».} \quad [\text{صحيح رواه أحمد}].$$

"Whoever goes to a fortuneteller or astrologer and believes what he says, he disbelieved in what was revealed to Muhammad." (*Ahmad*)

Occasionally the predictions of these fortunetellers do turn out true, but part of that is due to chance, because they are guessing and trying to extrapolate on what they already know. If they were really truthful in their claim to knowledge of the unseen, they would be right all the time, and they would have informed us of the secrets of the Jews, and they could have uncovered all the buried treasures of the earth, and they would not be dependent on the people for money, taking their wealth from them under false pretenses.

4. Defamation of Prophets nullifies *Imân*

This fourth category is the rejection of any of the Messengers of Allah or defaming their characters, these are the following :

1. To deny the Message of Muhammad صلى الله عليه وسلم because the testimony that 'Muhammad is the Messenger of Allah' is one of the pillars of Belief.

2. To disparage the Messenger of Allah صلى الله عليه وسلم or his truthfulness, or his faithfulness in discharge of what he was entrusted with, or his chasteness or to revile him or make fun of him, or make light of him, or to find fault with any of his documented behaviour.

3. To attack his authentic *Ahadîth* (transmitted sayings) and disbelieve them, or to reject the true news which he has described for us including his documented prophecies, such as the appearance of the *Dajjal* (the Antichrist) or the descent of Jesus عليه السلام who will rule by the *Shar'iah* of Muhammad صلى الله عليه وسلم and other prophecies documented in the Qur'ân and *Sunnah*, after accepting the attribution of the *Ahadith* to the Prophet صلى الله عليه وسلم as being authentic.

4. To deny any of the Messengers sent by Allah before Muhammad صلى الله عليه وسلم or to deny the stories and sayings in regards to them and their nations, as reported in the Qur'ân or by the Messenger of Allah صلى الله عليه وسلم in authentic *Ahadîth*.

5. To claim Prophethood after Muhammad صلى الله عليه وسلم for example Ghulam Ahmed, the *Qadiani*, who claimed Prophethood, while the Qur'ân says in this verse:

﴿ مَّا كَانَ مُحَمَّدٌ أَبَآ أَحَدٍ مِّن رِّجَالِكُمۡ وَلَٰكِن رَّسُولَ ٱللَّهِ وَخَاتَمَ ٱلنَّبِيِّـۧنَ ﴾

"Muhammad (صلى الله عليه وسلم) is not the father of any man among you, but he is the Messenger of Allah, and the Last (end) of the Prophets..." (V. 33: 40)

And the Messenger of Allah صلى الله عليه وسلم said:

« . . . أَنَا الْعَاقِبُ الَّذِي لَيْسَ بَعْدَهُ نَبِيٌّ . . . » . [متفق عليه].

"I am the last one, after whom there will be no Prophet." (Agreed upon).

And anyone who believes that there is a Prophet after Muhammad صلى الله عليه وسلم whether he is a *Qadiani* or from any other group, he disbelieved and nullified his Belief.

6. To describe the Prophet صلى الله عليه وسلم with attributes which belong to Allah only, such as unlimited knowledge of the unseen, as some *Sufi* claim. One of their poets said :

51

"O (total) knower of the unseen, we resorted to you;
O cure of the hearts, blessing upon you."

7. To supplicate to the Prophet صلى الله عليه وسلم for what only Allah has the power to bestow, such as supplicating for victory and help, cure of illness etc. as is happening today among the Muslims, especially among the *Sufi* as their poet, Al-Busairy said :

"Whoever, by the Messenger of Allah gets victory, if a lion meets him in the forest;

Never did time impose on me a hardship and I sought his protection except that I got his protection and no harm came to me."

This conception of the station of the Prophet صلى الله عليه وسلم is *Shirk*, contradicting the unequivocal announcement of the Qur'ân:

$$﴿ وَمَا ٱلنَّصْرُ إِلَّا مِنْ عِندِ ٱللَّهِ ﴾$$

"...And there is no victory except by the help of Allah..." (V. 8:10)

and contradicting the order of the Prophet صلى الله عليه وسلم :

« إِذَا سَأَلْتَ فَاسْأَلِ اللهَ وَإِذَا اسْتَعَنْتَ فَاسْتَعِن بِاللهِ » . [رواه الترمذي].

"When you ask, ask from Allah, and when you seek help, seek the help of Allah." (*Tirmidhi*)

So what should we think about those who attribute to "saints" knowledge of the unseen, or make a *Nadhr* (a vow to give charity or perform some other optional good deed) for their sake, or dedicate animal sacrifices to them or ask of them what may only be requested of Allah, such as sustenance or cure of illness, or victory, etc. ? No doubt, these are *Shirk*.

8. We do not deny the miracles that appeared from the Messengers of Allah nor those charismata that came out from the saints, but what we deny is making them partners with

Allah, supplicating them as we supplicate Allah, and dedicating sacrifies to them, and undertaking a regime of optional worship for their sake. It has gotten to the point that the graves of some ostensible "saints" are showered with donations which are appropriated by the custodians and servants of these shrines, who divide them among themselves, consuming people's money under false pretenses, while surrounded by multitudes of poor people who don't get enough to eat for a day.

One poet said :

"Our living don't even get a Dirham (a coin of silver), while thousands and thousands go to the dead."

Not all of these shrines and graves even contain the body of a saint. But swindlers erect some of them as a means of taking the money of the gullible.

For example, one of my fellow teachers related to me that a certain *Sufi Shaikh* came to his mother's house requesting a donation in order to erect a green flag to indicate the presence of a saint on a certain street, so she gave him some money. He bought some green cloth and fixed it to a wall and started telling people there is a *Wali* (saint) here, one of the friends of Allah. "I saw him in a dream." And thus he started collecting money. One day the government decided to widen that street, which would require removing the grave. The man who had started the whole story started telling people that they had tried to remove it, but the equipment used had broken, and some people believed him, and this rumor started circulating, which caused the government to proceed with caution. The *Mufti* of that country himself told me that government called him in the middle of the night to the site of the saint's grave. He found it surrounded by soldiers. Then the excavator was brought and the grave was dug up. The *Mufti* looked inside and found nothing there, and knew that the whole thing was a lie and a fabrication.

Another example, which I heard from a teacher in the *Haram* in Makkah: One poor man met another and they complained to each other of their poverty. Then they saw a saints' grave which was filled with wealth. One said to the other : "Come on, let's dig up a grave and put a saint in it, and the money will start rolling in." His friend agreed, so they set out until they came to a braying donkey. They killed it and laid it to rest in a pit, then raised a mausoleum with a dome over it. And then both of them proceeded to roll around in the dust of the grave, to get the *Barakat* (blessing) from it. When people passing by asked them "What's up?" They said: "This is the grave of the saint, Hubaish bin Tubaish, who worked miracles which defy description" People were taken in by their spell and they began laying donations before the grave, as charity and to fulfill vows, until they had gathered great wealth. When they started dividing it, they got into an argument and started shouting at each other, which attracted a crowd of spectators. One of the two said: "I swear to you by this saint I didn't take anything from you." His friend said: "You swear to me by this saint while both of us know there is a donkey in this grave, we buried him together." The people were astonished and felt sheepish at the donations they had made as vows, and took them back after beating the two men.

THE BOOK OF *TAHARAH* (PURIFICATION)

* The categories of water

* Etiquette of going to the bathroom

* How to perform *Wudu* (ablution)

* Factors which nullify *Wudu*

* Wiping over leather or cloth socks

* The *Ghusl* (obligatory bath) and the things which make it mandatory

* Things forbidden to a *Junub* (a person in need of a *Ghusl*)

* The fundamental constituents (*Arkân*) of *Ghusl*

* The *Sunnah* way of the *Ghusl*

* *Ghusl* which are *Mustahab* (desirable)

* Some issues concerning *Ghusl*

* *Mash* (wiping) over a bandage or cast

* *Tayammum* (purification with pure dust and clay) and the circumstances which make it permissible

* The dust to be used for *Tayammum*

* How to perform *Tayammum*

* Factors which nullify *Tayammum*

* The *Salat* of a person who has no access to water nor to pure dust

* *Haid* (menstruation) and *Nifas* (post-partum bleeding)

* Things forbidden to a menstruating woman or one in post-partum bleeding

* *Istihadah* (non-menstrual vaginal bleeding) and the rules associated with it

THE CATEGORIES OF WATER

First: Ordinary water is *Tahûr*, that is, it is pure in itself and purifies other things. Among its division are:

1. Rainfall, snow and hail; Allah said:

﴿ وَأَنزَلْنَا مِنَ ٱلسَّمَاءِ مَاءً طَهُورًا ﴾

"...And We send down pure water from the sky," (V. 25: 48)

2. Water of springs and rivers.

3. Sea water, as the Prophet ﷺ said:

هُوَ الطَّهُورُ مَاؤُهُ الحِلُّ مَيْتَتُهُ». [صحيح رواه الخمسة].

"Its water is purifying and its creatures are *Halal* (without the need to slaughter)."

4. Zam-zam water.

«لَمَّا ثَبَتَ أَنَّ الرَّسُولَ ـ ﷺ ـ دَعَا بِسَجْلٍ مِنْ مَاءِ زَمْزَمَ فَشَرِبَ مِنْهُ وَتَوَضَّأً». [حسن رواه أحمد].

It is established that the Prophet ﷺ called for a bucket of Zam-zam water, then drank from it and performed *Wudu* (*Ahmad*).

5. Water which has changed due to stagnation for a long time, or by tree leaves settling in it or moss growing in it, because it is still valid to call it "water" without qualifying the word, therefore it is valid to use it for purification. Allah said:

﴿ فَلَمْ تَجِدُوا مَاءً فَتَيَمَّمُوا ﴾

"And if you find no water, perform *Tayammum*" (V. 5:6).

Second: Used water, that is, water which flows off the limbs when performing *Wudu* or *Ghusl* pertains its purifying quality, just like ordinary water, based on the fact that it started out as

56

purifying and there is no *Dalîl* (reason) from the *Shari'ah* (Islamic Laws) indicating a change in its status.

Third: Water mixed with any clean substance, for instance soap or saffron, or flour, etc. remains purifying (*Tahûr*) as long as the quantity of the adulterant is not enough to cause us to stop calling the mixture "water". If it exceeds that limit when we can no longer call it simply water, then it is *Tahir*: pure in itself, but incapable of purifying anything else.

Fourth: Water mixed with *Najâsah* (filthy substance), this can occur in one of the two stages:

1. The taste or color or smell of the water changes due to the *Najâsah*, in which case, the water is not permissible to be used for purification by the consensus of the scholars.

2. None of the three qualities of the water changes: in this case it remains purifying whether its a little or a lot. As the Prophet صلى الله عليه وسلم said:

$$\text{«المَاءُ طَهُورٌ لاَ يُنَجِّسُهُ شَيْءٌ»} \quad . \text{[صحيح أخرجه أحمد وغيره]}$$

"Water is purifying, nothing makes it filthy." (*Ahmad* and others).

And in this case the water has retained the name "Water" without the need to qualify the word.

And the Prophet صلى الله عليه وسلم said:

$$\text{«إِذَا كَانَ المَاءُ قُلَّتَيْنِ لَمْ يَحْمِلِ الخَبَثَ» وفي رواية : «لَمْ يُنَجِّسُهُ}$$
$$\text{شَيْءٌ»} \quad . \text{[صحيح رواه الخمسة]}$$

"If the water is 2 *Qullah*, it doesn't carry impurity" and in a version "nothing makes it filthy." (*Ahmad* and others).

(A *Qullah* is a big water container made from the hide of an animal).

Some scholars used the contrapositive of the last *Hadîth* as evidence. That is, if the water is less than 2 *Qullah*, then contact with *Najâsah* renders it impure.

ETIQUETTE OF GOING TO THE BATHROOM

1. Don't take anything containing the Name of Allah into the bathroom, unless there is fear of losing it by leaving it outside, or if it is wrapped up.

2. To be away from people and screened, especially when defecating.

3. To say the following supplication before entering the bathroom, or if one is outdoors, before removing clothes, as the Prophet صلى الله عليه وسلم said:

«بِسْمِ اللهِ اللّٰهُمَّ إِنِّي أَعُوذُ بِكَ مِنَ الْخُبُثِ وَالْخَبَائِثِ».

"In the Name of Allah, O Allah I seek refuge with you from all the evils."

إِذَا خَرَجَ مِنَ الْخَلَاءِ قَالَ: « غُفْرَانَكَ ».

[صحيح رواه الترمذي انظر الإرواء ج ١/ ٩١].

And after leaving the toilet to say:

Your forgiveness (O Lord)." (*Tirmidhi*)

4. To refrain from speaking altogether, whether it be *Dhikr* (Remembrance of Allah) or anything else. One should not return *Salam* (greetings) nor repeat after the *Mu'adhdhin*, or anything else except what is unavoidable like guiding a blind man who would otherwise fall. If one sneezes one should say *Al hamdulillah* in one's mind without moving the tongue.

5. To respect the *Qiblah* by not facing it nor turning one's back directly towards it.

58

6. When outdoors, one should try to choose a place where the earth is soft and low-lying so that the likelihood of getting *Najâsah* on oneself is reduced.

7. When outdoors, avoid going in an animal's hole or burrow, as it could make life as uncomfortable for you as you did for it.

8. Avoid places where people take rest in the shade, or their paths, or places they sit to talk.

9. Do not urinate where you bathe or shower, or in still or running water.

10. Don't urinate in a standing position, as it is undignified, and goes against good customs, and there is the probability of urine splashing up from the ground onto your clothes. However, if one is reasonably sure there will be no splashing, then it is permitted.

11. One must remove all *Najâsah* from the private parts, front or back, at the very least with stones or anything that serves the purpose as long as the substance is solid, *Tahir*, and has a blotting or wiping effect; the use of toilet paper is all right, but one should not use paper with writing on it, as it is deserving of more respect than that or one can use water only, or a combination of toilet paper followed by water.

12. One should not use the right hand to clean one's private parts, as it is used for eating and other clean functions.

13. After cleaning the private parts, rub clean earth on the hand, or wash with soap, etc.

14. One should sprinkle water on one's penis and trousers after urinating. This is to stop the whispering of *Shaitân,*

15. When entering the bathroom put your left foot first, and when leaving it, take out your right foot first.

HOW TO PERFORM *WUDÛ* (ABLUTION)

Allah عز وجل said:

﴿يَـٰٓأَيُّهَا ٱلَّذِينَ ءَامَنُوٓاْ إِذَا قُمْتُمْ إِلَى ٱلصَّلَوٰةِ فَٱغْسِلُواْ وُجُوهَكُمْ وَأَيْدِيَكُمْ إِلَى ٱلْمَرَافِقِ وَٱمْسَحُواْ بِرُءُوسِكُمْ وَأَرْجُلَكُمْ إِلَى ٱلْكَعْبَيْنِ﴾

"O you who believe! When you intend to offer prayer, wash your faces and your hands (forearms) up to the elbows, rub (by passing wet hands over) your heads, and (wash) your feet up to ankles..." (V. 5: 6).

1. Before starting it one should intend to enter the state of ritual purity by the actions of the ablution and say *Bismillah*.

2. Wash your hands up to the wrists, rinse water in your mouth and draw water from your cupped hand into your nose up to the start of the nose bone—three times for each of these actions.

3. Wash your face three times.

4. Starting with the right hand, wash your forearms up to and including the elbows three times.

5. Wipe your wet hands over your hair or scalp (all of it) and wipe the inside and back of the ears with the forefingers and thumb.

6. Wash the feet up to and including the ankles three times each, starting with the right foot.

7. After completing the aforementioned, say :

اشهد ألاّ إله إلاّ الله وحده لاشريك له وأشهد أن محمداً عبده ورسوله

"I bear witness that none has the right to be worshipped but Allah Alone and without partners, and I bear witness that Muhammad is His slave and His Messenger."

FACTORS WHICH NULLIFY WUDÛ

There are some factors which nullify the ablution and destroy the object of purification like *Salât* etc. These are the following:

1. All things coming out of the private parts, front or back, including urine, excrement, and gas; whether it escapes silently or audibly. The Prophet ﷺ said:

«لاَ يَقْبَلُ اللهُ صَلاَةَ أَحَدِكُمْ إِذَا أَحْدَثَ حَتَّى يَتَوَضَّأَ». [رواه مسلم].

"Allah will not accept *Salât* (prayer) from anyone if he passes out anything from his private parts until he performs *Wudû* (ablution)." (*Muslim*).

2. The seeping out of *Madhî* or *Wadî*; *Madhî* is prostatic fluid which seeps out during sexual arousal, before ejaculation; and *Wadî* is a fluid which seeps out after urination without any accompanying sexual arousal. The Prophet ﷺ, when asked what one should do if *Madhî* is excreted, said:

«يَغْسِلُ ذَكَرَهُ وَيَتَوَضَّأُ». [متفق عليه].

"He should wash his penis and perform *Wudû*". (Agreed upon).

3. Deep sleep, the kind where no trace of wakeful consciousness remains; such that if one started out sitting up, he would end up slumping over onto the ground.

4. A loss of rational consciousness; whether by way of insanity or fainting or drunkenness or sedation.

5. To touch one's private parts without an intervening barrier (of cloth etc.). The Prophet ﷺ said:

«مَنْ مَسَّ ذَكَرَهُ فَلاَ يُصَلِّ حَتَّى يَتَوَضَّأَ». [صححه الترمذي وقال البخاري وهو أصح شيء في الباب].

61

"Whoever touches his penis, he should not pray until he performs *Wudû* (ablution)."

(Tirmidhi classed it as authentic, Bukhâri said it is the most authentic *Hadîth* related to the issue).

Things which do not nullify *Wudû*

1. Touching a woman with skin to skin contact. Aisha رضي الله عنها said:

$$﴿كُنْتُ أَنَامُ بَيْنَ يَدَيِ النَّبِيِّ - ﷺ - وَرِجْلَايَ فِي قِبْلَتِهِ فَإِذَا أَرَادَ أَنْ يَسْجُدَ غَمَزَ رِجْلَيَّ﴾ . [متفق عليه].$$

"I used to sleep in front of the Prophet صلى الله عليه وسلم and my feet would be between him and the *Qiblah* (the direction of Ka'bah), so when he performed *Sajdah* (prostration), he would touch my feet." (Agreed upon)

2. The flow of blood from anywhere other than the vagina, whether because of a wound or cupping or nosebleed. Hasan رضي الله عنه said:

$$﴿مَازَالَ الْمُسْلِمُونَ يُصَلُّونَ فِي جِرَاحَاتِهِم﴾ .$$

"The Muslims used to keep on praying while wounded." (*Bukhâri*)

3. Vomit, whether enough to fill the mouth or less.

4. Being doubtful regarding excretion (of stool, urine, gas etc., from private parts) after performing *Wudu*. This uncertainty does not require consideration whether one is in *Salât* or outside it, since certain knowledge cannot be superseded by uncertainty. In contrast, if he is sure of excretion, and he doubts whether he performed *Wudu* or not after it, his *Wudu* would not be treated as established.

5. Laughing aloud while in *Salât* does not invalidate *Wudû*. There is a weak *Hadîth* which states that it does invalidate

Wudû, but a weak *Hadîth* can not be used to establish a point of law.

6. To give a bath to a dead person does not require one to perform *Wudû* afterwards. There is some evidence which caused some scholars to rule that it does, but when all the evidence on the issue is considered, the result is that *Wudû* is recommended but not required.

WIPING OVER LEATHER OR CLOTH SOCKS

1. Evidence for the permissibility of wiping (*Mash* سح) over leather socks while performing *Wudû* (ablution), rather than removing them: The *Sunnah* is well established, that there is no need to remove one's leather socks, whether in travel or at home. Among the strongest *Hadîth* on the issue is what Bukhâri reported from Jarîr bin Abdullah رضي الله عنه ; he said:

عن جرير بن عبدالله قال رأيت رسول الله ـ ﷺ ـ «بَالَ ثُمَّ تَوَضَّأَ وَمَسَحَ عَلَى خُفَّيْهِ» . [رواه البخاري وغيره].

"I saw that the Messenger of Allah urinated, then performed *Wudû* and wiped over his leather socks."

2. Evidence for the permissibility of wiping over cloth and nylon socks: It was a practice of many *Sahâbah* (Companions of the Prophet صلى الله عليه وسلم), Abû Dâwûd said:

"Ali bin Abi Tâlib, 'Abdullah bin Mas'ûd, Bara' bin 'Âzib, and Anas bin Mâlik used to wipe over cloth socks, and it is reported also regarding 'Umar bin Al-Khattab and Ibn Abbâs."

Ibn Al-Qaiyim mentioned in his book *Tahdheeb As-Sunan* from Ibn Al-Mundir that Imam Ahmad clearly stated his view that wiping on cloth socks is permissible, which indicates his fairness. He relied in that on the practice of the *Sahâbah* and on the clear analogy (between cloth socks and leather socks).

63

Other scholars who considered it permissible were Sufyan Thauri, Abdullah bin Mubârak, Ata bin Rabah Hasan Basri, Sa'eed bin Musaiyab; and according to Abû Yûsuf and Muhammad bin Hasan, it is permissible if the socks are thick enough that the skin under them cannot be seen.

Abû Hanifah used to consider wiping on thick cloth socks not permissible but he changed his mind 3 or 4 days or a week before his death. He would wipe over his thick socks in his death-illness and he would tell his visitors, "I'm doing what I used to prohibit."

Mughirah bin Shu'bah reported:

«أَنَّ رَسُولَ الله ـ ﷺ ـ تَوَضَّأَ وَمَسَحَ عَلَى الْجُورَبَيْنِ وَالنَّعْلَيْنِ» .

[رواه أحمد وغيره والترمذي وقال حسن صحيح] .

"Allah's Messenger صلى الله عليه وسلم performed *Wudû* (ablution) and wiped over his cloth socks and sandals." (*Ahmad* and *Tirmidhi*, who graded it *Hasan Sahih*).

Conditions for wiping over leather and cloth socks

1. In order to be able to complete *Wudû* by wiping over socks, one must put on both of them while in a state of *Wudû*.

2. Where to wipe: Over the top of each sock, based on the following *Hadîth* from Ali رضي الله عنه , he said:

«لَوْ كَانَ الدِّينُ بِالرَّأْيِ لَكَانَ أَسْفَلَ الْخُفِّ أَوْلَى بِالْمَسْحِ مِنْ أَعْلَاهُ، لَقَدْ رَأَيْتُ رَسُولَ الله ـ ﷺ ـ يَمْسَحُ عَلَى ظَاهِرِ خُفَّيْهِ» .

[رواه أبوداود والدارقطني، وإسناده صحيح] .

"If the religion was according to opinion, it would be more fitting to wipe the bottom of the sock, rather than the top.

64

Surely, I saw Allah's Messenger ﷺ wiping over the tops of his socks." (*Abu Dawûd* and *Ad-Daraqutni*)

3. How long can you keep wiping over the socks without taking them off to wash the feet? The Prophet ﷺ said:

«لِلْمُسَافِرِ ثَلَاثَةَ أَيَّامٍ وَلَيَالِيهِنَّ، وَلِلْمُقِيمِ يَوْمٌ وَلَيْلَةٌ». [رواه مسلم].

"One day and one night, i.e. 24 hours for a resident, from the last *Wudû*, and three days and three nights for a traveller." (*Muslim*).

4. How to wipe: After performing a proper *Wudû* put on the leather or cloth socks, then anytime one wants to perform *Wudû*, instead of washing the feet, wipe over the socks. But if you need to perform a *Ghusl* (bath) you must remove the socks.

5. The following things nullify the permission to wipe over the socks:

a) The elapse of the permitted period.
b) The necessity of *Ghusl-e-Janabat*.
c) Taking off one or both of the socks.

If the permitted time limit ends or one takes off the socks while in a state of *Wudû*, it is sufficient to immediately wash the feet in order to stay in *Wudû* .

THE OBLIGATORY BATH (*GHUSL*) AND THE THINGS WHICH MAKE IT MANDATORY

Obligatory bath (*Ghusl*) means to apply water to every part of the body. Allah عز وجل said:

﴿ وَإِن كُنتُمْ جُنُبًا فَٱطَّهَّرُواْ﴾

"...If you are in a state of *Janâba* (i.e. had a sexual discharge), purify yourself (bathe your whole body)..." (V. 5: 6)

65

And Allah said:

$$﴿ وَيَسْأَلُونَكَ عَنِ ٱلْمَحِيضِ قُلْ هُوَ أَذًى فَٱعْتَزِلُواْ ٱلنِّسَاءَ فِى ٱلْمَحِيضِ وَلَا
تَقْرَبُوهُنَّ حَتَّىٰ يَطْهُرْنَ فَإِذَا تَطَهَّرْنَ فَأْتُوهُنَّ مِنْ حَيْثُ أَمَرَكُمُ ٱللَّهُ إِنَّ ٱللَّهَ يُحِبُّ
ٱلتَّوَّٰبِينَ وَيُحِبُّ ٱلْمُتَطَهِّرِينَ ﴾$$

"They ask you concerning menstruation. Say: that is an *Adha* (a harmful thing for a husband to have a sexual intercourse with his wife while she is having her menses), therefore keep away from women during menses and go not unto them till they have purified (from menses and have taken a bath). And when they have purified themselves, then go in unto them as Allah has ordained for you (go in unto them in any manner as long as it is in their vagina). Truly, Allah loves those who turn unto Him in repentance and loves those who purify themselves (by taking a bath and cleaning and washing thoroughly their private parts and bodies, for their prayers, etc.)." (V. 2 : 222)

There are five things which require one to perform a *Ghusl*:

1. Ejaculation or orgasm with an accompanying fluid discharge, whether sleeping or awake, for males and females. This is the opinion of the majority of scholars, based on the *Hadîth:*

$$«الْمَاءُ مِنَ الْمَاءِ» . [رواه مسلم].$$

   "The water (of the *Ghusl*) is due to the water (of sexual emission)." (*Muslim*)

   However, if seminal fluid flows due to sickness or medication without the accompaniment of sexual arousal, a *Ghusl* is not required. Similarly if one experiences a wet dream but do not find trace of an emission, no *Ghusl* is necessary.

2. Entrance of the head of penis inside the vagina, whether there is ejaculation or not; based on Allah's Statement:

66

$$\text{﴿ وَإِن كُنتُمْ جُنُبًا فَٱطَّهَّرُواْ ﴾}$$

"If you are in a state of *Janâba* (i.e. had a sexual discharge), purify yourself (bathe your whole body)." (V. 5:56)

And based on the statement of the Prophet صلى الله عليه وسلم :

$$\text{«إِذَا جَلَسَ بَيْنَ شُعَبِهَا الْأَرْبَعِ ثُمَّ جَهَدَهَا فَقَدْ وَجَبَ الْغُسْلُ أَنْزَلَ}$$
$$\text{أَمْ لَمْ يُنْزِلْ». [رواه مسلم وغيره].}$$

"If he sat between her four parts and exerted her, the *Ghusl* became mandatory, whether he ejaculated or not." (*Muslim* and others)

3. The termination of menses or post-partum bleeding; based on the Statement of Allah عز وجل :

$$\text{﴿ وَلَا تَقْرَبُوهُنَّ حَتَّىٰ يَطْهُرْنَ فَإِذَا تَطَهَّرْنَ فَأْتُوهُنَّ مِنْ حَيْثُ أَمَرَكُمُ ٱللَّهُ ﴾}$$

"...therefore keep away from women during menses and go not unto them till they have purified (from menses and have taken a bath). And when they have purified themselves, then go in unto them as Allah has ordained for you (go in unto them in any manner as long as it is in their vagina)..." (V. 2 : 222)

And based on the Prophet's statement to Fatimah bint Abi Hubaish:

$$\text{«دَعِي الصَّلَاةَ قَدْرَ الأَيَّامِ الَّتِي كُنْتِ تَحِيضِينَ فِيهَا، ثُمَّ}$$
$$\text{اغْتَسِلِي وَصَلِّي». [متفق عليه].}$$

"Leave *Salât* for the number of days you used to menstruate, then perform a *Ghusl* and offer *Salât*." (Agreed upon)

By this statement, even though it was made about menstruation only, post-partum bleeding gets the same ruling according to the consensus of the *Sahâbah*.

4. Death; if a Muslim dies, he must be given a *Ghusl* (before burial), by the consensus of the scholars.

5. A disbeliever; if he accepts Islam, must perform a *Ghusl*.

6. There is a sixth cause (which is not mandatory according to most scholars) one must perform *Ghusl* before attending *Jumu'ah* Prayers. The Prophet صلى الله عليه وسلم said:

«غُسْلُ الْـجُمُعَةِ وَاجِبٌ عَلَى كُلِّ مُحْتَلِمٍ». [رواه البخاري].

"The *Ghusl* on Friday is mandatory on all who have attained puberty."

(There are some other *Ahadîth* on the issue which make most scholars consider the command here to be conditional on whether one is sweaty and smelly).

THINGS FORBIDDEN TO A *JUNUB*
(a person in a state of major ritual impurity and is in need of a *Ghusl*)

1. *Salât;* based on Allah's عز وجل Statement:

﴿ وَإِن كُنتُمْ جُنُبًا فَٱطَّهَّرُواْ ﴾

"If you are in a state of *Janâba* (i.e. had a sexual discharge), purify yourself (bathe your whole body)." (V. 5: 6)

2. *Tawâf* (circumambulating the *Ka'bah* in Makkah); based on the statement of the Prophet صلى الله عليه وسلم :

«الطَّوَافُ بِالْبَيْتِ صَلَاةٌ إِلَّا أَنَّ اللهَ تَعَالَى أَحَلَّ فِيهِ الْكَلَامَ، فَمَنْ تَكَلَّمَ فَلَا يَتَكَلَّمَنَّ إِلَّا بِخَيْرٍ». [رواه الترمذي والدارقطني وصححه الحاكم وابن السكن وابن خزيمة].

"*Tawâf* around the House is *Salât*, except that Allah has permitted in it (ordinary) speech, so whoever speaks should speak nothing but good." (*Tirmidhi*)

3. To touch the Qur'ân or carry it; its prohibition is agreed upon by all the *Imam*.

4. To stay in the *Masjid*; based on Allah's Statement:

﴿ يَـٰٓأَيُّهَا ٱلَّذِينَ ءَامَنُوا۟ لَا تَقْرَبُوا۟ ٱلصَّلَوٰةَ وَأَنتُمْ سُكَـٰرَىٰ حَتَّىٰ تَعْلَمُوا۟ مَا تَقُولُونَ وَلَا جُنُبًا إِلَّا عَابِرِى سَبِيلٍ حَتَّىٰ تَغْتَسِلُوا۟ ﴾

"O you who believe! Approach not prayer when you are in a drunken state until you know (the meaning) of what you utter, nor when you are in a state of *Janâba*, (i.e. in a state of sexual impurity and have not yet taken a bath) except when travelling on the road (without enough water, or just passing through a mosque), till you wash your whole body..." (V. 4: 43).

The prohibition is relaxed for both of these classes (the drunk and the *Junub*) if they are just passing through that phase, based on this verse and the statement of the Prophet صلى الله عليه وسلم to Aisha رضي الله عنها :

«نَاوِلِينِي الْـخُمْرَةَ مِنَ الـمَسْجِدِ فَقَالَتْ: إِنِّي حَائِضٌ فَقَالَ: إِنَّ حَيْضَتَكِ لَيْسَتْ فِي يَدِكِ». [رواه الجماعة إلا البخاري].

"Get me the prayer mat from the *Masjid*." She said "I'm menstruating." He said, "Your menstruation is not in your hand." (A group of traditional reporters except Al-Bukhari).

THE FUNDAMENTAL CONSTITUENTS (*ARKAN*) OF *GHUSL*

The prescribed *Ghusl,* in accordance with the *Shari'ah,* is not complete without two components:

1. The intention, which distinguishes this prescribed *Ghusl* from an ordinary bath (that is, to intend by this bath to leave the state of major ritual impurity and to gain eligibility for acts of worship like *Salât*). The intention is related to the heart and does not require statement by the tongue which many people do these days. This is a heresy in the religion and should be avoided.

2. Washing every part of the body; based on Allah's Statement:

$$ \text{﴿ وَإِن كُنتُمْ جُنُبًا فَٱطَّهَّرُواْ ﴾} $$

"If you are in a state of *Janâba* (i.e. had a sexual discharge) purify yourself (bathe your whole body)." (V. 5: 6)

And His Statement:

$$ \text{﴿ يَٰٓأَيُّهَا ٱلَّذِينَ ءَامَنُواْ لَا تَقْرَبُواْ ٱلصَّلَوٰةَ وَأَنتُمْ سُكَٰرَىٰ حَتَّىٰ تَعْلَمُواْ مَا تَقُولُونَ وَلَا جُنُبًا إِلَّا عَابِرِى سَبِيلٍ حَتَّىٰ تَغْتَسِلُواْ ﴾} $$

"O you who believe! Approach not prayer when you are in a drunken state until you know (the meaning) of what you utter, nor when you are in a state of *Janâba*, (i.e. in a state of sexual impurity and have not yet taken a bath) except when travelling on the road (without enough water, or just passing through a mosque), till you wash your whole body." (V. 4: 43).

The second verse explains the first, indicating that the meaning of purification is the *Ghusl*, and the reality of *Ghusl* in the Arabic language is the flow of water over every part of the body, and this was made clear in the *Sunnah*, as well.

THE *SUNNAH* WAY OF THE *GHUSL*

It is best to observe the *Sunnah* of the Prophet صلى الله عليه وسلم in taking a ritual bath :

70

1. Start by washing hands three times.

2. Wash the private parts of the body.

3. Perform a complete *Wudû*, just like the *Wudû* of the *Sâlat*. Then pour water over the whole body, first the right side, then the left, passing the hands over what one can easily reach of the body, paying particular attention that water reaches all out of the way places like the inside of the ears, the belly button, between the toes, etc. The basis of this is what Âisha رضي الله عنها narrated:

«أنَّ النَّبِي ﷺ ـ كَانَ إِذَا اغْتَسَلَ مِنَ الجَنَابَة يَبْدَأُ فَيَغْسِلُ يَدَيْهِ، ثُمَّ يُفْرِغُ بِيَمِينِهِ عَلى شِمَالِهِ، فَيَغْسِلُ فَرْجَهُ، ثُمَّ يَتَوَضَّأُ وُضُوءَهُ لِلصَّلاةِ، ثُمَّ يَأْخُذُ المَاءَ، وَيُدْخِلُ أَصَابِعَهُ في أُصُولِ الشَّعْـرِ، حَتَّى إِذَا رَأَى أَنَّـهُ استَبْرَأً (أَيْ أَوْصَلَ المَاءَ لِلبَشَرَةِ) حَفَنَ عَلى رَأْسِهِ ثَلاثَ حَثَيَاتٍ ثُمَّ أَفَاضَ عَلى سَائِرِ جَسَدِهِ» .

[متفق عليه]. «انظر فقه السنة ج١/ ٧٢، ٧٣».

"When the Prophet صلى الله عليه وسلم used to take a bath while *Junub*, he would start by washing both hands, then with his right hand he would pour water into his (cupped) left hand and wash his private parts, then he would perform *Wudû*, like the *Wudû* of *Salât*, then he would take water and run his fingers through the roots of his hair until the water had reached the scalp, he would scoop water up with both hands and pour it over his head three times, then he would pour water over the rest of his body." (Agreed upon)

GHUSL WHICH ARE *MUSTAHAB* (DESIRABLE)

Mustahab: The person who does it is praiseworthy and will be rewarded for it, whereas one who doesn't do it is not blameworthy nor will he be punished for leaving it.

1. The *Ghusl* of *Jumu'ah* (Friday). Since Friday is the day of congregational prayer in a large assembly, the Prophet صلى الله عليه وسلم ordered us to perform the *Ghusl*, so that the Muslims should be in the best condition of cleanliness and purity.

The Prophet صلى الله عليه وسلم said:

«غُسْـلُ الجُمُعَةِ واجِبٌ على الـمُحتلِمِ ، وَالسِّـوَاكُ ، وأن يَمسَّ مِنَ الطّيبِ مَايقدِرُ عَليهِ» . [رواه البخاري].

"The *Ghusl* of Friday is obligatory on those who attained puberty, and (also the cleaning of their teeth with) the *Siwak* (tooth brush taken from the twigs of the *Arak* or other tree) and the use of perfume, if available." (*Bukhâri*).

The apparent meaning of the *Hadîth* is that the *Ghusl* of Friday is mandatory, not just *Mustahab*. And most *Hadîth* scholars understood the *Hadîth* according to the apparent meaning as opposed to the interpretation of the *Fuqahâ'* (scholars in the interpretation of religious matters in general- religious jurists).

2. *Ghusl* for the two 'Eid (festival) prayers, as was recommended by the scholars.

3. *Ghusl* for one who has bathed a dead person, the Prophet صلى الله عليه وسلم said:

«مَن غَسَّلَ مَيِّتاً فَلْيَغْتَسِلْ وَمَنْ حَمَلَهُ فَلْيَتَوَضَّأْ» . [حسنه الترمذي وابن حجر].

"Whoever gives bath to a dead person should perform a *Ghusl* and whoever carries him should perform *Wudû*." (*Tirmidhi*).

4. The majority of scholars consider it praiseworthy to perform

a *Ghusl* when entering in the state of *Ihrâm* (and putting ceremonial garment consisting of two unstitched pieces of cloth) for *Hajj* or *'Umrah*.

5. To take a bath upon entering Makkah is also recommended based upon the action of the Prophet صلى الله عليه وسلم .

SOME ISSUES CONCERNING *GHUSL*

1. One *Ghusl* covers two causes: For instance, if a woman had a wet dream just before finishing menstruation or if one took a bath for *Eid Salât* which happened to fall on a Friday, or if one was *Junub* on a Friday. But one should make the intention that the one bath is to take care of two reasons. As the Prophet صلى الله عليه وسلم said:

$$\text{«وَإِنَّما لِكُلِّ امْرِىءٍ مَا نَوَى» [متفق عليه].}$$

"Every person will be judged according to his intention." (Agreed upon)

2. If a person performed a *Ghusl* because he was *Junub* but did not perform the *Wudû*, the *Ghusl* is sufficient. Abu Bakr Ibn Arabi said that the scholars did not differ on the issue of *Wudû* coming under the jurisdiction of the *Ghusl*. And that the intention (*Niyah*) of purification from the major impurity covers the purification from the minor impurity.

3. There's no problem in attending public baths if one can do so without being exposed to the sight of others. Ahmad said: If you know that everyone in the public bath wears a *Izar* (a cloth wrapped around the waist), go ahead in; but if not, then don't.

A *Hadîth* states:

$$\text{«لَا يَنْظُرُ الرَّجُلُ إلى عَوْرَةِ الرَّجُلِ وَلاَ تَنْظُرُ المَرْأَةُ إلى عَوْرَةِ}$$
$$\text{المَرْأَةِ». [رواه مسلم].}$$

73

"A man should not look at another man's private parts nor a woman look at another woman's private parts." (*Muslim*).

4. A man may use the water left in a basin from which a woman has taken bath, and vice versa. Also it is permitted for a man & his wife to take a bath together, drawing water from one container; based on the statement of the Prophet صلى الله عليه وسلم :

«إِنَّ الماءَ لَا يَجْنُبُ» . [رواه الترمذي وقال حسن صحيح] .

"Verily water doesn't become *Junub* (impure)." (Tirmidhi).

5. It is not permissible to take a bath naked in front of people, since exposing one's private parts (to other than one's spouse) is forbidden. However, if one covers himself with a knee-length shirt or sarong etc., there is no problem, as there is also no prohibition on bathing naked where people can't see you.

«فَقَدِ اغْتَسَلَ مُوسىٰ عَلَيهِ السَّلامُ عُرْيَاناً»

It is mentioned in a *Hadîth* in *Bukhâri* that Prophet Moses عليه السلام bathed naked.

6. The *Ghusl* of a woman is just like the *Ghusl* of a man, but she doesn't have to undo her braids if the water can reach the roots of her hair. As was mentioned in the *Hadîth* related by Umm Salamah رضي الله عنها :

«أن امرأة قالت يارسول الله إني امرأة أشد ضفر رأسي، أفأنقضه للجنابة؟ قال : «إِنَّما يَكفِيكِ أَنْ تَحْثِى عَلَيهِ ثَلَاثَ حَثَيَاتٍ مِنْ مَاءٍ، ثُم تُفْضِي على سَائِرِ جَسَدِكِ، فَإِذاً أنتِ قَدْ طَهُرْتِ» . [رواه مسلم] .

A woman said, "O Messenger of Allah, I am a woman who keeps her braid tight. Do I have to undo it when performing a *Ghusl* for *Janâba*?" He said, "It is enough for you to pour three scoops of water over it, then pour water over your whole body, after that your purification is complete." (*Muslim*)

However, there is a *Hadîth* mentioned in the *Mughni* of Ibn Qudâma which indicates that a woman should undo her braid for the *Ghusl* after menses.

MASH (WIPING) OVER A BANDAGE OR CAST

1. It is permitted to wipe over a bandage or other material used to protect the limbs of an injured or sick person.

2. If one cannot wash a limb or the limbs for *Wudû*, then wiping over the bandage becomes mandatory.

3. When is the wiping normally mandatory ? When a person has a wound or broken bone or an injury, and he wants to perform a *Wudû* or a *Ghusl*, he would normally have to wash the affected limb as well, even if it requires heating the water to make it tolerable. However, if he fears harm from washing the afflicted limb, such that the water will increase the affliction, or make him sick, or increase the pain, or delay his recovery then what is required of him is wiping the limb with water. If he fears harm from wiping, he must wrap the limb with a bandage or have a cast put on, to the extent required to cover it and as much extra area as is necessary to secure the bandage. But unnecessary areas should remain uncovered. Then he must wipe over the whole bandage once in the course of his *Wudû* (ablution) or *Ghusl* (bath).

There is no requirement in the case of the bandage or cast that the person be in a state of purity when it is first applied, and there is no time limit on how long one can keep wiping over it. He can keep wiping over it in his *Wudû* and *Ghusl* as long as the reason for doing so remains.

4. The permission to wipe on the bandage ends when it is

removed or it falls off, or when the injury heals so that there is no further need for the bandage.

TAYAMMUM
(PURIFICATION WITH DUST OR CLAY) AND THE CIRCUMSTANCES WHICH MAKE IT PERMISSIBLE

Allah عز وجل said:

﴿ وَإِن كُنتُم مَّرْضَىٰٓ أَوْ عَلَىٰ سَفَرٍ أَوْ جَآءَ أَحَدٌ مِّنكُم مِّنَ ٱلْغَآئِطِ أَوْ لَـٰمَسْتُمُ ٱلنِّسَآءَ فَلَمْ تَجِدُواْ مَآءً فَتَيَمَّمُواْ صَعِيدًا طَيِّبًا فَٱمْسَحُواْ بِوُجُوهِكُمْ وَأَيْدِيكُمْ إِنَّ ٱللَّهَ كَانَ عَفُوًّا غَفُورًا ﴾

"...And if you are ill, or on a journey, or one of you comes after answering the call of nature, or you have been in contact with women (by sexual relations) and you find no water, perform *Tayammum* with clean earth and rub therewith your faces and hands (*Tayammum*). Truly, Allah is Ever Oft-Pardoning, Oft-Forgiving." (V. 4: 43).

Tayammum is permissible as a substitute for *Wudû* or *Ghusl*, whether on a journey or at home, if one of the following circumstances applies:

1. If water is unavailable, as the Prophet صلى الله عليه وسلم said:

«إِنَّ الصَّعِيدَ طَهُورٌ لِمَنْ لَمْ يَجِدِ الماءَ عَشَرَ سِنِينَ» . [رواه أصحاب السنن وقال الترمذي حديث حسن صحيح].

"Dust is purifier for a believer if he doesn't find water, even if it were for ten years." (*Tirmidhi*)

2. If one is wounded or sick and fears that water will increase the illness or delay the recovery, whether that is based on

personal experience or the advice of a reliable doctor.

3. If the water is very cold, and it seems likely to him that its use will harm him, on the condition that he is unable to warm it, even if he has to pay for that, and that it is hard on him to go to bathroom.

4. If water is nearby, but he fears for his life or honour or property or separation from his companions, or if an enemy is between him and the water whether human or nonhuman, or if he is imprisoned, or if he is unable to get it out of a well because he lacks the necessary means, such as a bucket and rope - in all these cases the presence of the water is not different from its absence, like wise; if he fears being accused of something he is innocent of, due to performing a *Ghusl*, then *Tayammum* becomes permissible.

5. If he has some water, but he needs it for drinking, now or later, or to give a drink to an animal, even to a non-biting dog, or he needs it to make dough, or in cooking, or to wash away *Najasah* (impurity), purification of which is essential from his body or clothes or place of prayer; in all these circumstances he can perform *Tayammum*, and save available water for those other uses.

THE DUST TO BE USED FOR *TAYAMMUM*

It is permissible to perform *Tayammum* with clean dust or anything else which is originally earth such as sand, rocks, pebbles; based on the Statement of Allah عزوجل:

﴿فَتَيَمَّمُواْ صَعِيدًا طَيِّبًا﴾

"Then perform *Tayammum* with clean earth." (V. 4: 43)

The scholars of the Arabic language are agreed that "*Sa'īd* صعيد" means the face of the earth, whether dirt or any other geological category.

HOW TO PERFORM *TAYAMMUM*

1. First, make the intention that by this action you want to purify yourself from a state of either minor or major impurity.

2. Say *Bismillah.*

3. Slap the dust with your palms, blow the excess dust off them, then wipe the face and both hands up to and including the wrist. The Prophet (صلى الله عليه وسلم) said:

«إِنَّـما كَانَ يَكْفِيكَ هَذَا وَضَرَبَ النَّبِيُّ ـ ﷺ ـ بِكَفَّيْهِ الأَرْضَ وَتَنفُخُ فِيهِمَا ثُمَّ مَسَحَ بِهِمَا وَجْهَهُ وَكَفَّيْهِ» . [متفق عليه].

"It would have sufficed you to do like this" then he slapped both palms on the earth, blew into them and wiped his face and both hands with them.(Agreed upon)

Things permissible to one who performs *Tayammum*

Tayammum is a substitute for *Wudû* and *Ghusl* when water is unavailable, so whatever one can do after *Wudû* or *Ghusl*, can do after *Tayammum*, such as offering *Salât* or touching the Qur'ân, etc. The entry of the time for *Salât* is not a condition for its validity. And after one *Tayammum,* one can pray as many *Salât* as he wants, whether obligatory or optional. It is in that exactly like *Wudû*, based on the statement of the Prophet صلى الله عليه وسلم :

«إِنَّ الصَّعِيدَ طَهُورُ الـمُسْلِم ، وَإِن لَمْ يَجِد الماءَ عَشرَ سِنِينَ ، فَإِذَا وَجَدَ الماءَ فَلْيُمسَّه بَشرَتَهُ ، فَإِن ذَلِكَ خَيرٌ» . [رواه أحمد والترمذي

"The clean earth is purifier for a Muslim, even if he didn't find water for ten years. But when he finds water he should use it (for *Wudû*) for that is better." (*Ahmad* and *Tirmidhi*).

FACTORS WHICH NULLIFY *TAYAMMUM*

1. Everything which nullifies *Wudû* also nullifies *Tayammum*, as it is its substitute. Also, the presence of water nullifies it, for those who made *Tayammum* due to its absence; and for those who were unable to use it for other excuses, when the excuse is no more and one is able to use water, the *Tayammum* becomes null and void.

2. However, if one performed *Salât* with *Tayammum*, then found water or regained the ability to use it, it is not required to repeat the *Salât*, even if there is time left for it.

THE *SALÂT* OF A PERSON WHO HAS
NO ACCESS TO WATER NOR TO PURE DUST

A person in this condition should go ahead and offer *Salât* as he is, and he is not obligated to repeat the *Salât* later. The proof for this is the *Hadîth* reported by Muslim on the authority of 'Âisha رضي الله عنها that:

«أَنَّهَا اسْتَعَارَتْ مِنْ أَسْمَاءَ قِلادَةً فَهَلَكَتْ، فَأَرْسَلَ رَسُولُ اللهِ ﷺ نَاسًا مِنْ أَصْحَابِهِ فِي طَلَبِهَا، فَأَدْرَكَتْهُمُ الصَّلاةُ فَصَلَّوْا بِغَيْرِ وَضُوءٍ، فَلَمَّا أَتَوا النَّبِيَّ ﷺ شَكَوْا ذَلِكَ إِلَيْهِ، فَنَزَلَتْ آيَةُ التَّيَمُّمِ، فَقَالَ أُسَيْدُ بْنُ حُضَيْرٍ : جَزَاكَ اللهُ خَيْرًا، فَوَاللهِ مَا نَزَلَ بِكَ أَمْرٌ قَطُّ إِلاَّ جَعَلَ اللهُ لَكَ مِنْهُ مَخْرَجًا وَجَعَلَ لِلْمُسْلِمِينَ مِنْهُ بَرَكَةً»

She had borrowed a necklace from her sister Asmâ, then it went missing during an expedition in which she accompanied the Prophet صلى الله عليه وسلم. The Prophet صلى الله عليه وسلم sent some of his Companions to look for it. The time for

Salât became due while they were in the desert so they offered the *Salât* without *Wudû*. When they returned to the Prophet ﷺ they reported it to him, as it bothered them. It was then that the verse of *Tayammum* was revealed. Usaid bin Hudair رضي الله عنه said to 'Âisha رضي الله عنها: "May Allah reward you, by Allah no incident occurs to you, except that Allah makes for you a way out of it, and puts *Barakât* (blessing) in it for the Muslims."

In this incident, the Companions prayed without *Wudû* when they did not had water, which was the one and only purifying agent prescribed for them at the time, and when they informed to the Prophet ﷺ about it he made no objection to what they had done, nor did he order them to repeat their *Salât*.

Imam Nawawî said: "This opinion is based on the strongest proof."

HAID (MENSTRUATION) AND NIFAS (POST-PARTUM BLEEDING)

Haid (حيض): Menstruation. This is a natural type of blood, which flows from the uterus of women after puberty at regular intervals.

Allah created the uterus to receive the fertilized egg, so each month a blood supply is provided for its nurturance. If no fertilized egg implants itself, the lining of the uterus is flushed out, which causes the menstrual flow. If the woman becomes pregnant, the lining is retained and develops further, so menstruation ceases during pregnancy.

Allah has laid down certain rules in connection with menstruation, as a concession to the woman, in consideration of her condition:

A. Menstruation usually lasts 6 or 7 days and nights; with some variation, from woman to woman. Most women have a regular number of days they menstruate each month, although the number of days may fluctuate and the period might come a little early or a little late. So when a woman sees menstrual blood then she should consider herself menstruating. And when it stops she should consider herself as clean. This is the most correct view on this issue, as elucidated by Shaikh Muhammad Salih Al-Uthaimîn in his book: "Natural bleeding of women," and that is the *Madhhab* of Shafi'i, and the choice of Shaikh-ul-Islam Ibn Taimiyah, and was supported by Ibn Qudamah in "*Al- Mughni*".

B. If the colour of the blood is yellowish, or a muddy shade between yellow and black, and it appears during the course of menstruation or in continuance of it before purification, it should be treated as menstrual blood. However, if it appears after complete cessation of the normal coloured menstrual blood, then it should not be considered as menstruation. Umm Atiyah رضي الله عنها said:

«كُنَّا لَا نَعُدُّ الصُّفْرَةَ والكُدْرَةَ بَعْدَ الطُّهْرِ شَيْئاً». [رواه أبو داود بسند صحيح].

"We didn't use to consider the yellowish or mud-coloured flow after the cessation of menses as a thing." (*Abû Dâwûd*).

Nifâs (نفاس): Post-partum bleeding (after the birth of a baby or during delivery, or two or three days before delivery accompanied by labor pains). These are the rules for *Nifâs*:

1. There is no minimum limit to the length of the bleeding; the upper limit is generally within 40 days.

2. Most of the rules of *Nifâs* are just like the rules of menstruation (*Haid*).

THINGS FORBIDDEN TO A MENSTRUATING WOMAN OR ONE IN POST-PARTUM BLEEDING

1. *Salât;* the Prophet صلى الله عليه وسلم said:

81

«إِذَا أَقْبَلَتِ الْحَيْضَةُ فَدَعِي الصَّلَاةَ». [متفق عليه].

"When menstruation starts, leave off *Salât*". (Agreed upon)

2. *Tawâf* of the *Ka'bah;* the Prophet صلى الله عليه وسلم said:

«إِفْعَلِي مَايَفْعَلُهُ الْحَاجُّ غَيْرَ أَلَّا تَطُوفِي بِالْبَيْتِ حَتَّى تَطْهُرِي».

[متفق عليه].

"Do everything the *Haji* (Pilgrim) does, but don't perform *Tawâf* of the house (*Ka'bah*) until you become purified." (Agreed upon)

3. Fasting; as 'Aisha رضي الله عنها narrated:

«كَانَ يُصِيبُنَا ذَلِكَ فَنُؤْمَرُ بِقَضَاءِ الصَّوْمِ وَلَا نُؤْمَرُ بِقَضَاءِ الصَّلَاةِ». [متفق عليه].

"When we menstruated (during the lifetime of the Prophet صلى الله عليه وسلم) we were ordered to make up for the left fasting (of the month of Ramadan) and we were not ordered to make up for *Salât*." (Agreed upon)

4. Sitting in the *Masjid*, or even at the place where 'Eid prayer is performed, based on the *Hadîth*:

«يَخْرُجُ وَذَوَاتُ الْخُدُورِ وَالْحُيَّضُ .. وَفِيهِ يَنْزِلُ الْحَيَّضُ الْمُصَلَّى». [متفق عليه].

"The unmarried virgins, and the mature girls and the menstruating women should come out; but the menstruating women should keep away from *Musalla* — praying place." (Agreed upon)

5. Intercourse; it is forbidden upon the husband to intercourse with a menstruating wife, as it is forbidden for her to let him,

82

based on the Statement of Allah عز وجل :

﴿ وَيَسْأَلُونَكَ عَنِ ٱلْمَحِيضِ قُلْ هُوَ أَذًى فَٱعْتَزِلُوا۟ ٱلنِّسَآءَ فِى ٱلْمَحِـيضِّ وَلَا نَقْرَبُوهُنَّ حَتَّىٰ يَطْهُرْنَّ فَإِذَا تَطَهَّرْنَ فَأْتُوهُنَّ مِنْ حَيْثُ أَمَرَكُمُ ٱللَّهُ ﴾

"They ask you concerning menstruation. Say: that is an *Adha* (a harmful thing for a husband to have a sexual intercourse with his wife while she is having her menses), therefore keep away from women during menses and go not unto them till they have purified (from menses and have taken a bath). And when they have purified themselves, then go in unto them as Allah has ordained for you (go in unto them in any manner as long as it is in their vagina)." (V. 2: 222)

The word (المحيض) *Al-Mahîd*, of the Verse, is equally valid for the time during which menstrual blood flows (menstruation period) and for the place from which it flows (the vagina). The Prophet صلى الله عليه وسلم said:

«إِصْنَعُوا كُلَّ شَيْءٍ إِلَّا النِّكَاحَ». [رواه مسلم].

"You may do everything with them (your menstruating wives) except intercourse." (*Muslim*)

Nawawi in *Al-Majmu* relates Imam Shafi'i's statement: "Whoever does that has committed a major sin" and Nawawi said: Our companions (i.e. the Shâfi'i scholars) and others said: "Whoever says that intercourse with a menstruating woman is legal should be ruled a disbeliever." It is permissible for the husband to kiss his wife or hug her or touch her anywhere besides the pubic region, but it's better to avoid the area between the navel and the knees; based on 'Âisha's statement:

«كَانَ النَّبِيُّ ﷺ يَأْمُرُنِي فَأَتَّزِرُ فَيُبَاشِرُنِي وأَنَا حَائِضٌ». [متفق عليه]. .

83

"The Prophet صلى الله عليه وسلم used to order me to wrap a skirt around my waist and he used to fondle me while I was menstruating." (Agreed upon)

6. Recitation of Qur'ân; Muhammad Salih Al-Uthaimîn says in his book "Natural bleeding of women": After acknowledging the difference of opinion among scholars on this issue: "It is better for a menstruating woman not to recite Qur'ân orally, except if there is a need for that. For instance, if she is teaching Qur'ân, she has to coach her pupils; or if a pupil has to take a test for her recitation or memorization of Qur'ân, etc."

As for *Dhikr*, or saying *Allahu Akbar* or *Subhan Allah*, or *Al-Hamdulillah* or *Bismillah* before eating or any other action, or reading *Hadîth* or *Fiqh*, or making *Du'â'* or saying *Âmîn* to someone else's *Du'a'* or listening to recitation of Qur'ân, none of that is prohibited:

لأن النبي ـ ﷺ ـ «كَانَ يَتَّكِئُ فِي حِجْرِ عَائِشَةَ وَهِي حَائِض فَيَقْرَأُ القُرآنَ». [متفق عليه].

The Prophet صلى الله عليه وسلم used to rest in 'Aisha's apartment while she was menstruating, and he would recite Qur'ân (Agreed upon)

Some instructions for menstruating women and those in *Nifâs*

A. It is obligatory for a menstruating woman, when her bleeding stops, to perform a complete *Ghusl*; based on the Prophet's صلى الله عليه وسلم statement to Fatimah bint Abi Hubaish رضي الله عنها :

«فَإِذَا أَقْبَلَتِ الـحَيضَةُ فَدَعِي الصَّلاةَ فَإِذَا أَدبَرَت فَاغتَسِلِي وَصَلِّي». . [رواه البخاري].

"When the menstruation starts, leave off *Salât*; and when it

84

is finished, then perform a *Ghusl* and offer *Salât.* " (*Bukhari*)

After the *Ghusl*, *Salât* and fasting become obligatory on the woman, and it is permitted for her to enter the *Masjid*, and make *Tawâf*, and recite Qur'ân, and have intercourse. And if she had missed some days of fasting in Ramadan, she must make them up, but not the *Salât*. The same rules apply to the women in *Nifâs*.

B. If the bleeding of menstruation or *Nifâs* stops during a night of Ramadan, fasting becomes obligatory upon her the following day, even if she doesn't perform a *Ghusl* before the break of dawn, since the circumstance which prevented her from fasting has ended.

ISTIHADAH
(NON-MENSTRUAL VAGINAL BLEEDING) AND THE RULES ASSOCIATED WITH IT

Istihâdah (استحاضه) is vaginal bleeding for reasons other than menstruation or childbirth. In some women bleeding never stops, in others it continues for longer than a normal period, but it does stop for a short period.

The woman affected by it is in one of three conditions:

1. She had a known regular menses before the onset of the *Istihâdah*. She should calculate when her period would normally come, and stop offering *Salât* during the days of her calculated period. And all the other rules of menstruation would apply to her during that calculated period. For the rest of the days, her bleeding should be treated as *Istihâdah*.

2. She did not have a regular period, or does not remember when it used to occur, but she can distinguish between the two kinds of blood based on colour, thickness and smell. (Menstrual blood is dark, thick, and with a strong odour; *Istihâdah* is bright red,

thin, and less disagreeable in smell).

3. She didn't have a regular period, and even cannot distinguish between the two types of blood, either because it's always the same, or because it's always changing, she should go by the average period of most women; so for 6 or 7 days, every month, she should consider herself as menstruating, and that should be calculated from the time she first noticed vaginal bleeding, the rest of the days should be treated as *Istihâdah*.

There is no difference between a woman beset by *Istihâdah* and a woman who has a complete cessation of menstrual flow, except as follows:

A) If the woman beset by *Istihâdah* wants to perform *Wudû*, she should wash the blood from her vaginal area then apply a menstrual pad or wrap the area with a clean rag on top of a wad of cotton to catch the blood; any blood coming out after that is of no account.

B) She must perform *Wudû* for every single *Fard* (obligatory) *Salât*, as the Prophet صلى الله عليه وسلم ordered a woman in this condition:

«تَوَضَّئِي لِكُلِّ صَلَاةٍ» . [رواه البخاري].

"Perform *Wudû* for every *Salât*" (*Bukhari*)

THE BOOK OF *SALÂT* (PRAYER)

* The *Adhân* and *Iqâmah* (calls to prayer)

* How to perform *Salât-ul-Fajr* (the Dawn Prayer)

* Some rules of *Salât*

* Conditions for the validity of *Salât*

* The basic elements (*Arkân*) of *Salât*

* Times in which *Salât* is forbidden

* The times of obligatory *Salât*

* How the Prophet صلى الله عليه وسلم used to pray

* *Salât Tatawwu'* (optional prayers)

* Those upon whom *Salât* is mandatory

* *Sujud As-Sahw*

* Attendance of woman for congregational *Salât* in the *Masjid*

* Who is most befitting to lead *Salât*?

* The virtues of *Salât,* and warning against abandoning it

* The mandatory nature of attending Friday Prayer and the daily *Salât* in congregation

* The virtues of praying in congregation and attending the Friday prayer

* How to offer Friday Prayer with its etiquettes

* *Ahâdith* on the subject of *Salât*

* The *Salât* of a traveller on land or sea or in an airplane

* *Salât* is mandatory on the sick person

* How a sick person can perform the acts of purification

* How a sick person can perform *Salât*

* *Du'â* (supplications) at the beginning of *Salât*
* *Du'â* at the end of *Salât*
* How to perform *Salât* on a dead person (Funeral Prayer)
* The admonishment of death
* *'Eid* Prayers
* Emphasis upon offering a sacrifice on the *'Eid* day
* *Salât* to supplicate for rain (*Istisqa*)
* *Salât* at the time of solar or lunar eclipse
* *Salât-ul-Istikhara*
* Beware of passing in front of a praying person
* The recitation of the Messenger صلى الله عليه وسلم and his performing the prayer.
* The Prophet's worship of Allah

THE *ADHAN* (CALL TO PRAYER) AND *IQAMAH* (CALL TO START THE PRAYER)

1. The *Adhân* is the announcement that the time of a particular *Salât* has begun. This is done with a specific wording, and for the purpose of calling the people to pray in congregation. It is a distinctive feature of Islamic society and its religious practice. It is obligatory for the Muslim society to establish it.

2. The wording of the *Adhân* :

اللهُ أَكْبَرُ اللهُ أَكْبَرُ، اللهُ أَكْبَرُ اللهُ أَكْبَرُ.

Allahu Akbar, Allahu Akbar; Allahu Akbar, Allahu Akbar

"Allah is the Most Great" (repeated 4 times).

أَشْهَدُ أَنْ لاَإِلٰهَ إِلاَّ اللهُ، أَشْهَدُ أَنْ لاَإِلٰهَ إِلاَّ اللهُ.

Ash-hadu an la ilaha illa-Allah, Ash-hadu an la ilaha illa-Allah

"I bear witness that none has the right to be worshipped but Allah" (twice).

أَشْهَدُ أَنَّ مُحَمَّدًا رَسُولُ اللهِ، أَشْهَدُ أَنَّ مُحَمَّدًا رَسُولُ اللهِ.

Ash-hadu anna Muhammadan Rasul-ullah, Ash-hadu anna Muhammadan Rasul-ullah

"I bear witness that Muhammad is the Messenger of Allah" (twice).

حَيَّ عَلَى الصَّلاَةِ، حَيَّ عَلَى الصَّلاَةِ.

Haiya 'alas-Salâh, Haiya 'alas-Salâh

"Hurry towards *Salât*" (twice).

حَيَّ عَلَى الْفَلاَحِ، حَيَّ عَلَى الْفَلاَحِ

Haiya 'alal-Falâh, Haiya 'alal-Falâh

"Hurry towards success" (twice).

89

اللهُ أَكْبَرُ، اللهُ أَكْبَرُ، لاَإِلَهَ إِلاَّ اللهُ.

Allahu Akbar, Allahu Akbar

"Allah is the Most Great" (twice).

La ilaha illa-Allah

"None has the right to be worshipped but Allah" (once).

Note: In the call to prayer for *Fajr* (the Dawn Prayer) the *Mu'adhdhin* (caller) adds after *Haiya 'alal-Falâh*:

(وَيَزِيدُ فِي الفَجْرِ «الصَّلاَةُ خَيْرٌ مِنَ النَّوْم» مَرَّتَيْن) .

As-Salatu Khairum minan naum, As-Salatu Khairum minan naum

"The *Salât* is better than sleep" (twice).

3. The *Iqâmah* is like the *Adhân* but it is pronounced immediately before the start of obligatory prayer, in order to assemble the people in the *Masjid* in orderly rows.

4. The wording of *Iqâmah*:

اللهُ أَكْبَرُ اللهُ أَكْبَرُ،

Allahu Akbar, Allahu Akbar

"Allah is the Most Great" [twice].

أَشْهَدُ أَنْ لاَإِلَهَ إِلاَّ اللهُ.

Ash-hadu an la ilaha illa-Allah

"I bear witness that none has the right to be worshipped but Allah" [once].

أَشْهَدُ أَنَّ مُحَمَّدًا رَسُولُ اللهِ،

Ash-hadu anna Muhammadan Rasul-ullah

"I bear witness that Muhammad is the Messenger of Allah" (once).

حَيَّ عَلَى الصَّلَاةِ،

Haiya 'alas-Salâh

"Hurry towards *Salât*" (once).

حَيَّ عَلَى الفَلَاحِ

Haiya 'alal-Falah

"Hurry towards success" (once).

قَدْ قَامَتِ الصَّلَاةُ، قَدْ قَامَتِ الصَّلَاةُ

Qad qâmatis-Salâh, Qad qâmatis-Salâh

"The time of *Salât* has come" (twice).

اللهُ أَكْبَرُ اللهُ أَكْبَرُ،

Allahu Akbar, Allahu Akbar

"Allah is the Most Great" (twice).

لَاإِلَهَ إِلاَّ اللهُ

La ilaha illa-Allah

"None has the right to be worshipped but Allah" (once).

5. It is praiseworthy for one who while hears the *Adhân* repeats each phrase after the *Mu'adhdhin*, except when he says "Hurry to *Salât*" and "Hurry to success," one should say:

لاحول ولا قوة إلا بالله.

La hawla wa la quwwata illa billah

"There is no power nor ability except by Allah."

6. One should ask Allah to bless the Prophet صلى الله عليه وسلم after the *Adhân*, in a low voice, then he should make the following *Du'â*

«مَنْ قَالَ حِينَ يَسْمَعُ النِّدَاءَ: اللَّهُمَّ رَبَّ هَذِهِ الدَّعْوَةِ التَّامَّةِ وَالصَّلَاةِ القَائِمَةِ، آتِ مُحَمَّداً الوَسِيلَةَ وَالفَضِيلَةَ، وَابْعَثْهُ مَقَاماً

مَحْمُوداً الَّذِي وَعَدتَهُ حَلَّتْ لَهُ شَفَاعَتِي يَومَ القِيَامَةِ». [رواه البخاري].

Allahumma rabba hadhi-hid da'wa tit-tâm-mati was-sala til qâ'imati ati Muhammada nil waseelata wal fadeelata wab 'ath-hu maqâmam mahmuda nil-ladhi wa'ad tahu.

"O Allah, the Lord of this perfect invitation and established *Salât*, grant Muhammad intercession (to You) and honour, and raise him to the position of praise on the Day of Judgement, which You promised him."

The Prophet صلى الله عليه وسلم said:

"Whoever supplicates with this *Du'a* after hearing the *Adhân* will be eligible for my intercession on the Day of Judgement." (*Bukhâri*)

7. The *Adhân* is an act of worship, and worship should be performed in accordance with the teachings of the Prophet صلى الله عليه وسلم without addition or omission. Some detestable heresies associated with the *Adhân* are as follows:

(A) To kiss the thumbs and wipe over the eyelids with them and to say: "Welcome my beloved, and the coolness of my eyes."

(B) Mispronunciation of the words of the *Adhân* by adding letters or changing vowels or stretching vowels where they should be short.

(C) Singling out *Fajr* (Dawn) and *Jumu'ah* (Friday) Prayers to regularly say *Tasbîh* (*Subhan Allah*) before the *Adhân*.

(D) To send blessings upon the Prophet صلى الله عليه وسلم in a loud voice after the *Adhân*.

HOW TO PERFORM *SALÂT-UL-FAJR*
(The Dawn Prayer)

1. Make the intention to pray two *Rak'at* (units) of *Fajr* (Dawn) *Salât*. This should be done in the mind without saying it by tongue.

2. Face the *Qiblah* (the direction of the *Ka'bah* in Makkah) raise your hands up to your ears and say:

اللهُ أَكْبَرُ

"Allah is the Most Great"*

3. Place your right hand on the back of your left hand on your chest and recite:

سُبْحَانَكَ اللّهُمَّ وَبِحَمْدِكَ وَتَبَارَكَ اسْمُكَ وَتَعَالَى جَدُّكَ وَلَا إِلهَ غَيْرُكَ .

"Glory to you O Allah, and with Your Praise, and Your Name is Blessed and none has the right to be worshipped but You."

(It is all right to recite any other *Du'a* reported from the *Sunnah*).

The First *Rak'a*

Recite in a low tone:

أَعُوذُ بِاللهِ مِنَ الشَّيْطَانِ الرَّجِيمِ ، بِسْمِ اللهِ الرَّحْمنِ الرَّحِيمِ

"I seek refuge with Allah from the accursed Satan, in the Name of Allah, the Most Gracious, the Most Merciful".

Recite the opening chapter of the Qur'ân (*Al-Fâtihah*):

﴿ الْحَمْدُ لِلّهِ رَبِّ الْعَالَمِينَ ٠ الرَّحْمَنِ الرَّحِيمِ ٠ مَالِكِ يَوْمِ

---

* Translator's note: I am not transliterating because the person who learns by transliteration without a teacher will learn incorrectly, then he will have to unlearn all the mistakes which have been fixed in his memory through constant repetition.

"All the praises and thanks are to Allah, the Lord of the *'Alamîn* (mankind, jinns and all that exists). The Most Gracious, the Most Merciful. The Only Owner (and the Only Ruling Judge) of the Day of Recompense (i.e. the Day of Resurrection). "You (Alone) we worship, and You (Alone) we ask for help (for each and everything). Guide us to the Straight Way. The Way of those on whom You have bestowed Your Grace, not (the way) of those who earned Your Anger (such as the Jews), nor of those who went astray (such as the Christians)." (V. 1: 1-7)

Recite: آمين *'Ameen*

Recite:

"In the Name of Allah, the Most Gracious, the Most Merciful."

Recite:

قُلْ هُوَ ٱللَّهُ أَحَدٌ ٥ ٱللَّهُ ٱلصَّمَدُ ٥ لَمْ يَلِدْ
وَلَمْ يُولَدْ ٥ وَلَمْ يَكُن لَّهُۥ كُفُوًا أَحَدٌ ٥

"Say: He is Allah, (the) One. The Self-Sufficient Master, Whom all creatures need, He neither eats nor drinks. He begets not, nor was He begotten. And there is none co-equal or comparable unto Him." (V. 112: 1- 4)

Note: Any other *Surah* (chapter) or even a long verse of the Qur'ân can also be recited, whatever is easy for you to memorize.

94

1. Raise your hands and saying: " الله اكبر Allah is the Most Great," bow at the waist with your legs straight, grasping your knees, your back should be in level. Say three times in this position:

" سبحان رب العظيم

Glory to my Lord, the Exalted."

2. Raise your head and hands until you are standing upright. Say, as you move: " سمع الله لمن حمده Allah hears those who praise Him", when upright, say: "ربنا لك الحمد O Lord, all Praise is to You."

3. Saying " الله اكبر Allah is the Most Great" go down on your hands and knees and place your forehead and nose on the ground. Your toes should also be on the ground, pointing toward the *Qiblah,* your elbows should be off the ground and away from your sides. Say three times: "سبحان ربي الأعلى Glory to my Lord, the Most High."

4. Raise your head up, saying " الله اكبر Allah is the Most Great", until you come to a sitting position with your legs folded beneath you. Place palms on your thighs with the fingers ending at the beginning of the knees and say:

«رَبِّ اغْفِرْ لِي وَارْحَمْنِي وَاهْدِنِي وَعَافِنِي وَارْزُقْنِي» .

"O Lord, forgive me, have mercy on me, guide me, protect me and provide me with sustenance."

5. Prostrate on the ground a second time, saying " الله اكبر Allah is the Most Great" as you move, and say three times: " سبحان ربى الأعلى Glory to my Lord, the Most High."

6. Raise your head a second time, saying " الله اكبر Allah is the Most Great" sit briefly as before, resting your haunches on the sole of your left foot, with the right foot propped up, the toes touching the ground and pointing towards the *Qiblah.*

This position is called *Jalsat-ul-Istirâhah* (the resting posture)."

The Second *Rak‘a*

1. Rise up to a standing position with your hands clasped as before. Recite بسم الله الرحمن الرحيم and say: " اعوذ بالله من الشيطان الرجيم In the Name of Allah, the Most Gracious, the Most Merciful" then recite *Surah Fâtihah* and any other *Surah* or whatever is easy for you of the Qur'ân.

2. Make *Rukû‘* (bowing) and two *Sajdah* (prostrations) as in the first *Rak'a*. After coming up from the second *Sajdah*, sit like before with your right foot propped up, close the fingers of the right hand, and extend the index finger, raise it and wiggle it, recite التحية (*At-Tahiyah*):

«التَّحِيَّاتُ لِلَّهِ، وَالصَّلَوَاتُ والطَّيِّبَاتُ، السَّلامُ عَلَيْكَ أَيُّهَا النَّبِيُّ وَرَحْمَةُ اللَّهِ وَبَـرَكَـاتُـهُ، السَّـلامُ عَلَيْنَا وَعَلَى عِبَادِ اللَّهِ الصَّالِحِينَ، أَشْهَدُ أَن لاَّ إِلهَ إِلاَّ اللَّهُ، وأَشْهَدُ أَنَّ مُحَمَّداً عَبْدُهُ وَرَسُولُهُ، اللَّهُمَّ صَلِّ عَلَى مُحَمَّدٍ وَعَلَى آلِ مُحَمَّدٍ، كَمَا صَلَّيْتَ عَلَى إِبْرَاهِيمَ وَعَلَى آلِ إِبْرَاهِيمَ، وَبَارِكْ عَلَى مُحَمَّدٍ وَعَلَى آلِ مُحَمَّدٍ، كَمَا بَارَكتَ عَلَى إِبْرَاهِيمَ وَعَلَى آلِ إِبْرَاهِيمَ، إِنَّكَ حَمِيدٌ مَجِيدٌ.

"All the compliments, prayers and good things are due to Allâh; peace be on you, O Prophet, and Allah's Mercy and Blessings be on you. Peace be on us and on the true pious devotees of Allah. I testify that none has the right to be worshipped but Allah and I also testify that Muhammad is His slave and His Messenger. O Allah! Send Your *Salât* (Blessings Graces, Honours and Mercy) on Muhammad and the family of Muhammad as You sent Your *Salât* on Ibrahim and the family of Ibrahim. O Allah! Send Your

Blessings on Muhammad and the family of Muhammad as You sent Your Blessings on Ibrahim and the family of Ibrahim. You are Praiseworthy, Most Gacious."

Then recite:

اللَّهُمَّ إِنِّي أَعُوذُ بِكَ مِنَ عَذَابِ جَهَنَّمَ وَمِنْ عَذَابِ القَبْرِ، وَمِنْ فِتْنَةِ المَحْيَا وَالمَمَاتِ، وَمِنْ فِتْنَةِ المَسِيحِ الدَّجَّالِ .

"O Allah, I seek refuge with You from the torment of Hell, and from the torment of the grave, and from the trial of life and death and from the trial of the *Dajjâl* (the Antichrist)."

3. Then turn your head right, saying:

«وَالسَّلامُ عَليكُمْ وَرَحمةُ اللَّهِ» .

"Peace be upon you and the Mercy of Allah."

Then turn your head to the left and say the same.

4. After *Salât* there are certain supplications of Allah's remembrance, which are recommended in the *Sunnah*. For instance: *Ayat-ul-Kursi* (the Verse of the *Kursi* - 2:256); the last 3 *Surah* of the Qur'ân; *Subhân Allah, Al-Hamdulillah,* and *Allahu Akbar*—33 times each; and then supplication like:

«اللَّهُمَّ أَعِنِّي عَلَى ذِكرِكَ وَشُكْرِكَ وَحُسْنِ عِبَادَتِكَ» .

"O Allah help me to remember You and express gratitude to You and to worship You in the best way."

And as well as other supplications.

Table of number of *Rak'at* of each *Salât*

Prayers	*Sunnah* before	*Fard* (obligatory) *Salât*	*Sunnah* after
Fajr (Dawn)	2	2	-
Zuhr (Noon)	2 + 2	4	2
'Asr (Afternoon)	2 + 2	4	-
Maghrib (Sunset)	2	3	2
'Ishâ (Night)	2	4	2 + 3 or 1 *Witr*
Jumu'ah (instead of *Zuhr* on Friday)	2 (Greeting the *Masjid*)	2	2 at home or 2 + 2 in the *Masjid*

SOME RULES OF *SALÂT*

1. There are certain supererogatory *Salât*, some just before and some just after the obligatory *Salât*. They are highly recommended by the Prophet صلى الله عليه وسلم and he used to offer them regularly (see chart).

2. Do not rush through your prayers, fix your sight in your prostration place and don't look here and there.

3. If the *Imâm* recites out loud, be quiet and listen; if the *Imâm* recites to himself, recite in a low voice so that you can hear yourself but others do not (except *Fatihah* which should be recited in both cases in low voices).

4. The obligatory *Salât* of *Jumu'ah* has two *Rak'â* which can not be offered anywhere but in the *Masjid* after the *Khutbah* (sermon).

5. The obligatory *Salât* of *Maghrib* is 3 *Rak'â*; the first two *Rak'â* are like *Fajr* but after sitting in the second *Rak'â* and

reciting the *Tahiyât* until " وأشهد أن محمداً عبده ورسوله and I bear witness that Muhammad is His slave and Messenger," do not recite anything further and do not make *Taslîm* (salutation), but say *Allahu Akbar* and stand up raising your hands to the shoulders. Then recite *Surah Fâtihah* only to yourself then the rest of the *Rak'a* is the same as the second. Finish the *Salât* by making *Taslîm* right then left.

6. The obligatory *Salât* of *Zuhr*, *'Asr*, and *'Ishâ* are each 4 *Rak'a*. The first two *Rak'a* are just like *Fajr*, but when sitting in the second *Rak'a* after reciting the *Tahiyât*, do not make *Taslîm*, but stand for the third *Rak'a*, and then for the fourth, reciting *Surah Fatihah* only in both of them, recite to yourself, not loud, and don't sit long between the third and fourth *Rak'a*. When you finish, make *Taslîm* to the right and left.

7. *Witr* is three *Rak'a*. Pray two *Rak'a* and end with *Taslîm* to right and left. Then pray a single *Rak'a* by itself, and it's best to invoke the following *Masnûn** *Du'a* before going to *Ruku'* by lifting the hands and saying:

«اللَّهُمَّ اهْدِنِي فِيمَنْ هَدَيتَ، وَعَافِنِي فِيمَن عَافَيتَ، وتَوَلَّنِي فِيمَن تَوَلَّيتَ، وبَارك لِي فِيمَا أعطَيتَ، وَقِني شَرَّ مَاقَضَيتَ، فَإنَّكَ تَقضِي ولاَ يُقضَى عَلَيكَ وإنَّهُ لا يَذِلُّ من وَالَيتَ، وَلاَ يَعِزُّ من عَادَيتَ، تَبَارَكتَ رَبَّنَا وتَعَالَيْتَ». [رواه أبوداود بسند صحيح].

"O Allah guide along with those whom You have guided, and grant me well-being along with those whom You have granted well-being, and take care of me along with those whom You have taken care, and bless me in what You have bestowed, and protect me from the evil You have decreed, for verily You decree and none can impose a decree upon You, and whomsoever You took as a friend will never be demeaned. And whomsoever You took as an

enemy will not be honoured. You are blessed our Lord,
High and Exalted." (*Abû Dâwûd*).

8. If you come late to the *Jamâ'at* (congregational prayer) stand
until you are shoulder to shoulder with the person beside.
Then say the *Takbîr* standing, even if the *Imâm* is in *Ruku'*.
Then say another *Takbîr* and assume the same position as the
Imâm is in. If he is in *Ruku'*, and you reach the position of the
Ruku' before he rises from it, you should consider yourself as
having prayed that whole *Rak'a;* but if you join after the
Ruku', then you will have to pray it after the *Imâm* finishes;
based on the *Hadîth:*

«إِذَا وَجَـدْتُمُ الإِمَـامَ سَاجِداً فَاسْجُدُوا أَوْ رَاكِعاً فَارْكَعُوا وَقَائِماً
فَقُومُوا وَلاَ تَعْتَدُّوا بِالسُّجُودِ إِذَا لَمْ تُدْرِكُوا الرَّكْعَةَ». [صحيح رواه
البيهقي . انظر سلسلة الأحاديث الصحيحة ١١٨٨].

"If you find the *Imâm* in *Sajdah*, prostate (with him), or if
he is in *Ruku'*, bow; or if he is standing, stand. And don't
count your *Sajdah* if you didn't catch the *Raka* .
(*Baihaqi*)

9. If you miss one or more *Rak'a* with the *Imâm*, follow him
until the end of the *Salât*, but do not make *Taslîm* when he
does, instead stand up and offer the remaining *Rak'a* .

10. Beware of performing *Salât* in a rush, because it causes it to
be invalidated. The Prophet صلى الله عليه وسلم saw a man performing
Salât in a hurry, he (صلى الله عليه وسلم) told him:

ارْجِعْ فَصَلِّ فَإِنَّكَ لَمْ تُصَلِّ» فَقَالَ لَهُ فِي الثَّالِثَةِ : عَلِّمْنِي يَارَسُولَ
اللهِ فَقَالَ : ارْكَعْ حَتَّى تَطْمَئِنَّ رَاكِعاً ثُمَّ ارْفَعْ حَتَّى تَسْتَوِي قَائِماً،
ثُمَّ اسْجُدْ حَتَّى تَطْمَئِنَّ سَاجِداً، ثُمَّ ارْفَعْ حَتَّى تَطْمَئِنَّ جَالِساً»
[متفق عليه].

"Go back and pray because you didn't pray (yet)." After he repeated it in a similar manner twice more and the Prophet صلى الله عليه وسلم ordered him to repeat the *Salât*. He said, "Teach me, O Messenger of Allah." He (صلى الله عليه وسلم) told him, "Bow until you come to rest in *Rukû'*. Then stand until you are fully upright, then prostrate until you come to rest, then sit until you come to rest, then prostrate until you come to rest in *Sajdah...*" (Agreed upon)

11. If you forgot to perform an action which is *Wâjib* (compulsory) in the *Salât*, like sitting at the end of the second *Rak'a* to recite *Tahiyat*, or if you're unsure how many *Rak'a* you prayed, build on the lower number (which is the number you're sure of) then at the end of the *Salât* make two extra *Sajdah*. These are called *Sujûd As-Sahw* (the prostrations for forgetfulness).

CONDITIONS FOR THE VALIDITY OF *SALÂT*

The following conditions must be met before you start the *Salât*, and if anyone of these is missing, the *Salât* will be invalid:

1. Knowledge that the time for a particular *Salât* has begun. It is sufficient to be reasonably certain.

2. To be in a state of purity, cleansed of the major and minor impurity, based on the statement of the Prophet صلى الله عليه وسلم :

$$\text{«لَا يَقْبَلُ اللهُ صَلَاةً بِغَيْرِ طَهُورٍ» . . [رواه مسلم وغيره].}$$

"Allah will not accept *Salât* without purification." (*Muslim* and others)

3. Cleanliness of one's body, clothing, and place of prayer (i.e., they should be free from physical impurities, like faeces, urine etc.), that is, if one has the power to achieve that. If one is unable to remove the impurity, go ahead and pray as it is.

4. Covering one's private parts; based on the Statement of Allah عز وجل:

﴿ يَبَنِيٓ ءَادَمَ خُذُواْ زِينَتَكُمْ عِندَ كُلِّ مَسْجِدٍ ﴾

"O children of Adam! Take your adornment (by wearing your clean clothes), while praying..." (V. 7: 31)

The Arabic word *Zinah* (زينة) translated as "adornment" is understood by the commentators to mean clothing sufficient to cover the private parts. The word *Masjid* literally means "the place of *Sajdah*" so it is interpreted as referring to *Salât*. So the sentence comes to mean "cover your private parts for every *Salât*."

The private part ('*Aurah* عورة) of a man is from the navel to the knees.

The private part ('*Aurah*) of a woman is her complete body, other than the face and hands, (in *Salât*) it is mandatory that the clothing screen the private parts. Sheer material, which allows the skin to be seen, is not good enough, and the *Salât* is not acceptable in it.

5. To face the *Qiblah*, which is the sacred *Masjid* in Makkah, as Allah عز وجل said:

﴿ فَوَلِّ وَجْهَكَ شَطْرَ ٱلْمَسْجِدِ ٱلْحَرَامِ وَحَيْثُ مَا كُنتُمْ فَوَلُّواْ وُجُوهَكُمْ شَطْرَهُۥ ﴾

"So turn your face in the direction of *Al-Masjid-al-Harâm* (at Makkah). And wheresoever you people are, turn your faces (in prayer) in that direction..." (V. 2: 144)

One who is close enough to the Ka'bah to see it, must look at it before starting his prayer to make sure he's really facing it. And one who cannot see it must face in its direction, since that is the most he is capable of.

6. Facing the *Qiblah* in *Salât* is an obligation which may not be waived except under the following circumstances:

A) Voluntary *Salât* of a traveller mounted on an animal or any conveyance: a car, ship, plane etc. The person can pray in whatever direction he is facing; and if sitting, he can make a gesture indicative of *Rukû'* and *Sajdah*. The lowering of his head in *Sajdah* should be more distinct than in *Rukû'*.

B) One who fears (of present danger) or one held against his will in a certain position or direction, or one so weak, from illness that he can not turn towards the *Qiblah*, in all of these cases the requirement of facing the *Qiblah* is waived due to inability.

7. The *Niyah* (intention), the person about to pray should know what *Salât* he's going to pray — whether *Fard* (obligatory) or *Nafl* (voluntary); and which prayer of the day– *Zuhr* or *'Asr* etc.; as the Prophet صلى الله عليه وسلم said:

«إِنَّمَا الأَعْمَالُ بِالنِّيَّاتِ وَإِنَّمَا لِكُلِّ امْرِيءٍ مَانَوَى» . [رواه

البخاري] .

"Deeds are only judged according to the intentions, and every person will get only what he has intended." (*Bukhari*)

THE BASIC ELEMENTS (*ARKAN*) OF *SALÂT*

The basic elements of *Salât* are its essential components, if one of them is missing, the *Salât* is unacceptable. These elements are as follows:

1. *Takbirat-ul-Ihrâm* (to say *Allahu Akbar* at the beginning of the *Salât*); the Prophet صلى الله عليه وسلم said:

«مِفْتَاحُ الصَّلاةِ الطُّهُورُ وتَحْريمُهَا التَّكْبِيرُ وَتَحْلِيلُهَا التَّسْلِيمُ» [رواه

الترمذي وغيره وقال هذا أصح شيء في هذا الباب وأحسن] .

"The key of *Salât* is purity. It starts with the *Takbir* and it ends with the *Taslîm*." (Tirmidhi and others, Tirmidhi said this is the most authentic *Hadîth* on this issue)

2. *Qiyâm* (standing) in obligatory *Salât*; Allah عزوجل said:

﴿ حَٰفِظُواْ عَلَى ٱلصَّلَوَٰتِ وَٱلصَّلَوٰةِ ٱلْوُسْطَىٰ وَقُومُواْ لِلَّهِ قَٰنِتِينَ ﴾

"Guard strictly the (five obligatory) prayers especially the middle (i.e. the best) ('*Asr*) prayer. And stand before Allah with obedience (and do not speak to others during the prayers)." (V. 2:238)

As for *Nafl* (voluntary) *Salât*, you can offer it sitting, even if you're able to stand. The Prophet صلى الله عليه وسلم said:

«صَلاةُ الرَّجُلِ قَاعِداً نِصفُ الصَّلاةِ». [متفق عليه].

"A man's *Salât* while sitting has half [the reward] of the [normal] *Salât*." (Agreed upon)

If one is unable to stand for *Fard Salât*, he should pray sitting, and if unable to pray sitting, he should pray on his side or as best as he can.

3. To recite *Surah Fatihah* in every *Rak'a* of every *Salât*, whether obligatory or voluntary. The Prophet صلى الله عليه وسلم said:

«لاَ صلاةَ لِمَن لَمْ يَقْرَأ بِفَاتِحَةِ الكِتَابِ». . [متفق عليه].

"There is no *Salât* for one who does not recite "The opening of the Book (*Surah Al-Fatihah*)" (Agreed upon).

4. *Rukû'* (bowing): All scholars are in agreement that *Rukû'* is a basic element of *Salât*. The minimum acceptable *Rukû'* is to bend at the waist until one's hands touch his knees, and he must come to rest in this position; based on the Prophet's statement:

«اركَعْ حَتَّى تَطمَئِنَّ راكِعاً. . [رواه البخاري].

"Bow until you come to rest in *Rukû'.*" (*Bukhâri*)

5. To resume standing after bowing: One should come to rest in an upright position; based on the Prophet ﷺ statement:

$$﴿ثُمَّ ارْفَعْ حَتَّى تَعْتَدِلَ قَائِماً﴾ . [رواه البخاري].$$

"Then rise up until you stand straight and upright." (*Bukhâri*)

6. Two *Sajdah* in each *Rak'a* and sitting up between them, coming to rest in each position. The Prophet ﷺ said:

$$﴿ثُمَّ اسْجُدْ حَتَّى تَطْمَئِنَّ سَاجِداً، ثُمَّ ارْفَع حَتَّى تَطْمَئِنَّ جَالِساً﴾ . [رواه البخاري].$$

"Then prostrate until you come to rest in *Sajdah*. Then sit up until you come to rest in sitting." (*Bukhâri*)

There are special wordings of remembrance in between the two *Sajdah* and the sitting between them, whether in obligatory (*Fard*) *Salât* or voluntary (*Nafl*).

The parts of the body on which *Sajdah* must be made are: the face, both hands, both knees, and the toes of both feet. The Prophet ﷺ said:

$$﴿أُمِرتُ أَنْ أَسْجُدَ عَلَى سَبْعَةِ أَعْظُمٍ : عَلَى الـجَبْهَةِ وَأَشَارَ بِيَدِهِ عَلَى أَنْفِهِ وَالْيَدَيْنِ وَالرُّكْبَتَيْنِ وَأَطْرَافِ القَدَمَيْنِ﴾ . . [متفق عليه].$$

"I was ordered to make *Sajdah* on seven parts of the body; the forehead - (and he ﷺ pointed to his nose) - both hands, both knees, and the toes of both feet." (Agreed upon)

7. The final sitting and recitation of *Tashahhud* while sitting. The Prophet ﷺ said:

«فَإِذَا رَفَعْتَ رَأْسَكَ مِنْ آخِرِ سَجْدَةٍ، وَقَعَدتَّ قَدرَ التَّشهُّدِ فَقَد تَمَّت صَلَاتُكَ». [رواه البخاري].

"If you raised your head from the final *Sajdah* and sat the length of time it takes to recite *Tashahhud*, your *Salât* gets complete." (Agreed upon)

8. *Taslîm*: (to say *As-Salamu Alaikum* to the right then the left). The *Taslîm* is established through the way the Prophet صلى الله عليه وسلم prayed and according to his statement:

«مِفتَـاحُ الصَّـلَاةِ الـطُّهُـورُ، وَتَحـرِيمُها التَّكبِيرُ، وَتَحلِيلُها التَّسلِيمُ» . . [رواه الترمذي وغيره، وقال هذا أصح شيء في الباب وأحسنه، انظر فقه السنة ج١/١٣٣ إلى ١٤١ باختصار].

"The key to *Salât* is purity, it starts with *Takbir* and it ends with *Taslîm*." (*Tirmidhi* and others)

9. The proper order: Start with *Takbirat-ul-Ihrâm* standing, recite *Fatihah*, then bow in *Rukû'*, then rise up from it to standing, then perform *Sajdah*, then rise up from it to sitting, then perform the second *Sajdah*. In the second *Rak'a* and in the final *Rak'a,* one should sit for *Tashahhud*, and in the final *Rak'a* make *Taslîm*. The proof for the order is the *Hadîth* in which the Prophet صلى الله عليه وسلم taught the order of the elements of *Salât* to the man who was hastily offering *Salât*.

TIMES IN WHICH *SALAT* IS FORBIDDEN

1. After the obligatory *Salât* of *Fajr* (Dawn) until the sun has risen.

2. At the moments the sun is cresting the horizon until it reaches a spear's length about it. (5° ‑ 10°).

3. At high noon until it passes the zenith by a few minutes.

106

4. After the obligatory *Salât* of *'Asr* (Afternoon) until the sun sets. The Prophet ﷺ said:

«لاَ صَلاَةَ بَعْدَ صَلاَةِ العَصْرِ حَتَّى تَغْرُبَ الشَّمْسُ وَلاَ صَلاَةَ بَعْدَ صَلاَةِ الفَجْرِ حَتَّى تَطْلُعَ الشَّمْسُ». [متفق عليه].

"No *Salât* (prayer) is valid after the *'Asr* Prayer till the sun sets and no *Salât* (prayer) is valid after the *Fajr* Prayer till the sun rises." (Agreed upon)

5. It is permissible to offer a *Salât,* one had previously forgotten or slept through, at any time; based on the Prophet's statement:

«مَنْ نَسِيَ صَلاَةً أَوْ نَامَ عَنْهَا، فَكَفَّارَتُهَا أَنْ يُصَلِّيَهَا إِذَا ذَكَرَهَا». . [رواه مسلم].

"Whoever forgot a *Salât* or slept through it, its expiation is to offer it when one remembers it." (*Muslim*)

6. Imam Shâfi'î was of the opinion that it is permissible to pray a voluntary *Salât* which has a specific cause, in the forbidden times, for instance two *Rak'a* as a greeting to the mosque whenever one enters into it and before sitting there; or two *Rak'a* after making *Wudû*. And his opinion is the closest to the truth.

7. When the obligatory *Salât* in congregation is announced, it is not permissible to get busy with voluntary *Salât*, the Prophet ﷺ said:

«إِذَا أُقِيمَتِ الصَّلاَةُ، فَلاَ صَلاَةَ إِلَّا الـمَكْتُوبَةَ». [رواه مسلم].

"When the *Salât* in congregation commences, there is no *Salât* other than the prescribed one (i.e. the obligatory *Salât* in the congregation)." (*Muslim*)

THE TIMES OF OBLIGATORY *SALAT*

Each *Salât* has the prescribed time in which it must be performed. Allah عز وجل said:

﴿ إِنَّ ٱلصَّلَوٰةَ كَانَتْ عَلَى ٱلْمُؤْمِنِينَ كِتَابًا مَّوْقُوتًا ﴾

"...Verily the *Salât* is enjoined on the believers at fixed hours." (V. 4: 103)

The Qur'ân indicated these times in a general way, and the *Sunnah* explained them in detail. Abdullah bin 'Amr رضي الله عنهما said that Allah's Messenger صلى الله عليه وسلم said:

«وَقْتُ الظُّهْرِ إِذَا زَالَتِ الشَّمْسُ، وَكَانَ ظِلُّ الرَّجُلِ كَطُولِهِ مَالَمْ يَحْضُرِ العَصْرُ وَوَقْتُ العَصْرِ مَالَمْ تَصْفَرَّ الشَّمْسُ. وَوَقْتُ صَلاةِ الـمَغْرِبِ مَا لَمْ تَغِبِ الشَّفَقُ. وَوَقْتُ العِشَاءِ إِلَى نِصْفِ اللَّيْلِ الأَوْسَطِ. وَوَقْتُ صَلاةِ الصُّبْحِ مِنْ طُلُوعِ الفَجرِ مَا لَمْ تَطْلُعِ الشَّمْسُ، فَإِذَا طَلَعَتِ الشَّمْسُ فَأَمْسِكْ عَنِ الصَّلاةِ فَإِنَّهَا تَطْلُعُ بَيْنَ قَرْنَيْ شَيْطَانٍ». [رواه مسلم].

"The time of *Zuhr* (the Noon Prayer) is when the sun passes the zenith, until the shade of a man equals his length whence time for *'Asr* commences. And the time of *'Asr* (the Afternoon Prayer) is as long as the sun's light has not turned yellow. And the time of *Maghrib* (the Sunset Prayer) lasts as long as the redness has not vanished from the sky. And the time of *'Isha* (the Night Prayer) is until the middle of the night. And the time of *Fajr* (the Dawn Prayer) is from the first appearance of dawn (and lasts) as long as the sun has not yet risen. If the sun starts to crest the horizon, refrain from praying because it rises between *Satan's* two horns." (*Muslim*)

From this *Hadîth* and others it becomes clear that the times of *Salât* are as follows:

Zuhr: starts right after the sun passes its zenith, and continues until the shadow of an object equals the same length as the object.

'Asr: starts as soon as the shadow of the object becomes equal to the object after deducting the length of the shadow at noon. And it lasts until the sun sets (although it should not be postponed until the sun's rays turn yellowish without a valid excuse).

Maghrib: starts when the sun disappears below the horizon, and extends until the last trace of redness disappears from the sky.

'Ishâ: starts when the last trace of redness has disappeared from the sky, and lasts until the middle of the night.

Fajr: starts with the appearance of the "true dawn" until the sun starts to crest the horizon.

HOW THE PROPHET صلى الله عليه وسلم USED TO PRAY

There are many *Ahadîth*, either in words of the Prophet صلى الله عليه وسلم, or his Companions' descriptions of his *Salât* which make clear how one should perform *Salât* in the best way. Among these *Ahadîth* are the following :

1. «إِذَا قُمْتَ إِلَى الصَّلاةِ فَأَسْبِغِ الْوُضُوءَ، ثُمَّ اسْتَقْبِلِ الْقِبْلَةَ فَكَبِّرْ، ثُمَّ اقْرَأْ مَاتَيَسَّرَ مَعَكَ مِنَ الْقُرْآنِ، ثُمَّ اركَعْ حَتَّى تَطْمَئِنَّ رَاكِعاً، ثُمَّ ارْفَعْ حَتَّى تَعْتَدِلَ قَائِماً، ثُمَّ اسْجُدْ حَتَّى تَطْمَئِنَّ سَاجِداً، ثُمَّ ارْفَعْ حَتَّى تَطْمَئِنَّ جَالِساً ثُمَّ اسْجُدْ حَتَّى تَطْمَئِنَّ سَاجِداً، ثُمَّ افْعَلْ ذَلِكَ فِي صَلَاتِكَ كُلِّها» . [متفق عليه].

"When you stand to pray, perform a perfect *Wudû*, then face the *Qiblah*; say *Takbir* then recite what is easy for

109

you of the Qur'ân that is with you (i.e. memorized), then bow until you come to rest in *Rukû'*, then rise up till you are standing straight, then prostrate until you come to rest in *Sajdah*, then raise (your head) until you come to rest in sitting. Then prostrate until you come to rest in *Sajdah*. Then do that in all of your *Salât*." (Agreed upon)

[By the words "To recite what is easy for you of the Qur'ân," some scholars interpret to mean *Surah Al-Fatihah* (the opening chapter of the Qur'ân)].

٢. «كَانَ رَسُولُ اللهِ ـ ﷺ ـ إذَا قَامَ إلى الصَّلاةِ يَرْفَعُ يَدَيْهِ حَتَّى يُحَاذِي بِهِمَا مَنْكِبَيْهِ، ثُمَّ كَبَّرَ حَتَّى يَقِرَّ كُلُّ عَظْمٍ في مَوْضِعِهِ مُعْتَدِلاً، ثُمَّ يَقْرَأُ، ثُمَّ يُكَبِّرُ فَيَرْفَعُ يَدَيْهِ حَتَّى يُحَاذِي بِهِمَا مَنْكِبَيْهِ، ثُمَّ يَرْكَعُ وَيَضَعُ رَاحَتَيْهِ على رُكْبَتَيْهِ، ثُمَّ يَعْتَدِلُ فَلا يَصُبُّ رَأْسَهُ وَلا يُقْنِعُ ثُمَّ يَرْفَعُ رَأْسَهُ فَيَقُولُ: سَمِعَ اللهُ لِمَنْ حَمِدَهُ، ثُمَّ يَرْفَعُ يَدَيْهِ حَتَّى يُحَاذِي مَنْكِبَيْهِ مُعْتَدِلاً، ثُمَّ يَقُولُ اللهُ أَكْبَرُ، ثُمَّ يَهْوِي إلى الأرضِ فَيُجَافِي يَدَيْهِ عَنْ جَنْبَيْهِ، ثُمَّ يَرْفَعُ رَأْسَهُ وَيَثْنِي رِجْلَهُ اليُسْرَى فَيَقْعُدُ عَلَيْهَا وَيَفْتَحُ أَصَابِعَ رِجْلَيْهِ إذَا سَجَدَ، ثُمَّ يَسْجُدُ، ثُمَّ يَقُولُ: اللهُ أَكْبَرُ، وَيَرْفَعُ رَأْسَهُ وَيَثْنِي رِجْلَهُ اليُسْرَى فَيَقْعُدُ عَلَيْهَا حَتَّى يَرْجِعَ كُلُّ عَظْمٍ إلى مَوْضِعِهِ، ثُمَّ يَصْنَعُ في الأُخْرَى مِثْلَ ذَلِكَ ثُمَّ إذَا قَامَ مِنَ الرَّكْعَتَيْنِ كَبَّرَ وَرَفَعَ يَدَيْهِ حَتَّى يُحَاذِي بِهَا مَنْكِبَيْهِ كَمَا كَبَّرَ عِنْدَ افْتِتَاحِ الصَّلاةِ، ثُمَّ يَصْنَعُ ذَلِكَ في بَقِيَّةِ صَلاتِهِ، حَتَّى إذَا كَانَتِ السَّجْدَةُ الَّتِي فِيهَا التَّسْلِيمُ أَخَّرَ رِجْلَهُ اليُسْرَى وَقَعَدَ مُتَوَرِّكاً على شِقِّهِ الأَيْسَرَ». [أخرجه البخاري مختصراً، ورواه أبوداود وغيره، وقال الترمذي حديث حسن صحيح].

110

"When the Prophet ﷺ would stand up to perform *Salât*, he would raise his hands on a level with his shoulders. Then he would say *Takbir* until every bone came to rest in its place with him standing straight upright. Then he would recite. Then he would say *Takbir*, raising his hands on a level with his shoulders, then he would bow at the waist, placing his palms on his knees, coming to rest without raising his head nor letting it droop. Then he would raise his head up saying: "Allah hears those who praise Him." Then he would raise his hands on a level with his shoulders, coming to rest, then he would say "*Allahu Akbar*" then he would descend to the earth, keeping his hands away from his side. Then he would raise his head, with his left leg folded under him, sitting on it. He would spread his toes when he would make *Sajdah*, after the *Sajdah* he would say *Allahu Akbar* rising up with his left leg folded under him, sitting on it, until every bone had returned to its place. Similarly he would do in the second *Rak'a* as he did in the first. When he would rise after the first two *Rak'a*, he would say *Takbir* and raise his hands on a level with his shoulders, like at the start of *Salât*, and he would perform the rest of the *Rak'a* like the first two. Then when sitting after the last *Sajdah* before the *Taslim*, he would move his left leg back a bit so that he would be sitting on his left haunch."

(Reported by *Bukhâri* in a shorter version, and reported by Abû Dawûd and others, Tirmidhi classed it *Hasan Sahih*).

3. The Prophet ﷺ said:

«لَا يُصَلِّي أَحَدُكُم فِي الثَّوبِ الوَاحِدِ لَيسَ عَلَى عَاتِقِه مِنْهُ شَيءٌ» «متفق عليه» وفي رواية مسلم: «لَيْسَ عَلَى عَاتِقَيْهِ شَيءٌ».

111

"None of you should perform *Salât* in a single piece of clothing which leaves his shoulder bare," (Agreed upon)

Muslim reported one version with the wording:

"his two shoulders."

SALÂT TATAWWU' (OPTIONAL PRAYERS)

1. Its place in the *Shari'ah*: Optional *Salât* was prescribed to make up for deficiencies which might occur in obligatory *Salât*; and in view of the special merits of *Salât* which other forms of worship are lacking. The Prophet ﷺ said:

«إنَّ أوَّلَ مَايُحَاسَبُ بِهِ العَبْدُ يَومَ القِيَامَةِ مِنْ عَمَلِهِ الصَّلاةِ، فَإِن صَلُحَتْ فَقد أفلَحَ وَأَنْجَحَ، وَإِنْ فَسَدَتْ فَقَدْ خَابَ وَخَسِرَ، وَإِن انتقصَ مِنْ فَرِيضَةٍ قَالَ الرَّبُّ: انظُرُوا هَل لِعَبْدِي مِن تَطَوُّعٍ؟ فَيُكَمَّلُ بِهَا مَاانتقصَ مِنَ الفَرِيضَةِ، ثُمَّ يَكُونُ سَائِرَ عَمَلِهِ عَلى ذَلِكَ». [صحيح رواه الترمذي وغيره انظر صحيح الجامع رقم ٢٠٢٠].

"The first thing to be taken account of from the deeds of the slave on the Day of Judgement will be the *Salât*. If it is satisfactory, he will be successful and pass; and if it is not so, he will fail and lose, and if something is deficient in his obligatory prayers, the Lord will say: 'Check if my slave has any optional *Salât* to his credit.' The deficiency will be made good from that. After that, the rest of his deeds will be examined in a similar way." (Reported by Tirmidhi and others as authentic).

The Prophet ﷺ said to Rabi'ah bin Malik Al-Aslami:

«سَلْ، فَقُلْتُ: أَسْأَلُكَ مُرَافَقَتَكَ في الـجَنَّةِ. فَقَالَ: أو غَيْرَ

112

ذَلِكَ قُلْتُ: هُوَ ذَاكَ؟ قَالَ: فَأَعِنِّي عَلَى نَفْسِكَ بِكَثْرَةِ السُّجُودِ».

[رواه مسلم].

"Ask me for something." He said, "I ask you your company in Paradise." He said, "Is there anything besides that?" He replied, "That's it." The Prophet (صلى الله عليه وسلم) said, "Help me (in that) by making lots of *Sajdah* for yourself." (*Muslim*)

2. The best place to offer voluntary *Salât* is in your own home. The Prophet صلى الله عليه وسلم said:

«أَفْضَلُ الصَّلَاةِ صَلَاةُ الْمَرْءِ فِي بَيْتِهِ إِلَّا الْـمَكْتُوبَةَ». . [متفق عليه].

"The best *Salât* is that of a man in his house, except for the obligatory *Salât*." (Agreed upon).

The Prophet صلى الله عليه وسلم said:

«صَلَاةُ الْمَرْءِ فِي بَيْتِهِ أَفْضَلُ مِنْ صَلَاتِهِ فِي مَسْجِدِي هَذَا إِلَّا الْـمَكْتُوبَةَ». [رواه أبو داود بإسناد صحيح].

"The *Salât* of a man in his house is more meritorious than his prayer in my *Masjid* except the obligatory *Salat*." (*Abû Dawûd*)

Imam Nawawi said: "Stress was placed on praying optional *Salât* in the home because it further removes the chance of praying just to show off (*Ar-Riya*), and it brings blessing to the house and mercy descends upon it as well as angels; and the Satan clears out."

3. In optional *Salât*, it is permitted to sit, even if one has the ability to stand, and it is also permissible to stand for part of it and sit for part even in one *Rak'a*, and it makes no difference whether the sitting precedes the standing or vice versa; all is permitted with no aversion. And one can sit anyway he likes, although

cross legged is the best. Just one thing:

«صلاةُ الرَّجُلِ قاعداً نصفُ الصلاةِ» . [حديث رواه مسلم] .

"The reward of a *Salât* performed while sitting is half the reward of a *Salât* performed while standing." (*Muslim*)

4. Optional *Salât* encompasses the *Sunnah* (supererogatory) *Salât* of *Fajr*, *Zuhr*, *'Asr*, *Maghrib* and *'Ishâ*, and *Witr*, and *Salât* offered after *Wudu*, and *Tahajjud*, and others.

THOSE UPON WHOM *SALÂT* IS MANDATORY

Salât is mandatory on every adult and sane Muslim. The Prophet صلى الله عليه وسلم said:

«رُفِعَ القَلَمُ عن ثلاثةٍ: عَنِ الـمَجنُونِ المغلوبِ عَلَى عَقْلِهِ حَتَّى يَبْرَأَ، وَعَنِ النَّائِمِ حَتَّى يَستيقظَ، وَعَنِ الصَّبِي حَتَّى يَحْتَلِمَ» . [صحيح رواه أحمد وأبوداود، انظر صحيح الجامع ٣٥٠٦] .

"The pen is lifted from three [persons (i.e. they will not be taken to account)]: the insane whose rationality has been overcome until he recovers, the sleeper until he wakes, and the children until they attain puberty." (*Ahmad* and *Abû Dawûd*)

The father and mother should teach their children how to perform *Salât* and order them (in a gentle manner) to do so, when they reach seven years; and punish them for neglecting it when they reach ten years, so that they get used to it, and it becomes a natural practice that they will uphold after puberty. The Prophet صلى الله عليه وسلم said:

«عَلِّمُوا أولادَكُمُ الصَّلاةَ إذَا بَلَغُوا سَبعاً وَاضرِبُوهُم عَلَيهَا إذَا بَلَغُوا عَشراً، وَفرِّقُوا بَينَهُم في الـمَضَاجِعِ » . [صحيح رواه أحمد] .

3. If one forgets the first *Tashahhud*: The proof is:

صَلَّى ﷺ بِهِمُ الظُّهرَ، فَقَامَ فِي الرَّكعتينِ الأُولَيينِ

فَقَامَ النَّاسُ مَعَهُ، حَتَّى إِذَا قَضَى الصَّلَاةَ وَانتَظَرَ

كَبَّرَ وَهُوَ جَالِسٌ، وَسَجَدَ سَجدَتينِ قَبلَ أَن يُسَلِّمَ

[البخاري].

"The Prophet ﷺ led them in *Zuhr* [...]
second *Rak'a* he stood up a[...]
sitting; the people stood u[...]
was (almost) over and th[...]
he said *Takbîr* while sit[...]
before the *Taslîm*, then made t[...]

And it is mentioned in a *Hadîth* tha[...]
the *Tashahhud*, then remembered befo[...]
up, he should return to the sitting posture[...]
standing before he remembers, he should not s[...]
the end of the *Salât*, he should perform the *Sujud As-*[...]

4. If one is unsure how much *Rak'a* he prayed: The Prophe[...] الله عليه وسلم said:

«إِذَا شَكَّ أَحَدُكُم فِي صَلَاتِهِ، فَلَم يَدرِ كَم صَلَّى ثَلَاثًا أَم

أَربَعًا فَليَطرَحِ الشَّكَّ وَليَبنِ عَلَى مَااستَيقَنَ، ثُمَّ يَسجُدُ سَجدَتَينِ

قَبلَ أَن يُسَلِّمَ، فَإِن كَانَ صَلَّى خَمسًا شَفَعنَ لَهُ صَلَاتَهُ، وَإِن كَانَ

صَلَّى تَمَامًا كَانَت تَرغِيمًا لِلشَّيطَانِ». [رواه مسلم].

"If one of you becomes uncertain in his *Salât*, so that he doesn't know how much he prayed— three *Rak'a* or four? He should cast off what he is uncertain about, and build on what he's sure of, then perform two *Sajdah* before making

117

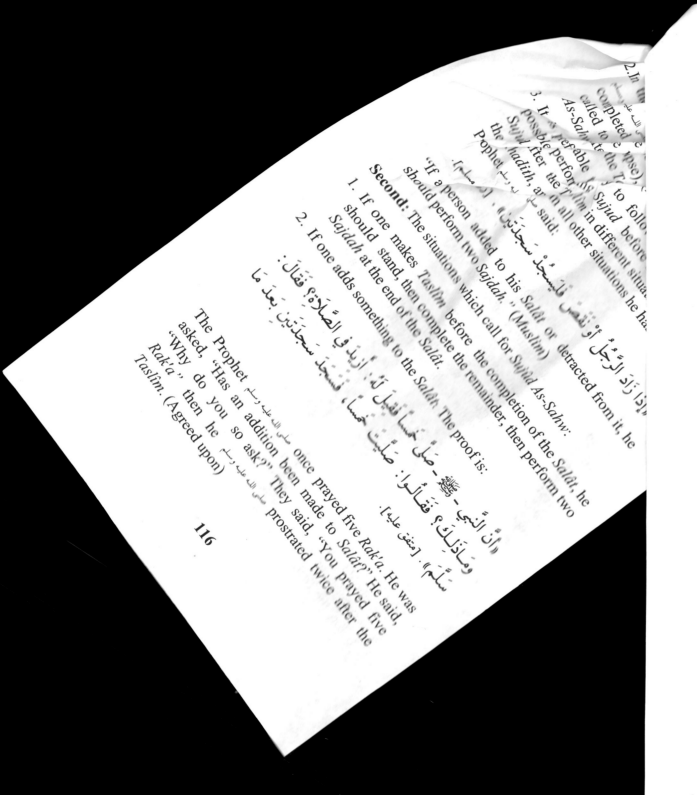

the *Taslîm*. So if he ends up praying five *Rak'a*, his *Salât* will be taken as complete and if he prayed correctly it is like rubbing *Shaitan's* nose in the dust." (*Muslim*)

5. If you're unsure how many *Rak'a* you prayed, go with the lower number. The Prophet ﷺ said:

«إِذَا شَكَّ أَحَدُكُم في الاثنَتَين وَالواحِدةِ فَلْيَجْعَلْها وَاحِدةً، وَإِذَا شَكَّ في الاثنَتَين وَالثَّلاثِ، فَليجعَلْها اثنَتَينِ، وَإِذَا شَكَّ في الثَّلاثِ والأربع فَلْيَجْعَلْهَا ثَلاثاً، حَتَّى يَكُونَ الوَهمُ في الزِّيَادَة ثُمَّ لِيتُمَّ مَابقِيَ من صَلاتِه، ثُمَّ يَسجُدْ سَجدتَينِ وَهوَ جَالِسٌ قَبْلَ أن يُسَلِّم». [صحيح رواه أحمد وغيره وانظر الجامع الصحيح ٦٤٣].

"If one of you is not sure between two and one, he should treat it as one (*Rak'a*); and if he is not sure between two and three, he should treat it as two; and if he's not sure between three and four, he should treat it as three. Because the uncertainty is in the extra *Rak'a*. Then he should complete what is left of his *Salât* and perform two *Sajdah* while sitting before he makes *Taslîm*." (*Ahmad* and others)

ATTENDANCE OF WOMEN FOR CONGREGATIONAL *SALÂT* IN THE *MASJID*

It is permissible for women to go out to the *Masjid* to attend daily congregational *Salât*, on condition that they avoid clothing, ornament, or perfume that will attract attention of the opposite sex or invite to turmoil or confusion.

The Prophet ﷺ said:

«لَا تَمنَعُوا النِساءَ حُظُوظَهُنَّ مِنَ المساجِدِ إِذَا استَأذَنَّكُم».

[رواه مسلم].

"Do not prevent the women from their share in the *Masjid* when they seek your permission." (*Muslim*)

This *Hadîth* indicates that a married woman should ask the permission of her husband and the unmarried girl should ask the permission of her father or guardian.

The Prophet صلى الله عليه وسلم said:

«أَيُّمَا امرأةٍ أصابت بُخُوراً فَلاَ تَشهدْ مَعَنَا العِشَاءَ الآخرةِ».

[رواه مسلم] .

"Any woman who puts on perfume should not attend *Ishâ* (prayer) with us." (*Muslim*)

He صلى الله عليه وسلم also said:

«أيما امرأةٍ تَطَيَّبَتْ: ثُمَّ خَرَجَتْ إلى الـمسجدِ لَمْ تُقْبَلُ لَها صَلاةٌ حَتَّى تَغْتَسِلَ». [صحيح رواه ابن ماجه، انظر الجامع الصحيح ٢٧٠٠].

"Any women who puts on perfume and goes to *Masjid* for prayers, her *Salât* will not be accepted until she washes (it off)." (*Ibn Mâjah*).

The Prophet صلى الله عليه وسلم said:

«لا تمنعوا نساءَكم المساجِدَ، ويُبوتُهُنَّ خَيرُ لَهُنَّ». [صحيح رواه أبوداود، انظر المشكاة ١٠٦٢].

"Do not forbid your women from (attending to congregational prayers in) the *Masjid*, and their homes are better for them." (*Abû Dawûd*)

This indicates that the *Salât* of a women in her house is better for her then her *Salât* in the *Masjid*.

A woman's dress in *Salât*

The Prophet صلى الله عليه وسلم said:

«لَا يَقْبَلُ اللهُ صَلَاةَ حَائِضٍ إِلَّا بِخِمَارٍ». [صحيح رواه أبوداود
وغيره انظر المشكاة ١٠٦٢].

"Allah will not accept the *Salât* of a woman who is of menstruating age except with a *Khimâr* (a long scarf which covers her hair, neck, and chest)." (*Abû Dawûd* and others)

This *Hadîth* indicates that of a woman who has attained puberty, Allah will not accept her *Salât* unless she covers her head and neck and wears a long dress which will cover her legs and feet, or wears heavy socks which will cover her feet and legs, so that nothing of her skin can be seen underneath them, in addition to a dress which will cover her whole body. And it is permitted for her to expose her face and hands in *Salât* if there is no male stranger to see her, as there is no proof which requires her to cover those parts in *Salât*. As for outside of *Salât*, all of the woman's body is *'Aurah*, that is, a male stranger should not be able to see any part of her.

WHO IS MOST BEFITTING TO LEAD *SALÂT* ?

The most befitting to be *Imâm* (the one who leads the *Salât*) is the most adept at reciting the Book of Allah. [This has two aspects: one is how much he has memorized and knows its meanings, the other is how well he follows *Tajweed* (the rules of recitation)]. If they are equal in recitation, then the most learned in the *Sunnah*; if they are equal in that, then the one who made *Hijrah* (migrated) earlier; if equal in that, then the one who is older.

1. The Prophet صلى الله عليه وسلم said:

«يَؤُمُّ الْقَومَ أَقْرَؤُهُمْ لِكِتَابِ اللهِ فَإِن كَانُوا فِي القِرَاءةِ سَوَاءً

120

فَأَعْلَمُهُمْ بِالسُّنَّةِ، فَإِن كَانُوا فِي السُّنَّةِ سَوَاءً فَأَقْدَمُهُمْ هِجْرَةً، فَإِنْ كَانُوا فِي الهِجْرَةِ سَوَاءً فَأَقْدَمُهُمْ سِنّاً، وَلَا يَؤُمَّنَّ الرَّجُلُ الرَّجُلَ فِي سُلْطَانِهِ، وَلَا يَقْعُدْ فِي بَيْتِهِ عَلَى تَكْرِمَتِهِ إِلَّا بِإِذْنِهِ» . [رواه مسلم].

"The one to lead the people in *Salât* should be the most adept at reciting the Book of Allah; if they are equal in recitation, then the most learned in the *Sunnah*; and if they are equal in the *Sunnah*, then the one who made *Hijrah* earlier. And if they are equal in *Hijrah*, then the one who is older; and a man should certainly not lead where the other has authority, nor sit in his house on his furnishings without his permission." (*Muslim*)

A man's authority covers political authority or a man in his own house, or the *Imâm* of a *Masjid*. Any of these has more right to lead *Salât* where he has authority than anyone else, unless he grants to other permission.

Those who are eligible to be *Imâm*

1. It is acceptable that a child who has reached the age of discernment be *Imâm*, since 'Amr bin Salamah رضي الله عنه used to lead his people in *Salât* when he was six or seven years old because he knew more Qur'ân than any of them.

2. It is acceptable that a blind man may lead *Salât*, since the Prophet صلى الله عليه وسلم deputed Ibn Umm Maktûm as Governor of Al-Madinah in his absence, and he used to lead the people in *Salât*, and he was blind.

3. It is acceptable that a person praying *Fard* (obligatory) *Salât* may lead a person offering *Nafl* (voluntary) *Salât* as it is permissible for a person offering *Nafl* to lead a person performing *Fard* since Mu'adh رضي الله عنه used to pray '*Isha* with the Prophet صلى الله عليه وسلم then return to his tribe and lead

121

them in the same *Salât*, so for him that *Salât* was optional or voluntary, and for them it was obligatory.

4. It is permissible for a man who performed *Tayammum* to lead others in *Salât*. As 'Amr bin Al-Âs led people in *Salât* after performing *Tayammum* and the Prophet صلى الله عليه وسلم when hearing about that did not rebuke him, which indicates what he did was not wrong.

5. It is permissible for a traveller to be *Imâm* for resident. The Prophet صلى الله عليه وسلم led the people in *Salât* in Makkah at the time of its conquest, and he made all his prayers two *Rak'a* except *Maghrib* and he would say:

$$\text{يَا أَهْلَ مَكَّةَ قُومُوا فَصَلُّوا رَكْعَتَيْنِ أُخْرَيَيْنِ فَإِنَّا قَوْمٌ سَفَرٌ}.$$

"O people of Makkah, stand and pray two more *Rak'a* because we are travellers."

If a traveller prays behind an *Imâm* who is a resident, he must pray a complete *Salât* (four *Rak'a* for *Zuhr*, *'Asr* and *'Ishâ*), even if he did not catch a full *Rak'a* behind the *Imâm*, before the *Imâm* made *Taslîm* (salutation).

6. It is permissible for an *Imâm*, who cannot stand, to pray sitting; the Prophet صلى الله عليه وسلم said:

$$\text{إِنَّمَا جُعِلَ الإِمَامُ لِيُؤْتَمَّ بِهِ، فَإِذَا كَبَّرَ فَكَبِّرُواْ، وَلاَ تُكَبِّروا حَتَّى}$$
$$\text{يُكَبِّرَ، فَإِذَا رَكَعَ فَارْكَعُواْ وَلاَ تَرْكَعُواْ حَتَّى يَرْكَعَ، وإذا قَالَ سَمِعَ}$$
$$\text{اللهُ لِمَنْ حَمِدَه فَقُولُوا رَبَّنَا وَلَكَ الْحَمْدُ وَإِذَا سَجَدَ وَلا تَسجدو حَتَّى}$$
$$\text{يَسْجُدَ، وَإِذَا صَلَّى قِيَاماً فَصَلُّوا قِيَاماً وَإِذاَ صَلَّى قاعداً فَصَلُّواْ}$$
$$\text{قُعُوداً أَجْمَعِينْ}. \text{[رواه البخاري]}.$$

"The *Imâm* is appointed in order to be followed, so when

122

he says *Takbir*, say *Takbir* and do not say *Takbir* until he does so, and when he goes to *Rukû'*, go to *Rukû'* and do not go to *Rukû'* until he does so; and when he says, "Allah hears those who praise Him", say, "Our Lord, and all praise is Your due"; and when he performs *Sajdah*, perform *Sajdah*, and do not perform *Sajdah* until he does so; and if he prays standing, pray standing, and if he prays sitting all of you should pray sitting."* (*Bukhâri*)

THE VIRTUES OF *SALÂT*, AND WARNING AGAINST ABANDONING IT

1. Allah عز وجل said:

﴿ وَٱلَّذِينَ هُمْ عَلَىٰ صَلَاتِهِمْ يُحَافِظُونَ ٠ أُوْلَٰٓئِكَ فِى جَنَّٰتٍ مُّكْرَمُونَ ﴾

"And those who guard their prayers well, such shall dwell in the gardens (i.e. Paradise) honoured." (V. 70: 34, 35)

2. And Allah عز وجل said:

﴿ وَأَقِمِ ٱلصَّلَوٰةَ إِنَّ ٱلصَّلَوٰةَ تَنْهَىٰ عَنِ ٱلْفَحْشَاءِ وَٱلْمُنكَرِ ﴾

"...and offer prayers perfectly (*Iqâmat-as-Salât*). Verily, prayer prevents from *Al-Fâhsha* (i.e. great sins of every kind, unlawful sexual intercourse etc.) and *Al-Munkar* (i.e. disbelief, polytheism, and every kind of evil wicked deed etc.)..." (V. 29: 45)

3. And Allah عز وجل said:

﴿ فَوَيْلٌ لِّلْمُصَلِّينَ ٠ ٱلَّذِينَ هُمْ عَن صَلَاتِهِمْ سَاهُونَ ﴾

---

* It is better for *Muqtadi* to pray standing when the *Imam* leads them sitting as approved by the Prophet صلى الله عليه وسلم in his last illness, when he prayed sitting and people prayed standing. (See *Fath Al-Barî*, 1/219)

"So woe unto those performers of prayers (hypocrites), who delay their prayer from its fixed time." (V. 107: 4, 5)

4. And Allah عز وجل said:

﴿ قَدْ أَفْلَحَ ٱلْمُؤْمِنُونَ ۝ ٱلَّذِينَ هُمْ فِي صَلَاتِهِمْ خَٰشِعُونَ ﴾

"Successful indeed are the believers. Those who offer their prayers with all solemnity and full submissiveness." (V. 23: 1, 2)

5. And Allah عز وجل said:

﴿ ۞ فَخَلَفَ مِنۢ بَعْدِهِمْ خَلْفٌ أَضَاعُوا۟ ٱلصَّلَوٰةَ وَٱتَّبَعُوا۟ ٱلشَّهَوَٰتِ فَسَوْفَ يَلْقَوْنَ غَيًّا ﴾

"Then, there has succeeded them a posterity who have given up prayers (i.e. made their prayers to be lost, either by not offering them or by not offering them perfectly or by not offering them in their proper fixed times, etc.) and have followed lusts. So they will be thrown in Hell." (V. 19: 59)

6. And the Prophet صلى الله عليه وسلم said:

«أَرَأَيْتُمْ لَوْ أَنَّ نَهَراً بِبَابِ أَحَدِكُمْ يَغْتَسِلُ مِنْهُ كُلَّ يَوْمٍ خَمْسَ مَرَّاتٍ، هَلْ يَبْقَى مِنْ دَرَنِهِ شَيْءٌ؟ قَالُوا لَا يَبْقَى مِنْ دَرَنِهِ شَيْءٌ قَالَ فَذَلِكَ مِثْلُ الصَّلَوَاتِ الْخَمْسِ يَمْحُو اللَّهُ بِهِنَّ الْخَطَايَا».

[متفق عليه].

"What do you think if one of you had a river running past his door and he bathed in it five times a day, would any dirt remain on him?" They said, "No dirt would remain on him." He said, "Likewise is the similitude of the five times daily Salât, Allah obliterates thereby the sins." (Agreed upon)

7. And the Prophet صلى الله عليه وسلم said:

«اَلْعَهْدُ الَّذِيَ بَيْنَنَا وَبَيْنَهُمُ الصَّلَاةُ، فَمَنْ تَرَكَهَا فَقَدْ كَفَرَ».

[صحيح رواه أحمد وغيره].

"The covenant (which distinguished) between us and them is *Salât*, so whoever abandoned it became a *Kâfir*."

[Translator's note: This is the most straight forward translation of the Arabic text, though there are other interpretations of the final phrase which are linguistically acceptable, for instance: "Whoever abandoned it committed an act of disbelief."]

8. And he صلى الله عليه وسلم said:

«بَيْنَ الرَّجُلِ وَبَيْنَ الشِّرْكِ وَالْكُفْرِ تَرْكُ الصَّلَاةِ». [رواه مسلم].

"Between a man and '*Kufr* and *Shirk*' is the abandonment of *Salât*." (*Muslim*)

THE MANDATORY NATURE OF ATTENDING FRIDAY PRAYER AND THE DAILY *SALÂT* IN CONGREGATION

Congregational Salat five times a day and *Salât-ul-Jumu'ah* on Friday are obligatory on men, based on the following evidence:

1. Allah the Exalted said:

﴿ يَٰٓأَيُّهَا ٱلَّذِينَ ءَامَنُوٓاْ إِذَا نُودِيَ لِلصَّلَوٰةِ مِن يَوْمِ ٱلْجُمُعَةِ فَٱسْعَوْاْ إِلَىٰ ذِكْرِ ٱللَّهِ وَذَرُواْ ٱلْبَيْعَ ذَٰلِكُمْ خَيْرٌ لَّكُمْ إِن كُنتُمْ تَعْلَمُونَ﴾

"O you who believe (Muslims)! When the call is proclaimed for the *Salât* (prayer) on the day of Friday (*Jumu'ah* prayer), come to the remembrance of Allâh [*Jumu'ah* religious talk (*Khutbah*) and *Salât* (prayer)] and leave off business (and every other thing), that is better for you if you did but know!" (V. 62:9)

2. And the Prophet صلى الله عليه وسلم said:

«مَنْ تَرَكَ ثَلاثَ جُمَعٍ جُمَعٍ تَهَاوُناً بِهَا طَبَعَ اللهُ عَلَى قَلْبِهِ»

"Whoever leaves three *Jumua'h* (prayers) consecutively considering it not very important, Allah will seal his heart". (Ahmad)

3. And the Prophet صلى الله عليه وسلم said:

«لَقَدْ هَمَمْتُ أَنْ آمُرَ فِتْيَانِيْ، فَيَجْمَعُواْ لِيْ حُزْماً مِنْ حَطَبٍ، ثُمَّ آتِيْ قَوْمَاً يُصَلُّوْنَ فِيْ بُيُوْتِهِمْ لَيْسَتْ بِهِمْ عِلَّةٌ، فَأُحَرِّقُهَا عَلَيْهِمْ» . [رواه مسلم].

"I had a strong inclination to order the boys to gather firewood for me, then go to the houses of those who pray in their homes without excuse (like illness) and burn their houses down." (*Muslim*)

4. And it is reported that he (صلى الله عليه وسلم) said:

«مَنْ سَمِعَ النِّدَا، فَلَمْ يَأْتِهِ، فَلاَ صَلاَةَ لَهُ إِلاَّ مِنْ عُذْرٍ» .

"Whoever hears the *Adhân*, then doesn't come to the *Masjid* (but prays at home), then he has no *Salât* (acceptable) unless he has an excuse (a valid one - for instance, fear or illness)." (*Ibn Mâjah*)

5. A blind man came to the Prophet صلى الله عليه وسلم and said:

«أَتَى رَسُوْلَ اللهِ ﷺ رَجُلٌ أَعْمَى ، فَقَالَ: يَارَسُوْلَ اللَّهِ، إِنَّهُ لَيْسَ لِي قَائِدٌ يَقُوْدُنِيْ إِلَى المَسْجِدِ، فَسَأَلَ رَسُوْلَ اللَّهِ ﷺ أَنْ يُرَخِّصَ لَهُ، فَلَمَّا وَلَّىْ دَعَاهُ فَقَالَ: « هَلْ تَسْمَعُ النِّدَاءَ (الأذَانَ)؟ قَالَ نَعَمْ، قَالَ فَأَجِبْ» . [رواه مسلم].

"O Messenger of Allah, I have no guide to lead me to the *Masjid*," so grant me a leave from attending the congregational prayer in *Masjid*, which the Prophet صلى الله عليه وسلم did. But after he turned away, he (صلى الله عليه وسلم) called him back, and said, "Do you hear the call to prayer?" He said, "Yes." He (صلى الله عليه وسلم) said, "Then respond to it." (*Muslim*)

6. Abdullah bin Masûd رضي الله عنه said:

«مَنْ سَرَّهُ أَنْ يَلْقَى اللَّهَ غَداً مُسْلِماً فَلْيُحَــافِظْ عَلَى هَذِهِ الصَّلَوَاتِ الْخَمْسِ ، حَيْثُ يُنَادَى بِهِنَّ ، فَإِنَّ اللَّهَ شَرَعَ لِنَبِيِّكُمْ سُنَنَ الْهُدَى، وَإِنَّهُنَّ مِنْ سُنَنِ الْهُدَى وَلَوْ أَنَّكُمْ صَلَّيْتُمْ فِي بُيُوتِكُمْ كَمَا يُصَلِّي الْـمُتَخَلِّفُ فِي بَيْتِهِ لَتَرَكْتُمْ سُنَّةَ نَبِيِّكُمْ وَلَوْ تَرَكْتُمْ سُنَّةَ نَبِيِّكُمْ لَضَلَلْتُمْ ، وَلَقَدْ رَأَيْتُنَا وَمَا يَتَخَلَّفُ عَنْهَا إِلَّا مُنَافِقٌ مَعْلُومُ النِّفَاقِ، وَلَقَدْ كَانَ الرَّجُلُ يُؤْتَى بِهِ يُهَادَى بَيْنَ الرَّجُلَيْنِ حَتَّى يُقَامَ فِي الصَّفِّ».

"Whoever likes to meet Allah tomorrow as a Muslim, he should guard these five times daily *Salât* by praying them where the *Adhân* is called. Allah has prescribed for your Prophet (صلى الله عليه وسلم) practices of guidance, and if you pray in your homes, as some laggards do, you would abandon the *Sunnah* of your Prophet; and if you were to abandon the *Sunnah* of your Prophet, you will go astray. We used to see no one lagging behind from *Salât* in the *Masjid* except the known *Munâfiq* (hypocrite); and a sick person used to be helped to the *Masjid* supported between two men, until he would stand up in the row."

THE VIRTUES OF PRAYING IN CONGREGATION AND ATTENDING THE FRIDAY PRAYER

1. The Prophet صلى الله عليه وسلم said:

«مَنِ اغْتَسَلَ، ثُمَّ أَتَى الْجُمُعَةَ، فَصَلَّى مَا قُدِّرَ لَهُ ثُمَّ أَنْصَتَ حَتَّى يَفْرُغَ الإِمَامُ مِنْ خُطْبَتِهِ، ثُمَّ يُصَلِّي مَعَهُ غُفِرَ لَهُ مَا بَيْنَهُ وَبَيْنَ الْجُمُعَةِ الأُخْرَى، وَزِيَادَةُ ثَلَاثَةِ أَيَّامٍ، وَمَنْ مَسَّ الْحَصَى فَقَدْ لَغَا» . [رواه مسلم].

"Whoever bathes, then comes to *Jumu'ah* (Friday prayer) then prayed whatever was written for him, then listened silently until the *Imâm* finishes the *Khutbah* (sermon) then prays with the *Imâm*, Allah will forgive his sins which he had committed between the previous *Jumu'ah* and the present one, plus three more days after that and whoever touches the pebbles, he committed a futile act." (*Muslim*)

2. And he صلى الله عليه وسلم said:

«مَنِ اغْتَسَلَ يَوْمَ الْجُمُعَةِ غُسْلَ الْجَنَابَةِ، ثُمَّ رَاحَ فَكَأَنَّمَا قَرَّبَ بَدَنَةً، وَمَنْ رَاحَ فِي السَّاعَةِ الثَّانِيَةِ، فَكَأَنَّمَا قَرَّبَ بَقَرَةً، وَمَنْ رَاحَ فِي السَّاعَةِ الثَّالِثَةِ، فَكَأَنَّمَا قَرَّبَ كَبْشاً أَقْرَنَ، وَمَنْ رَاحَ فِي السَّاعَةِ الرَّابِعَةِ فَكَأَنَّمَا قَرَّبَ دَجَاجَةً، وَمَنْ رَاحَ فِي السَّاعَةِ الْخَامِسَةِ، فَكَأَنَّمَا قَرَّبَ بَيْضَةً، فَإِذَا خَرَجَ الإِمَامُ حَضَرَتِ الْمَلَائِكَةُ يَسْتَمِعُونَ الذِّكْرَ» . [رواه مسلم].

"Whoever performs a *Ghusl* (bath) on Friday, like the *Ghusl* for *Janâba* (post discharge state) then set out for the

128

Masjid, it is as if he sacrificed a camel; and whoever set out in the second time, it is as if he sacrificed a cow; and whoever set out in the third time, it is as if he sacrificed a ram with horns; and the one who went in the fourth time, it is as if he sacrificed a chicken; and whoever went in the fifth time, it is as if he has given an egg in charity; and, when the *Imâm* comes out, the angels gather to listen to the sermon." (*Muslim*)

3. And he (صلى الله عليه وسلم) said:

«مَنْ صَلَّى الْعِشَاءَ فِي جَمَاعَةٍ فَكَأَنَّمَا قَامَ نِصْفَ اللَّيْلِ ، وَمَنْ صَلَّى الصُّبْحَ فِي جَمَاعَةٍ ، فَكَأَنَّمَا قَامَ اللَّيْلَ كُلَّهُ» .

[رواه مسلم] .

"Whoever prays 'Ishâ in congregation, it is as if he stood half the night (in *Salât*); and whoever prays *Fajr* (Dawn) in congregation, it is as if he stood the whole night." (*Muslim*)

4. And he (صلى الله عليه وسلم) said:

صَلَاةُ الرَّجُلِ فِي جَمَاعَةٍ تَزِيدُ عَلَى صَلَاتِهِ فِي بَيْتِهِ وَصَلَاتُهُ فِي سُوقِهِ بِضْعاً وَعِشْرِينَ دَرَجَةً، وَذَلِكَ أَنَّ أَحَدَهُمْ إِذَا تَوَضَّأَ فَأَحْسَنَ الْوُضُوءَ ثُمَّ أَتَى الْمَسْجِدَ لَايَنْهِزُهُ إِلَّا الصَّلَاةُ (لَا يُرِيدُ إِلَّا الصَّلَاةَ) فَلَمْ يَخْطُ خُطْوَةً إِلَّا رُفِعَ لَهُ بِهَا دَرَجَةٌ، وَحُطَّ عَنْهُ بِهَا خَطِيئَةٌ، ، حَتَّى يَدْخُلَ الْمَسْجِدَ، فَإِذَا دَخَلَ الْمَسْجِدَ كَانَ فِي الصَّلَاةِ مَا كَانَتِ الصَّلَاةُ هِيَ تَحْبِسُهُ، وَالْمَلَائِكَةُ يُصَلُّونَ عَلَى أَحَدِهِمْ مَادَامَ فِي مَجْلِسِهِ الَّذِي صَلَّى فِيهِ يَقُولُونَ: اللَّهُمَّ ارْحَمْهُ، اللَّهُمَّ اغْفِرْ لَهُ، اللَّهُمَّ تُبْ عَلَيْهِ مَا لَمْ يُؤْذِ فِيهِ مَالَمْ يُحْدِثْ فِيهِ» .

[رواه البخاري ومسلم واللفظ لمسلم] .

"The *Salât* of a man in congregation excels *Salât* in house or *Salât* in a business centre, 23 to 29 times in reward. That is because when anyone performed *Wudû*, and performed it well, then came to the *Masjid*, with no other motive except the *Salât*, he takes no step without being raised thereby a degree, and a sin is removed from his account, until he enters the *Masjid*, once he enters the *Masjid* he is counted as being in prayer as long as he is waiting for the *Salât*, and the angels keep praying for him as long as he is sitting where he prayed; they say, 'O Allah have mercy on him, O Allah forgive him, O Allah accept his repentance.' They do that as long as he bothers no one and as long as he keeps his *Wudû*". (*Bukhâri* and *Muslim*, the wording is according to *Muslim*)

HOW TO OFFER FRIDAY PRAYER WITH ITS ETIQUETTES

1. Take a bath on Friday, and trim your nails, and apply some perfume and wear clean clothes after performing *Wudû*.

2. Don't eat raw onion or garlic and don't smoke. Clean your mouth with a *Siwak* (toothstick) or a toothbrush with toothpaste.

3. Pray two *Rak'a* upon entering the *Masjid* even if the *Khatîb* (orator) is on the *Minbar* (pulpit) in accordance with the order of the Prophet صلى الله عليه وسلم when he said:

«إِذَا جَاءَ أَحَدُكُم الْجُمُعَةَ والإِمَامُ يَخْطُبُ، فَلْيَرْكَعْ رَكْعَتَيْنِ، وَلْيَتَجَوَّزْ فِيهِمَا (أَيْ يُخَفِّفها)». [متفق عليه].

"When one of you comes to *Jumu'ah* and the *Imâm* is giving the *Khutbah*, he should perform two *Rak'a*, and make them short." (Agreed upon)

4. Sit quietly listening to the *Imâm*.

5. Pray the two obligatory *Rak'a* of *Jumu'ah* behind the *Imâm* (the intention should be in the heart).

6. Pray four *Rak'a Sunnah*, afterwards, in the *Masjid* or two *Rak'a* in the home, which is better.

7. Supplicate for the Prophet صلى الله عليه وسلم i.e. ask Allah to bless him. This should be more plentiful than on other days.

8. Supplicate to Allah as much as you can on Friday. The Prophet صلى الله عليه وسلم said:

«إِنَّ فِي الْجُمُعَةِ لَسَاعَةً لَا يُوافِقُهَا مُسْلِمٌ يَسْأَلُ اللَّه فِيهَا خَيْراً إِلَّا أَعْطَاهُ إِيَّاهُ». [متفق عليه].

"Verily, there is an hour on Friday, no Muslim would ask Allah for what is good but He would give it to him." (Agreed upon)

AHADÎTH ON THE SUBJECT OF SALÂT

1. «صَلُّوا كَمَا رَأَيْتُمُونِي أُصَلِّي». [رواه البخاري].

"Pray as you have seen me praying." (*Bukhâri*)

2. «إِذَا دَخَلَ أَحَدُكُمْ الْمَسْجِدَ فَلْيَرْكَعْ رَكْعَتَيْنِ قَبْلَ أَنْ يَجْلِسَ» [رواه البخاري].

"When one of you enters the *Masjid*, he should pray two *Rak'a* before sitting down." (This prayer is called greeting of *Masjid*). (*Bukhâri*)

3. «لَا تَجْلِسُوا عَلَى الْقُبُورِ، وَلَا تُصَلُّوا إِلَيْهَا». [رواه مسلم].

"Do not sit upon the graves and do not pray towards them." (*Bukhâri*)

4. «إِذَا أُقِيمَتِ الصَّلَاةُ، فَلَا صَلَاةَ إِلَّا الْـمَكْتُوبَةَ». [رواه مسلم].

"When the *Fard* (obligatory) *Salât* starts, there is no *Salât* except the obligatory one." (*Muslim*)

5. أُمِرْتُ أَنْ لَا أَكُفَّ ثَوْباً». [رواه مسلم].

"I was ordered not to pray with rolled up sleeves." (*Muslim*)

6. «أَقِيمُوا صُفُوفَكُمْ وَتَرَاصُّوا»، «وَكَانَ أَحَدُنَا يُلْزِقُ مَنْكِبَهُ بِمَنْكِب صَاحِبِه، وَقَدَمَهُ بِقَدَمِه». [رواه البخاري].

"Make your rows straight and get close together",

and in a version of the *Hadîth* the *Sahâbi* (Companion of the Prophet ﷺ) who narrated it added:

"We used to have our shoulders touching the shoulders of our adjoining person, and our feet touching their feet." (*Bukhâri*)

7. إِذا أُقِيمَتِ الصَّلَاةُ فَلَا تَأْتُوهَا وَأَنْتُمْ تَسْعَوْنَ، وَأْتُوهَا وَأَنْتُمْ تَمْشُونَ، وَعَلَيْكُمُ السَّكِينَةَ، فَمَا أَدْرَكْتُمْ فَصَلُّوا، وَمَا فَاتَكُمْ فَأَتِمُّوا». [متفق عليه].

"When the *Iqâmah* of *Salât* is called, do not come to *Salât* rushing. Come walking calmly. Whatever you find of the *Salât*, pray; and whatever you miss, complete it." (Agreed upon)

8. «ارْكَعْ حَتَّى تَطْمَئِنَّ رَاكِعاً، ثُمَّ ارْفَعْ حَتَّى تَعْتَدِلَ قَائِماً، ثُمَّ اسْجُدْ حَتَّى تَطْمَئِنَّ سَاجِداً». [رواه البخاري.]

"Perform *Rukû'* until you come to rest in *Rukû'*, then rise up until you are standing [fully] upright. Then perform *Sajdah* until you come to rest in *Sajdah.*" (*Bukhâri*)

9. «إِذَا سَجَدتَ فَضَعْ كَفَّيْكَ، وَارْفَعْ مِرْفَقَيْكَ» .[رواه مسلم]

When you perform *Sajdah*, place your hands down, and raise your elbows up." (*Muslim*)

10. «إِنِّي إِمَامُكُمْ فَلَا تَسْبِقُونِي بِالرَّكُوعِ وَالسُّجُودِ»[رواه مسلم].

"Verily I am your *Imâm* (leader), so don't perform *Rukû'* or *Sajdah* before I do." (*Muslim*)

11. «أَوَّلُ ما يُحَاسَبُ بِهِ العَبْدُ يَوْمَ القِيَامَةِ الصَّلاةُ فَإِنْ صَلُحَتْ صَلُحَ سَائِرُ عَمَلِهِ، وَإِنْ فَسَدَتْ فَسَدَ سَائِرُ عَمَلِهِ» . [رواه الطبراني]

"The first thing of the slave to be reckoned on the Day of Judgement will be his *Salât*. If it is good the rest of his deeds will be (accounted as) good. And if it is rotten the rest of his deeds will be rotten." (*Tabarâni*)

THE *SALÂT* OF A TRAVELLER ON LAND OR SEA OR IN AN AEROPLANE

1. Allah عز وجل said:

﴿ وَإِذَا ضَرَبْتُمْ فِى ٱلْأَرْضِ فَلَيْسَ عَلَيْكُمْ جُنَاحٌ أَن تَقْصُرُوا۟ مِنَ ٱلصَّلَوٰةِ ﴾

"And when you (Muslims) travel in the land, there is no sin on you if you shorten your prayer..." (V. 4: 101)

2. Ibn 'Abbas رضي الله عنهما said:

«فَرَضَ اللَّهُ الصَّلاةَ عَلَى لِسَانِ نَبِيِّكُم ﷺ فِي الحَضَرِ أَرْبَعاً، وَفِي السَّفَرِ رَكْعَتَيْنِ، وَفِي الخَوْفِ رَكْعَةً» . [رواه مسلم].

"Allah prescribed for you on the tongue of your Prophet صلى الله عليه وسلم four *Rak'a Salât* for a resident, two *Rak'a* in a journey and one *Rak'a* in a state of fear (war)." (*Muslim*)

3. And the Prophet صلى الله عليه وسلم said, "Shortening the prayer is:

«صَدَقَةٌ تَصَدَّقَ اللهُ بِهَا عَلَيْكَ فَاقْبَلُوْا صَدَقَتَهُ». [رواه مسلم].

A charity from Allah upon you, so accept his charity." (*Muslim*)

4. Ibn Qaiyim said: "The Prophet صلى الله عليه وسلم used to shorten four *Rak'a Salât* when he would set out on a journey, praying them as two *Rak'a* until he returned to Al-Madinah, and it is not proved that he ever prayed four *Rak'a Salât* complete during a journey. (*Maghrib* remains unchanged, to be prayed three *Rak'a*), and none of the *Imâm* differed on that."

5. Joining two *Salât*: It is permissible for a traveller to pray *Zuhr* and *'Asr* together, either by offering *'Asr* earlier or delaying *Zuhr,* and in the same way, he can join *Maghrib* and *'Ishâ*. This is permissible in the following circumstances:

(A) In *Hajj*, at Arafat and Muzdalifah. All scholars agree that *Zuhr* and *'Asr* should be prayed together during the time of *Zuhr* at Arafat; and that *Maghrib* and *'Isha* should be prayed together at the time of *'Isha* at Muzdalifah; that is the proven *Sunnah* of the Prophet صلى الله عليه وسلم .

(B) Joining two *Salât* during a journey in the time of one of them is permissible, as is proven by the statement of Anas bin Malik رضي الله عنه that:

«كَانَ الرَّسُوْلُ ﷺ إِذَا ارْتَحَلَ فِي سَفَرِهِ قَبْلَ أَنْ تَزِيغَ الشَّمْسُ (أَيْ قَبْلَ الزَّوَالِ) أَخَّرَ الظُّهْرَ إِلَى وَقْتِ الْعَصْرِ ثُمَّ نَزَلَ فَجَمَعَ بَيْنَهُمَا، فَإِنْ زَاغَتِ الشَّمْسُ (أَيْ بَعْدَ الـزَّوَالِ) قَبْلَ أَنْ يَرْتَحِلَ

صَلَّى الظُّهْـرَ، ثُـمَّ رَكِـبَ». [متفق عليه].

"When the Prophet ﷺ would travel before the sun passed the zenith, he would delay *Zuhr* until the time of *'Asr*, then he would pray both together. And if the sun passed the zenith before he set out, he would pray *Zuhr*, then mount his animal to travel." (Agreed upon)

«كَانَ ﷺ إِذَا كَانَ فِي سَفَرِهِ فَزَالَتِ الشَّمْسُ (أَيْ دَخَلَ وَقْتُ الظُّهْرِ) صَلَّى الظُّهْرَ وَالْعَصْرَ جَمْعاً، ثُمَّ ارْتَحَلَ». [أنظر سبل السلام ٤٢].

(C) Abu Nu'aim reported in his *Mustakhraj* on the *Hadîth* collection of Muslim:

"The Prophet ﷺ, when he was in a journey, used to pray *Zuhr* and *'Asr* together if the sun passed the zenith, and then he would set out."

The last *Hadîth* indicates that joining two *Salât* during the time of the earlier one is permissible. The *Hadîth* before that indicates the permissibility of delaying a *Salât* to join it to the one next to it.

(D) *Salât* is alright on ship or train or plane, in a manner a man finds it easier for him to perform, and it is permissible to join two *Salât* on them. The Prophet ﷺ was asked about *Salât* in a boat. He ﷺ said:

«صَـلِّ فِيهَـا قَائِماً إِلَّا أَنْ تَخَافَ الغَـرَقَ». [صححه الحاكم].

"Pray standing, unless you fear it might cause you to drown." (Declared authentic by Hakîm)

SALÂT IS MANDATORY ON THE SICK PERSON

1. Beware, O my Muslim brother, from abandoning *Salât*, even in

a state of sickness, because it is obligatory upon you; and Allah has even made it mandatory on the *Mujahideen* during war.

And know that *Salât* brings an inner tranquillity to the sick person which will help them get well. Allah said:

$$﴿ وَٱسۡتَعِينُواْ بِٱلصَّبۡرِ وَٱلصَّلَوٰةِ ﴾$$

"And seek help with patience and prayer..." (V. 2: 45)

And the Prophet صلى الله عليه وسلم used to say:

«يَا بِلَالُ أَقِم الصَّلَاةَ أَرِحْنَا بِهَا» . [رواه أبو داود وحسن إسناده الألباني]

"O Bilal call the *Iqâmah* for *Salât*, bring us relaxation by it" (*Abû Dâwûd*, Albâni declared its *Isnad* to be *Hasan*).

And it is better for a sick person if his life is drawing to an end, to die as one who prays, and not to die disobedient by abandoning *Salât*. And Allah has made things easy for the sick person. He can make *Tayammum* if he can't manage to use water for *Wudû* and *Janaba* so that he doesn't abandon *Salât*. Allah عز وجل said:

$$﴿ وَإِن كُنتُم مَّرۡضَىٰٓ أَوۡ عَلَىٰ سَفَرٍ أَوۡ جَآءَ أَحَدٌ مِّنكُم مِّنَ ٱلۡغَآئِطِ أَوۡ لَٰمَسۡتُمُ ٱلنِّسَآءَ فَلَمۡ تَجِدُواْ مَآءً فَتَيَمَّمُواْ صَعِيدًا طَيِّبًا فَٱمۡسَحُواْ بِوُجُوهِكُمۡ وَأَيۡدِيكُم مِّنۡهُ مَا يُرِيدُ ٱللَّهُ لِيَجۡعَلَ عَلَيۡكُم مِّنۡ حَرَجٍ وَلَٰكِن يُرِيدُ لِيُطَهِّرَكُمۡ وَلِيُتِمَّ نِعۡمَتَهُۥ عَلَيۡكُمۡ لَعَلَّكُمۡ تَشۡكُرُونَ ﴾$$

"...And if you are ill or on a journey or any of you comes from answering the call of nature, or you have been in contact with women (i.e. sexual intercourse) and you find no water, then perform *Tayammum* with clean earth and rub therewith your faces and hands. Allah does not want to place you in difficulty, but He wants to purify you, and to complete His Favour on you that you may be thankful." (V. 5: 6)

136

HOW A SICK PERSON CAN PERFORM
THE ACTS OF PURIFICATION

1. It is obligatory on the sick person to purify himself with water, that is to perform *Wudû* for the minor ritual impurity (passing wind or urine or answering the call of nature) and to perform a *Ghusl* for the major ritual impurity (sexual discharge).

2. If he is unable to use water for purification due to his weakness or he fears that the illness will get worse as a result, or that his recovery will be delayed, then he must perform *Tayammum*.

3. How to perform *Tayammum*: Strike clean earth with both hands one time. then wipe your whole face and wipe your hands, one over the other, leaving no part unwiped.

4. If he is unable to perform the purification act by himself, someone should help him perform *Wudû* or *Tayammum*.

5. If he has a wound on one of his limbs (which are washed for the purification act) he should wash it with water. If washing with water affects him (adversely) then he can wipe over the affected area with his wet hand. If wiping also affects him, then he should perform *Tayammum*.

6. If he has a bandage or cast over some portion of his limbs, he should wipe over it with a wet hand in place of washing the limb and he doesn't need to perform *Tayammum* since the wiping took the place of washing.

7. It is permissible to perform *Tayammum* on a wall or any clean place that has dust on it. If the wall has been covered by paint or some other substance that is not of the category of earthy substance, it shouldn't be used for *Tayammum* unless there is a coating of dust on it.

8. If *Tayammum* can't be easily performed on the face of the earth or a wall or other object having a dusty surface, there is

no harm in putting some clean dirt in a container or a handkerchief, etc. and performing *Tayammum* on that.

9. If he performed *Tayammum* for one *Salât*, then kept in that state until the next *Salât* comes in, he can pray with the first *Tayammum*, and doesn't need to perform a new *Tayammum*, because he is still in a state of purification and nothing occurred to cause its nullification.

10. It is obligatory for the sick person to clean his body of physical filth. If he is unable, he should go ahead and pray as he is, his *Salât* is valid, and he doesn't have to repeat the *Salât* later.

11. It is obligatory for the sick person to pray in clean clothes. If physical filth gets on his clothes, he must wash it off or change into clean clothes. If he is unable to, he should go ahead and pray as he is, his *Salât* is valid, and he doesn't have to repeat the *Salât* later.

12. It is obligatory for the sick person to pray on something clean, if the place becomes impure, washing it clean is obligatory or replacing it with some thing clean, or putting something clean over it. If he is unable, he should go ahead and pray as he is, his *Salât* is valid, and he doesn't have to repeat later.

13. It is not permitted for the sick person to postpone *Salât* from its time because he is too weak to purify himself, rather he should purify himself as much as he is able to do, and perform the *Salât* in time, even if there is some filth on his body or clothes or his place which he is incapable to clean away.

HOW A SICK PERSON CAN PERFORM *SALÂT*

1. It is obligatory for the sick person to pray standing, even if leaning, or propped against a wall or on a crutch or staff, if he

needs the support.

2. If he cannot stand, he should pray sitting, and the best thing is for him to sit cross-legged in the positions of *Qiyâm* and *Rukû'*.

3. If he cannot sit, he should lie on his side, facing *Qiblah*; and the right side is better to lie on. If he can't manage to face the *Qiblah*, he should face wherever he's facing, and his *Salât* is valid, and he doesn't have to repeat it later.

4. If he cannot offer the *Salât* lying on his side, he should lie on his back with his feet towards the *Qiblah* and if he's able, it is better for him to have his head propped up a bit so that he has got his face towards *Qiblah*; again, if he can't get his feet facing *Qiblah*, he should pray wherever he's facing and he doesn't have to repeat later.

5. It is obligatory for the sick person to perform *Rukû'* and *Sajdah* in his *Salât*. If he is unable, he can make a gesture with his head, making the gesture for *Sajdah* more prominent than the gesture for *Rukû'*. If he is able to perform *Rukû'* but not *Sajdah*, he should perform *Rukû'* normally then make the substitute gesture for *Sajdah*. And if he is able to perform *Sajdah*, he should perform *Sajdah* where called for and make the substitute gesture for *Rukû'*, and it is not necessary to get a pillow to perform *Sajdah* on.

6. If he cannot move his head, he should make the signal for *Rukû'* and *Sajdah* with his eyes, lowering his eyelids slightly for *Rukû'*, and more for *Sajdah*. As for gesturing with one's finger, as some sick people do, it is not correct, and I know of no basis for it in the Qur'ân or *Sunnah* or statements of the scholars.

7. If he is unable to gesture with his head nor with his eyes, he should pray in his heart, saying *Takbîr* and reciting, and making intention for *Rukû'* and *Sajdah* and standing and sitting in his heart, and everyone will be rewarded according

139

to their intention.

8. It is mandatory for the sick person to pray every *Salât* at its appointed time, and to perform every act of it according to his ability. If it proves difficult for him to pray each *Salât* on time, he can join *Zuhr* and *'Asr,* and *Maghrib* and *'Isha* together by delaying the first or offering second earlier, whatever is easier for him. As for *Fajr*, it must be prayed at its regular time, without joining it to what is before it nor to what is after it.

9. If the sick person travels for medical treatment to another country or city, he may shorten his four *Rak'a Salât*, praying *Zuhr, Asr* and *'Isha*, each as two *Rak'a*, until he returns to his own place, whether the period of his journey is long or short (this is according to Shaikh Muhammad Salih Uthaimîn).

DU'Â (SUPPLICATIONS) AT THE BEGINNING OF *SALÂT*

1. «اللَّهُمَّ بَاعِدْ بَيْنِي وَبَيْنَ خَطَايَايَ كَمَا بَاعَدْتَ بَيْنَ الـمَشْرِقِ وَالـمَغْرِبِ، اللَّهُمَّ نَقِّنِي مِنْ خَطَايَايْ كَمَا يُنَقَّىْ الثَّوْبُ الأَبْيَضُ مِنَ الـدَّنَسِ، اللَّهُمَّ أَغْسِلْ خَطَايَايَ بِالمَاءِ والثَّلْجِ وَالْبَرَدِ».

[متفق عليه].

"O Allah, put a distance between me and my sins like the distance you put between the east and the west. O Allah forgive me of my sins like the white robe is purified from dirt. O Allah, wash my sins with water and snow and hail." (Agreed upon)

2. «اللَّهُمَّ أَنْتَ الملكُ، لاَ إِلهَ إِلاَّ أَنْتَ أَنْتَ رَبِي، وَأَنَا عَبْدُكَ، ظَلَمْتُ نَفْسِي وَاعْتَرَفْتُ بِذَنْبِي، فَاغْفِرْ لِي ذُنُوبِي جَمِيعاً، إِنَّهُ

140

لَا يَغْفِرُ الذُّنُوبَ إِلَّا أَنْتَ، اللَّهُمَّ اهْدِنِي لِأَحْسَنِ الْأَخْلَاقِ، لَا يَهْدِي لِأَحْسَنِهَا إِلَّا أَنْتَ، وَاصْرِفْ عَنِّي سَيِّئَهَا فَإِنَّهُ لَايَصْرِفُ عَنِّي سَيِّئَهَا إِلَّا أَنْتَ». [رواه مسلم].

[He (صلى الله عليه وسلم) used to say it in the *Fard Salât*].

"O Allah, you are the King, none has the right to be worshipped but You, You are my Lord, and I am Your slave. I wronged my soul and I admit my sin, so forgive me of all my sins, indeed, no one forgives sins except You. O Allah, guide me to the best character, none can guide to the best of it except You, and divert from me the evil (character), for verily none can divert from me the evil of it except You". (*Muslim*)

[He (صلى الله عليه وسلم) used to say it in *Fard* and *Nafl Salât* at the beginning of it].

DU'Â AT THE END OF *SALÂT*

1. «اللَّهُمَّ إِنِّي أَعُوذُ بِكَ مِنْ عَذَابِ جَهَنَّمَ، وَمِنْ عَذَابِ الْقَبْرِ، وَمِنْ فِتْنَةِ الْمَحْيَا وَالْمَمَاتِ، وَمِنْ شَرِّ فِتْنَةِ الْمَسِيحِ الدَّجَّالِ». [رواه مسلم].

"O Allah, verily I seek refuge with You from the torment of Hell, and from the torment of the grave, and from the trial of life and death and from the evil of the trial of the *Dajjâl* (the Antichrist)." (*Muslim*)

[He (صلى الله عليه وسلم) used to make this *Du'â* at the end of *Tashahhud*].

2. «اللَّهُمَّ إِنِّي أَعُوذُ بِكَ مِنْ شَرِّ مَا عَمِلْتُ، وَمِنْ شَرِّ مَالَمْ أَعْمَلْ». [رواه النسائي بسند صحيح].

141

"O Allah I seek refuge with you from the evil of what I have done and from the evil of what I haven't done." (*Nasa'i*)

HOW TO PERFORM *SALÂT* ON A DEAD PERSON (FUNERAL PRAYER)

Make the intention for Funeral (*Janazah)* Prayer in your heart and say four *Takbîr.*

1. After the first *Takbîr*, say *A'udhu billahi* ... i.e. seek refuge with Allah from *Shaitan* and say *Bismillahir Rahmanir Rahim* then recite *Surah Al-Fâtihah.*

2. After the second *Takbîr,* recite *Salât-ul-Ibrahimia* on the Prophet صلى الله عليه وسلم just as you do in *Salât*:

اللّٰهُمَّ صَلِّ عَلَى مُحَمَّدٍ وَعَلَى أَلِ مُحَمَّدٍ كَمَا صَلَّيْتَ عَلَى إِبْرَاهِيمَ

Allahumma salli 'Ala Muhammadin wa 'ala âli Muhammadin kama sallaita 'ala Ibrahima ...

"O Allah have mercy on and reward Muhammad and the family of Muhammad as You had mercy and rewarded Ibrahim ... etc."

3. After the third *Takbîr* supplicate the following *Du'â* reported from the Prophet صلى الله عليه وسلم :

«اللَّهُمَّ اغْفِرْ لِحَيِّنَا وَمَيِّتِنَا، وَشَاهِدِنَا وَغَائِبِنَا، وَصَغِيرِنَا وَكَبِيرِنَا، وَذَكَرِنَا وَأُنْثَانَا، اللَّهُمَّ مَنْ أَحْيَيْتَهُ مِنَّا فَأَحْيِهِ عَلَى الإِسْلَامِ ، وَمَنْ تَوَفَّيْتَهُ مِنَّا فَتَوَفَّهُ عَلَى الإِيمَانِ اللَّهُمَّ لاَتَحْرِمْنَا أَجْرَهُ، وَلاَ تَفْتِنَّا بَعْدَهُ». [رواه أحمد والترمذي وقال حسن صحيح].

"O Allah, forgive our living and our dead, and those of us present and those of us absent, and our young and our old, and our male and female. O Allah, whomsoever You caused

142

to live among us, make them live on Islam, and those whom You cause to die among us, make him die on *Imân* (belief), O Allah, do not hold back from us his reward, and do not test us after him." (*Ahmad* and *Tirmidhi*).

4. After the fourth *Takbîr*, supplicate as you wish, then end with *Salâm* to the right.

THE ADMONISHMENT OF DEATH

Allah عز وجل said:

﴿ كُلُّ نَفْسٍ ذَآئِقَةُ ٱلْمَوْتِ وَإِنَّمَا تُوَفَّوْنَ أُجُورَكُمْ يَوْمَ ٱلْقِيَٰمَةِ فَمَن زُحْزِحَ عَنِ ٱلنَّارِ وَأُدْخِلَ ٱلْجَنَّةَ فَقَدْ فَازَ وَمَا ٱلْحَيَوٰةُ ٱلدُّنْيَا إِلَّا مَتَٰعُ ٱلْغُرُورِ ﴾

"Everyone shall taste death. And only on the Day of Resurrection shall you be paid your wages in full. And whoever is removed away from the Fire and admitted to Paradise, he indeed is successful. The life of this world is only the enjoyment of deception (a deceiving thing)." (V. 3: 185)

And the poet said:

"Make provision for the inevitable, for death has an appointment with every slave.

And repent for the sin you committed while alive, and be aware before the final sleep.

You will be sorry if you travel without provision, and you will be miserable when the caller calls.

Do you want to be in the company of people, who have provision while you have none?"

'EID PRAYERS AT MUSALLA (PRAYER PLACE)

١. كَانَ رَسُولُ اللهِ ﷺ يَخْرُجُ يَوْمَ الْفِطْرِ وَالْأَضْحَى إِلَى الْـمُصَلَّى،
فَأَوَّلُ شَيْءٍ يَبْدَأُ بِهِ الصَّلَاةُ . . . » . [رواه البخارى].

"The Prophet ﷺ used to go out to an open area for *Salât* on the festival at the end of Ramadan (*Eid-ul-Fitr*) and the feast of the sacrifice (*Eid-ul-Adha*), and the first thing he would start with would be *Salât.*" (Bukhâri)

2. The Prophet ﷺ said:

«التَّكْبِيرُ فِي الْفِطْرِ : سَبْعٌ فِي الْأُولَى، وَخَمْسٌ فِي الْآخِرَةِ، وَالْقِرَاءَةُ
بَعْدَهُمَا كِلْتَيْهِمَا» . [حسن رواه أبوداود].

"The number of extra *Takbîr* for *Salât* of *Eid-ul-Fitr* is seven in the first *Rak'a* and five in the second, then recitation after them in both *Rak'a.*" (*Abû Dâwûd*)

3. The Prophet ﷺ would order us to have all the women come out for *Eid-ul-Fitr* and Eid-ul-Adha:

«الْعَوَائِقَ، وُالْحُيَّضَ، وَذَوَاتِ الْخُدُورِ، فَأَمَّا الْـمَحِيضُ فَيَعْتَزِلْنَ
الصَّلَاةَ، وَيَشْهَدْنَ الْخَيْرَ وَدَعْوَةَ الْـمُسْلِمِينَ، قُلْتُ يَارَسُولَ اللهِ،
إِحْدَانَا لَايَكُونُ لَهَا جِلْبَابٌ ؟ قَالَ : لِتَلْبِسْهَا أُخْتُهَا مِنْ جِلْبَابِهَا.
[متفق عليه].

"Including the unmarried, the menstruating and the virgins; as for those menstruating, they should stay aside from the place of *Salât*. And they would witness the blessing and the supplications of the Muslims." I said to him, "One of us may not have an outer garment." He said,

"One of her sisters should clothe her with one of her outer garments." (Agreed upon)

What can be deduced from the *Ahadîth*:

1. *Salât* of the two *'Eid* (festivals) is part of the religion and it is two *Rak'a*. One should say seven *Takbîr* in the beginning of the first *Rak'a* and five in the beginning of the second *Rak'a*. Then recite *Fâtihah* and whatever is easy.

2. *'Eid* prayer should be in an open ground near the city and the Prophet صلى الله عليه وسلم used to go out for the two *'Eid* prayers and even the children and women and girls would go out with him and even women who couldn't pray because of menstruation.

   Ibn Hajar said in *Fath-ul-Bâri*: "It indicates that one should go out to an open space to pray. And the prayer shouldn't be in the *Masjid* except if there is no alternative."

EMPHASIS UPON OFFERING A SACRIFICE ON THE *'EID-UL-ADHA*

1. Allah's Messenger صلى الله عليه وسلم said:

«إنَّ أَوَّلَ مَانْبْدَأُ بِهِ فِي يَوْمِنَا هَذَا أَنْ نُصَلِّيَ ، ثُمَّ نَرْجِعَ فَنَنْحَرَ، فَمَنْ فَعَلَ ذَلِكَ فَقَد أَصَابَ سُنَّتَنَا، وَمَنْ نَحَرَ قَبْلَ الصَّلَاةِ، فَإِنَّما هُوَ لَحْمٌ قَدَّمَهُ لِأَهْلِهِ، وَلَيْسَ مِنَ النُّسُكِ فِي شَيْءٍ». [متفق عليه].

"Verily, the first thing we start with on this day of ours is *Salât*, then we go back and sacrifice an animal. Whoever did so, he is in accord with our *Sunnah*. And whoever slaughters before the prayer, it is only meat he provided for his family, and it is not part of the rites in the least." (Agreed upon)

2. And he (صلى الله عليه وسلم) said:

145

«يَاأَيُّهَا النَّاسُ : إِنَّ عَلَى كُلِّ بَيْتٍ أُضْحِيَةٌ» . [رواه أحمد والأربعة،

وقواه الحافظ في الفتح].

"O people, on every house there is a sacrifice (due)." (*Ahmad* and *Arba'ah*, Ibn Hajar brought evidence strengthening it in *Fath-ul-Bâri*).

3. And he (صلى الله عليه وسلم) said:

«مَنْ وَجَدَ سَعَةً لأَنْ يُضَحِّي فَلَمْ يُضَحِّ فَلَا يَقْرَبَنَّ مُصَلَّانَا» .

[رواه أحمد وغيره وحسنه محقق جامع الأصول].

"Whoever has the means to sacrifice but doesn't do so, he needs not come to where we pray the *'Eid*." (*Ahmad* and others, declared *Hasan* in the verification of *Jami'-ul-Usûl*)

SALÂT TO SUPPLICATE FOR RAIN (*ISTISQA*)

1. «خَرَجَ النَّبِيُّ - ﷺ - إِلَى الـمُصَلَّى يَسْتَسْقِي ، فَدَعَا وَاسْتَسْقَى ثُمَّ اسْتَقْبَلَ القِبْلَةَ ، فَصَلَّى رَكعتينِ ، وَقَلَّبَ رِدَاءهُ وجَعَلَ اليَمِينَ عَلَى الشِّمَالِ» . [رواه البخاري].

"The Prophet صلى الله عليه وسلم went out to the open ground to pray for rain, first he made *Du'â* asking for rain, then he turned towards the *Qiblah* and prayed two *Rak'a*, he turned his cloak, and the right side of his cloak was on his left." (*Bukhâri*)

2. «أن عُمَرَ بن الخطَّابِ كَانَ إذَا قَحَطُوا استسقَى بالعَبَّاسِ فَقَالَ : اللَهُمَّ إنَّا كُنَّا نَتَوَسَّلُ إليكَ بنبيِّكَ فَتسقِينا، وَإنَّا نَتوسَّلُ

146

إلَيكَ بِعَمِّ نَبِيِّكَ ـ ﷺ ـ فَاسْقِنَا فَيِسْقَوْنَ». [رواه البخاري].

Anas bin Malik عنه الله رضي narrates that when Umar bin Al-Khattâb was *Khalifah* (caliph) and there was a drought, he would ask 'Abbâs to lead the prayer for rain, saying:

"O Allah we used to seek the intercession of Your Prophet وسلم عليه الله صلى, and You would send us rain, and now we seek intercession of the uncle of Your Prophet وسلم عليه الله صلى so send us rain," and the rain would come. (*Bukhâri*)

This *Hadîth* proves that the Muslims used to seek intercession to Allah through the Messenger وسلم عليه الله صلى during his lifetime, asking him to make *Du'â* for them for the descent of rain, and when he (وسلم عليه الله صلى) departed this world, they did not continue to ask him to make *Du'â* rather they requested his uncle 'Abbâs for it, who was still alive, and so 'Abbâs would stand to make *Du'â* to Allah for them.

SALÂT AT THE TIME OF SOLAR OR LUNAR ECLIPSE

1. 'Aisha عنها الله رضي narrated:

«خَسَفَتِ الشَّمْسُ عَلَى عَهْدِ رَسُولِ اللهِ ـ ﷺ ـ فَبَعَثَ مُنَادِياً: «الصَّلَاةُ جَامِعَةٌ» فَقَامَ فَصَلَّى أَرْبَعَ رَكَعاتٍ فِي رَكْعَتَيْنِ وَأَرْبَعَ سَجَدَاتٍ». [رواه البخاري].

"The sun was eclipsed during the lifetime of Allah's Messenger وسلم عليه الله صلى, he sent a caller to announce '*As-Salât-u-Jumia* (*Salât* in congregation),' then he stood and prayed two *Rak'a* with four *Rukû'* and four *Sajdah*." (*Bukhâri*)

2. And 'Aisha عنها الله رضي said:

147

«كَسَفتِ الشَّمسُ في عَهدِ النَّبيِّ ﷺ ـ فَقامَ النَّبيُّ ﷺ ـ
فَصلى بالنَّاس ، فَأَطالَ القِراءةَ، ثُمَّ رَكعَ فَأَطالَ الرُّكُوعَ، ثُمَّ رَفَعَ
رَأسَهُ، فَأَطالَ القِراءةَ، ثُمَّ رَكعَ فَأَطالَ الركُوعَ ثُمَّ رَفعَ رَأسَهُ،
فَأَطالَ القِراءةَ ـ وهي دون قِراءته الأولى ـ ثُمَّ رَكعَ فَأَطالَ الرُّكُوعَ
دُونَ رُكُوعه الأول ، ثُمَّ رَفعَ رَأسَهُ، فَسَجدَ سَجدتيـن، ثُمَّ قامَ
فَصَنعَ في الرَّكعة الثَّانية مِثلَ ذَلكَ، فَسَلَّمَ، وَقَد تَجَلَّتِ الشَّمسُ
فَخطبَ الناس فَقَالَ :

إنَّ الشَّمس والقَمرَ لاَ يَنْكَسِفان لِـموتِ أحدٍ وَلاَ لِحياته ، وَلكنَّهما
آيتـان مِن آياتِ الله يُريهِما عِبادَه ، فإذا رأيتُم ذَلكَ فافزَعُوا إلى
الصَّلاة . . وَادعُوا الله وَصلُّوا وتَصدَّقُوا . . »

يَاأُمَّة مُحَمَّدٍ مَامِن أَحَدٍ أغيرُ مِنَ الله أَنْ يَزني عَبدُه، أوتَزني أَمَتُهُ،
يَاأُمَّـةَ مُحَمـدٍ والله لَوْ تَعلَمُونَ مَاأَعلَمُ لَضَحِكتُم قَليلاً وَلَبَكَيْتُم
كَثيراً، ألاَ هَلْ بَلَّغتُ». [هذه رواية البخاري ومسلم باختصار].

The sun was eclipsed during the lifetime of the Prophet ﷺ
صلى الله عليه وسلم , so the Prophet stood and led the people in *Salât*,
and his recitation was long. Then he performed *Rukû‘* and
he stayed bowing for a long time. Then he raised his head and
recited for a long time, but less than the first. Then he
performed *Rukû‘* and stayed bowing a long time, but less
than the first *Rukû‘*. Then he raised his head, then he
performed two *Sajdah*. Then he stood and prayed a second
Rakâ‘ like the first. Then he made *Taslîm*; by that time the
sun had reappeared. He then addressed the people, saying:

"The sun and the moon do not go into eclipse because of

148

anyone's death nor his life. Rather they are two signs from among the signs of Allah, which He shows to his slaves. So when you see that, leave everything for *Salât*, and pray to Allah and perform *Salât* and give charity."

"O followers of Muhammad no one is more jealous than Allah that His slave commits adultery, male or female. O followers of Muhammad, by Allah, if you only know what I know, you would laugh little and cry a lot. Did I convey (the Message)?" (Reported by Bukhâri by this wording and by Muslim in a condensed version)

SALÂT-UL-ISTIKHÂRA
(Prayer to seek guidance for what is better)

Jâbir رضي الله عنه said:

«كَانَ رَسُولُ الله ـ ﷺ ـ يُعَلِّمُنَا الاستِخَارَة في الأُمُورِ كُلِّها، كَما يُعَلِّمُنَا السُّورةَ مِنَ القُرآنِ، يَقُولُ: «إذَا هَمَّ أَحَدُكم بالأمرِ فَلْـيَرْكَعْ رَكعَتينِ مِن غَيرِ الفَريضَة، ثُم لِيَقُلْ: اللهُمَّ إني استَخِيرُك بعِلمِكَ، واستقدِرُك بِقُدرتِكَ، وأسألُكَ مِن فَضلِكَ العَظِيمِ، فَإنَّكَ تَقدِرُ وَلاَ أَقدِرُ، وَتَعلَمُ وَلاَ أَعلَمُ، وأنْتَ عَلاَّمُ الغُيُوبِ. اللهُمَّ إنْ كُنتَ تَعلَمُ أنَّ هَذا الأمرَ(1) خَيرٌ لي في دِيني وَمَعَاشي وَعَاقِبة أمري، (أو قَالَ في عَاجِلِ أمري وآجِلِه) فَاقْدُرْهُ لي وَيَسِّـرهُ لي ثُم بَارِك لي فيه، وَإِن كُنتَ تَعلَمُ أنَّ هَذا الأمرَ(1) شَرٌّ لي في دِيني وَمَعَاشي وَعَاقِبة أمري (أو قَالَ في عَاجِلِ أمري وآجِلِه) فَاصْرِفهُ عَنِّي واصرِفني عَنهُ واقْدُرْ لي الـخَيرَ حَيثُ كَانَ ثُمَّ أَرْضِني به(2) (قَالَ وَيُسمِّي حَاجَتَهُ). [رواه البخاري].

149

The Prophet صلى الله عليه وسلم used to teach us *Istikhâra* in all affairs in the way he would teach us a *Surah* of the Qur'ân. He would say:

"If one of you is concerned about something and is in need of guidance from Allah, he should make two *Rak'a* optional *Salât*, then say:

'O Allah, verily I seek the good from You by Your Knowledge, and I seek the Decree from You by Your Power and I ask of You, Your tremendous bounty. Because You decree and I do not, and You know and I do not know; and You are the Total Knower of the unseen.

'O Allah, if You know this affair [and he should name it] is good for me, in my religion and my livelihood and the final outcome of my affairs [or he (صلى الله عليه وسلم) said: In my immediate affairs and my long term ones] then decree it for me, and make it easy for me, and bless me in it, and if You know this affair [and he should name it] is evil for me in my religion and my livelihood and in the final outcome of my affairs [or he (صلى الله عليه وسلم) said: In my immediate affairs and my long term ones], then divert it away from me, and divert me away from it, and decree for me the good wherever it may be, then make me content with that." (*Bukhâri*)

This *Salât* and *Du'â* should be done by the person for himself just as he takes medicine for himself, with the certainty that his Lord, Whom he consulted for the right choice, will direct him to what is best for him. And the sign that the thing is good is that Allah will make the means of its attainment easy for him. And beware of seeking guidance in one's affairs by methods outside the *Sunnah*, such as dream interpretation or numerology (for instance, checking the compatibility of prospective spouses by the numerical values of their names) or other methods which have no basis in the religion.

BEWARE OF PASSING IN FRONT OF A PRAYING PERSON

Allah's Messenger صلى الله عليه وسلم said:

«لَو يَعلمُ المَارُّ بَينَ يَدَي الـمُصَلِّي, مَاذَا عَلَيْهِ لَكَانَ أَنْ يَقِفَ أَربَعِينَ خَيراً لَهُ مِنْ أَن يَمُرَّ بَيْنَ يَدَيْهِ» . [رواه البخاري في باب إثم المار بين يدي المصلي الجزء الأول].

"If the person passing in front of someone offering *Salât* knew what he was incurring, he would prefer to wait 40 rather than pass in front of him."

One of the narrators, Abu Nadr, said, "I don't know if he said 40 days or months or years". (*Bukhâri*)

In the version related by Ibn Khuzaimah it is mentioned "40 years" and Ibn Hajar declared it authentic.

This *Hadîth* indicates that passing in front of one offering *Salât* in the area where he makes *Sajdah* is a sin and a menace there for. And if he only knew what kind of sin he was committing and the punishment for it, he would rather wait 40 years than to pass. However, to pass in front of the one at a distance is no sin, in accordance with the contrapositive of the *Hadîth* which stipulates the place where the praying person places his hands in *Sajdah*.

The one offering *Salât* is required to put a *Sutrah* (obstruction block) in front of him, so that the passer-by notices and can pass on the other side of it [the *Sutrah* is any solid object, such as a stick or spear or a column or wall etc., preferably higher than a cubit (the length of your arm from the elbow to the finger tips)].

The Prophet صلى الله عليه وسلم said:

«إِذَا صَلَّى أَحَدُكم إلى شَيْءٍ يَسْتُرهُ مِنَ النَّاسِ ، فَإِذَا أَرَادَ أَحَدٌ أَنْ يَجْتَازَ بَيْنَ يَدَيْهِ، فَلْيَدْفَعْ فِي نَحْرِهِ، فَإِنْ أَبَى فَلْيُقَاتِلهُ، فَإِنَّمَا هُوَ شَيْطَانٌ» . [متفق عليه].

"When one of you prays behind anything which screens him from the people, then if someone wants to pass between him and the *Sutrah*, he should repel him by pushing at his chest. And if he refuses to defer then fight him, for he is a devil." (Agreed upon)

This authentic *Hadîth* which Bukhâri reported and which warns against passing in front of a praying person includes the Sacred *Masjid* in Makkah and the Prophet's *Masjid* in Al-Madinah, as it is a general statement. And the Prophet صلى الله عليه وسلم said it either in Makkah or Al-Madinah. And the proof for that is as follows:

Bukhâri titled one chapter in this regard:

CHAPTER. The person offering *Salât* should repulse that person who tries to pass in front of him.

He said: "Ibn Umar repelled someone passing in front of him while he was in *Tashahhud* in front of the Ka'bah and he said: 'If he refuses every alternative except fighting, then fight him'." Hafiz Ibn Hajar said: "Mentioning the Ka'bah specifically is because no one should assume that passing is excusable there because it - is a crowded place. This report which Bukhâri mentioned was also reported by a connected chain of narrators by his Shaikh Abû Nu'aim in his "*Book of Salât*."

To sum up: To pass in front of a person praying *Salât* within the area where he performs *Sajdah* is *Harâm*, there is sin in doing so, and it carries a severe threat, if the person has placed a *Sutrah* in front of himself, whether in Makkah or Al-Madinah or anywhere else, based on the preceding *Ahadîth*. And perhaps it is excusable for one who has a pressing need in a very crowded place.

THE RECITATION OF THE MESSENGER
صلى الله عليه وسلم

1. Allah تعالى said:

﴿ وَرَتِّلِ ٱلۡقُرۡءَانَ تَرۡتِيلًا ﴾

"...And recite the Qur'ân (aloud) in a slow, (pleasant tone and) style." (V. 73: 4)

2. «كان ـ ﷺ ـ لاَ يَقْرَأُ القُرْآنَ في أَقَلَّ مِن ثَلاثَةِ أَيَّامٍ». [صحيح رواه ابن سعد].

"The Prophet صلى الله عليه وسلم would not complete a recitation of Qur'ân in less than 3 days." (According to an authentic report collected by Ibn Sa'ad).

3. «كـان ـ ﷺ ـ يُقَـطِّعُ قِراءَتَـهُ آيَةً آيَةً (الـحَمْـدُ لله رَبِّ العَالَـمِين) ثم يقف (الرَّحْمَن الرَّحِيم) ثم يقف .

He صلى الله عليه وسلم used to recite each *Ayat* (verse) separately such as: "All the praises and thanks are to Allah, the Lord of the *'Alamîn* (mankind, jinns and all that exists)." Then he would pause. "The Most Beneficent, the Most Merciful." Then he would pause. (*Tirmidhi*).

4. «زَيِّنُوا القُرْآنَ بأصواتِكُمَ، فإنَّ الصَّوتَ الحَسَـنَ، يَزِيـدُ القُـرآنَ حَسْنـاً». [صحيـح رواه أبوداود].

He صلى الله عليه وسلم used to say:

"Adorn the Qur'ân with your voices, (reciting the Qur'ân in a) fair voice will increase the beauty of the Qur'ân." (*Abû Dâwûd*)

5. «كَانَ يَمُدُّ صَوتَهُ بِالقُرآنِ مَدًّا». [صحيح رواه أحمد].

"He (صلى الله عليه وسلم) used to stretch the vowels of the Qur'ân" (which are appropriate to be stretched). (*Ahmad*)

6. «كَانَ يَقُومُ إِذَا سَمِعَ الصَّارِخَ» (الديك) [متفق عليه].

"He (صلى الله عليه وسلم) used to rise up when he heard the rooster crow." (Agreed upon)

7. «كَانَ يُصَلِّي فِي نَعْلَيْهِ» (أحياناً) [متفق عليه].

"He (صلى الله عليه وسلم) used to pray in his sandals" (some times) (Agreed upon)

8. «وكَانَ يَعْقِدُ التَّسْبِيحَ (بيمينه). [صحيح رواه الترمذي وأبوداود].

"He (صلى الله عليه وسلم) used to count the *Tasbih*" (with his right hand). (*Tirmidhi* and *Abû Dâwûd*)

9. «وكَانَ إِذَا حَزَبَهُ أَمْرٌ صَلَّى (حزبه: كربه) [حسن رواه أحمد وأبوداود].

"When anything troubled him, he (صلى الله عليه وسلم) used to offer *Salât.*" (*Ahmad* and *Abû Dâwûd*)

10. «كَانَ إِذَا جَلَسَ فِي الصَّلَاةِ وَضَعَ يَدَيْهِ عَلَى رُكْبَتَيْهِ، وَرَفَعَ إِصْبَعَهُ الْيُمْنَى الَّتِي تَلِي الإِبْهَامَ فَدَعَا بِهَا». [رواه مسلم في صفة الجلوس في الصلاة ٥/ ٨٠].

"When he (صلى الله عليه وسلم) sat in his *Salât*, he would keep his hands on his knees, and he would raise his right (index) finger while making *Du'â.*" (*Muslim*)

11. «وكَانَ يُحَرِّكُ إِصْبَعَهُ الْيُمنى يَدعُو بها». [صحيح رواه النسائي]

154

12.ويقول : «لَهِيَ أَشَدُّ عَلَى الشَّيطانِ مِنَ الْحَدِيدِ» (يعني السبابة).

[حسن رواه أحمد].

"He (صلى الله عليه وسلم) used to move his right (index) finger while making *Du'â."* (*Nasa'i*)

And the Prophet صلى الله عليه وسلم said:

"That is harder on *Shaitan* (devil) than being beaten with iron."

«وَكَـــانَ يَضَـعُ يَدَهُ الْيُمنى عَلَى الْيُسرَى عَلَى صَدْرِهِ» (في الصَّلاةِ). [رواه ابن خزيمة وغيره وحسنه الترمذي].

"And he (صلى الله عليه وسلم) used to place his right hand over his left hand on his chest." (Ibn Khuzaimah and others)

13. All the four *Imâm* stated: "If the *Hadîth* is authentic then that's my *Madhhab* (way)", so moving the finger and placing the hands on the chest in the *Salât* is part of their *Madhhab*, and is *Sunnah* in the *Salât*.

14. *Imâm* Mâlik and *Imâm* Ahmad and some Shâfi'î scholars explicitly recommended moving the index finger in *Salât*, as being *Sunnah*. And the Prophet صلى الله عليه وسلم mentioned the wisdom behind it in the previously mentioned *Hadîth*, because the movement of the single finger is symbolic of *Tauhîd*: i.e. Allah's Oneness and his unique right to be worshipped. That is harder on *Shaitân* than being beaten with iron as he hates *Tauhîd*.

So it is obligatory on the Muslim to follow the Prophet صلى الله عليه وسلم and not to object to his *Sunnah*, for he (صلى الله عليه وسلم) said:

«صَلُّوا كَمَا رَأَيْتُمُوني أُصَلِّي» . [رواه البخاري].

"Pray as you have seen me praying." (*Bukhâri*)

155

THE PROPHET'S WORSHIP OF ALLAH

1. Allah عز وجل said:

﴿ يَـٰٓأَيُّهَا ٱلۡمُزَّمِّلُ ۝ قُمِ ٱلَّيۡلَ إِلَّا قَلِيلًا ﴾

"O you, wrapped in garments (i.e. Prophet Muhammad صلى الله عليه وسلم). Stand (to pray) all night, except a little." (V. 73:1,2)

2. 'Âisha رضي الله عنها said:

«مَاكَانَ رَسُولُ اللهِ ﷺ ـ يَزِيدُ فِي رَمَضَانَ وَلَا فِي غَيْرِهِ عَلَى إِحْـدَى عَشْرَةَ رَكْعَـةً، يُصَلِّي أَرْبَعاً، فَلَا تَسْأَلْ عَنْ حُسْنِهِنَّ وطُولِهِنَّ، ثُمَّ يُصَلِّي أَرْبَعاً ، فَلَا تَسْأَلْ عَنْ حُسْنِهِنَّ وطُولِهِنَّ، ثُمَّ يُصَلِّي ثَلاثاً. فَقُلْتُ: أَتَنَامُ قَبْلَ أَنْ تُوتِرَ؟ فَقَالَ يَاعَائِشَةُ: إِنَّ عَيْنِيَّ تَنَامَانِ؟ وَلَا يَنَامُ قَلْبِي». [متفق عليه].

The Prophet صلى الله عليه وسلم did not use to exceed eleven *Rak'a* in Ramadan or in other months. He would pray four; don't ask about how long and how fine they were. He would pray another four; do not ask me for how long and how fine they were; then he would pray three. I asked him: "Do you sleep before you offer *Witr*?" He said, "'Aisha, my eyes sleep but my heart is awake." (Agreed upon)

3. Aswad bin Yazîd said: I asked 'Aisha رضي الله عنها about the *Salât* of Allah's Messenger صلى الله عليه وسلم at night. She said:

«كَانَ يَنامُ أَوَّلَ اللَّيْلِ ، ثُمَّ يَقُومُ، فَإِذَا كَانَ مِنَ السَّحَرِ أَوْتَرَ، ثُمَّ أَتَى فِرَاشَـهُ، فَإِذَا كَانَ لَهُ حَاجَةٌ.. أَلَمَّ بِأَهْلِهِ، فَإِذَا سَمِعَ الأَذَانَ وَثَبَ، فَإِذَا كَانَ جُنُباً أَفَاضَ عَلَيْهِ مِنَ المَاءِ (اغْتَسَلَ) وَإِلَّا تَوَضَّأَ، وَخَرَجَ إِلَى الصَّلاةِ». [رواه البخاري ومسلم وغيرهما].

"He used to sleep the first part of the night, then he would rise [and pray], when dawn was near he would offer *Witr*, then come to bed. If he had need of his wife he would have sex with her, then when he heard the *Adhân* he would jump up, if he was *Junub,* he would take a bath, and, if not, he would make *Wudû*, then go out for *Salât*." (*Bukhâri, Muslim* and others)

4. Abû Hurairah رضي الله عنه said:

«كَانَ رَسُولُ الله ـ ﷺ ـ يَقُومُ حَتى تَنْتفخَ قَدَمَاهُ، فَيُقالُ لَه : يَارسولَ الله لِم تَفعَل هَذا وَقد غَفرَ الله لَكَ ماتَقَدَّم مِن ذَنْبِكَ وَمَا تَأَخَّرَ؟ قَالَ : أفَلاَ أكُونُ عَبْداً شَكُوراً» . [متفق عليه].

Allah's Messenger صلى الله عليه وسلم used to stand until his feet would swell. It was said to him, "O Messenger of Allah! you do all that when Allah has forgiven you your past and future sins?" He said, "Shouldn't I be a grateful slave?" (Agreed upon)

5. Allah's Messenger صلى الله عليه وسلم said:

«حُبّبَ إليَّ مِن دُنْياكُم : النّساءُ والطّيبُ وجُعِلت قُرّةُ عَيْني في الصَّلاةِ» . [صحيح رواه أحمد].

"What was made dear to me of your world is women and perfume; and the coolness of my eyes is in *Salât*." (Ahmad)

THE BOOK OF ZAKÂT

* *Zakât* and its importance in Islâm
* The wisdom in the legislation of *Zakât*
* The kinds of wealth on which *Zakât* is required
* The *Nisâb* (minimum amount of property) on which *Zakât* is due
* How *Zakât* should be distributed
* Some benefits of paying *Zakât*
* Warnings to those who don't pay *Zakât*
* Some important information regarding *Zakât*

ZAKÂT AND ITS IMPORTANCE IN ISLÂM

Zakât is an obligatory charity due on wealth, with certain conditions, and to be distributed to specific groups of people at specific time.

Zakât is a pillar of Islâm and one of its most important components. It is mentioned and linked to *Salât* in a great number of places in the Book of Allah عز وجل .

The Muslims have agreed indisputably that *Zakât* is obligatory. Whoever denies its obligatory nature after knowing this, is a *Kâfir*, outside the fold of Islâm. And whoever is miserly, withholding some or all of it, then he is an unjust oppressor, befitting of punishment.

Among the proofs of its obligatory nature are the Statements of Allah عز وجل :

﴿ وَأَقِيمُوا۟ ٱلصَّلَوٰةَ وَءَاتُوا۟ ٱلزَّكَوٰةَ ﴾

"And offer prayers perfectly (*Iqamat-as-Salât*) and give *Zakât...*" (V. 2: 110)

And Allah عز وجل said:

﴿ وَمَآ أُمِرُوٓا۟ إِلَّا لِيَعْبُدُوا۟ ٱللَّهَ مُخْلِصِينَ لَهُ ٱلدِّينَ حُنَفَآءَ وَيُقِيمُوا۟ ٱلصَّلَوٰةَ وَيُؤْتُوا۟ ٱلزَّكَوٰةَ وَذَٰلِكَ دِينُ ٱلْقَيِّمَةِ ﴾

"And they were commanded not, but that they should worship Allah, and worship none but Him Alone (abstaining from ascribing partners to Him), and offer prayers perfectly (*Iqâmat-as-Salât*) and give *Zakât* and that is the right religion." (V. 98: 5)

Ibn Umar رضي الله عنهما said:

«قَالَ رَسُولُ اللهِ ـ ﷺ ـ: بُنِيَ الإِسْلَامُ عَلَى خَمْسٍ ـ فَذَكَرَ مِنْهَا ـ إِيتَاءِ الزَّكَاةِ».

159

The Prophet صلى الله عليه وسلم said: "Islâm is based on five" and he mentioned ... "to give *Zakât.*"

Bukhâri reported that when the Prophet صلى الله عليه وسلم sent Mu'âdh to Yemen, he said:

«فَـانْ هُمْ أَطَـاعُوا لِذَلِكَ فَاعَلِمِهُمْ أَنَّ اللهَ افْتَرَضَ عَلَيْهِم صَدَقَةً تُؤْخَذُ مِن أَغْنِيَائِهِم فَتُرَدُّ عَلَى فُقَرَائِهِم» .

"And if they obey you in that, inform them that Allah has obligated them with *Zakât* to be taken from their rich and distributed among their poors."

And it is disbelief of the one who refuses to pay it claiming it not necessary, as Allah عز وجل said:

﴿ فَإِن تَابُوا۟ وَأَقَامُوا۟ ٱلصَّلَوٰةَ وَءَاتَوُا۟ ٱلزَّكَوٰةَ فَإِخْوَٰنُكُمْ فِى ٱلدِّينِ ﴾

"But if they repent, offer prayers perfectly (*Iqâmat-as-Salât*) and give *Zakât,* then they are your brethren in religion." (V. 9: 11)

It can be understood from these verses that the one who doesn't establish *Salât* nor does he pay *Zakât*, he is not our brother in the religion, rather he is a disbeliever. For that reason Abû Bakr رضي الله عنه fought those who differentiated between *Salât* and *Zakât* regarding their obligatory nature. And the *Sahabah* agreed with his decision and carried it out, so it proves their consensus on the issue.

THE WISDOM IN THE LEGISLATION OF *ZAKAT*

There is great wisdom in the institution of *Zakât*, as it fulfills many major aims of the *Shari'ah* resulting general benefits, which becomes clear to one who ponders the texts of the Qur'ân and *Sunnah* that order for its payment; for instance, the *Ayat* of

Surah At-Taubah which explains where the *Zakât* should be distributed, and other verses and *Ahadîth* which encourage charity and spending for good causes in general. Among the aspects of this wisdom are:

1. Purification of the believer's soul from the stains of sins and transgressions and their negative effects on the hearts, and the cleansing of his soul from the despicable qualities of miserliness and stinginess and their effects. Allah عز وجل said:

﴿ خُذْ مِنْ أَمْوَٰلِهِمْ صَدَقَةً تُطَهِّرُهُمْ وَتُزَكِّيهِم بِهَا ﴾

   "Take *Sadaqah* (alms) from their wealth in order to purify them and sanctify them." (V. 9: 103)

2. To fulfill the requirements of the poor Muslim and to preserve his honour from the humiliation of asking other than Allah.

3. Lightening the burden of the Muslim debtor by helping to pay off his debts.

4. To join disparate hearts on belief and Islâm, bringing them from a state of doubts and spiritual uneasiness and weak faith to firmly rooted faith and complete certainty.

5. Equipping fighters in the way of Allah and preparing the military equipment and material for the spread of Islâm and for the defeat of disbelief and corruption, and for the establishment of justice between the people until there is no more *Fitnah* (*Shirk* in its beguiling and confusing manifestations) so that religion (worship) be exclusive for Allah Alone in the whole of the world.

6. Helping the stranded Muslim traveller to complete his journey; he is given from the *Zakât* what he needs to get back home.

7. Purification of wealth and its increase and protection from ruin through the blessing incurred by the obedience of Allah, and the aggrandizement of His order; and kindness to His creation.

161

This is some of the sublime wisdom and noble purposes for which *Zakât* was mandated. And there are much more, no one comprehends all of them except Allah عز وجل .

THE KINDS OF WEALTH
ON WHICH *ZAKÂT* IS REQUIRED

Zakât is mandatory on four things:

First: The produce of the earth of grain and fruits; as per the Statement of Allah عز وجل :

﴿يَٰٓأَيُّهَا ٱلَّذِينَ ءَامَنُوٓاْ أَنفِقُواْ مِن طَيِّبَٰتِ مَا كَسَبْتُمْ وَمِمَّآ أَخْرَجْنَا لَكُم مِّنَ ٱلْأَرْضِ وَلَا تَيَمَّمُواْ ٱلْخَبِيثَ مِنْهُ تُنفِقُونَ وَلَسْتُم بِـَٔاخِذِيهِ إِلَّآ أَن تُغْمِضُواْ فِيهِ﴾

"O you who believe! Spend of the good things which you have (legally) earned, and of that which We have produced from the earth for you, and do not aim at that which is bad to spend from it, (though) you would not accept it save if you close your eyes and tolerate therein..." (V. 2: 267)

And the Statement of Allah عز وجل :

﴿وَءَاتُواْ حَقَّهُۥ يَوْمَ حَصَادِهِۦ﴾

"...but pay the due thereof (its *Zakât*, according to Allah's orders ¹/₁₀th or ¹/₂₀th) on the day of its harvest..." (V. 6:141)

And the greatest of dues on wealth is the *Zakât*, the Prophet صلى الله عليه وسلم said:

«فِيمَا سَقَتِ السَّمَاءُ أَوْ كَانَ عَثَرِيًّا الْعُشْرُ وَفِيمَا سُقِىَ بِالنَّضْحِ نِصْفُ الْعُشْرِ». [رواه البخاري].

"On a land irrigated by rain water or by natural water

162

channels or if the land is wet due to a nearby water channel, *Ushr* (i.e. one-tenth) is compulsory (as *Zakât*); and on the land irrigated by the well, half of the *Ushr* (i.e. one-twentieth) is compulsory (as *Zakât*) on the yield of the land."

Second: Gold, silver and money; Allah عز وجل said:

﴿ وَٱلَّذِينَ يَكْنِزُونَ ٱلذَّهَبَ وَٱلْفِضَّةَ وَلَا يُنفِقُونَهَا فِي سَبِيلِ ٱللَّهِ فَبَشِّرْهُم بِعَذَابٍ أَلِيمٍ ﴾

"...And those who hoard up gold and silver and spend it not in the way of Allah—announce unto them a painful torment." (V. 9: 34)

And in *Sahih Muslim*, Abû Hurairah رضي الله عنه reported that the Prophet صلى الله عليه وسلم said:

«مَا مِنْ صَاحِب ذَهب وَلَا فِضَّةٍ لَا يُؤَدِّي مِنها حَقَّهَا إلَّا إذَا كَانَ يَوْمُ القِيَامَة صُفِحَتْ لَهُ صَفائحُ من نار فَأُحْمِي عَلَيها مِنْ نار جَهَنَّم فَيُكوى بها جَنْبُهُ وجَبِينُهُ وظَهْرُهُ، كُلَّما بَردَتْ أُعِيدَتْ لَهُ في يَوم كَانَ مِقْدَارُهُ خَمْسينَ ألْفَ سَنَةٍ، حَتى يُقْضِيَ بَينَ العِبادِ» .

«مَا مِنْ صَاحِب كنز لَا يُؤَدِّي زَكَاتَه» . [رواه مسلم].

"There is no possessor of gold and silver who does not pay the due on them except that on the Day of Judgement, the gold and silver will be beaten into sheets of fire which will be further heated in the fire of Hell, then his flanks and forehead and back will be branded with them; every time they cool down they will be replaced with heated sheets. That will go on for a day which will last 50,000 years, until all the slaves have been judged."

The "due" referred to is *Zakât*, as it is mentioned in another version:

"There is no possessor of a hoarded treasure who does not pay its Zakât. (*Muslim*).

Third: Business inventory: That is, goods owned to be sold. This includes real estate, animals, foods, drinks, cars, etc. The owner should calculate their value at the end of his first year of business (and every year after that), and pay 2.5% of their current value, whether their value is the same as when he bought them or has gone up or down.

It is mandatory for the business owners like grocers, auto dealers, parts stores, to conduct a detailed account each year and pay the required *Zakât* on it; if that is hard on them, they can play safe and pay enough to be sure they have discharged their responsibility.

Fourth: Livestock, that is camels, cattle, sheep and goats, on the condition that they are free grazing, not fed with grain or specially prepared foods, raised for breeding and milk production, and the number of head reaches the minimum payable level.

Note: If the cattle is fed with grain or specially prepared food, and is being raised for sale, *Zakât* must be paid on it, not because it is livestock but because it is a commodity for sale (the third category). Payable at 2.5% of its sale value if it reaches the minimum payable value for merchandise (either by itself or in conjunction with other merchandise for sale).

THE *NISAB* (MINIMUM AMOUNT OF PROPERTY) ON WHICH *ZAKÂT* IS DUE

1. Grains and fruit: five *Awsuq* which equal 618 kilograms.

   The *Zakât* due is 10% on what is irrigated by rainfall, or springs, or other natural means, 5% if it is irrigated by methods which require labour and/or capital.

2. Gold, silver and currency :

   a) Gold: 20 Dinars or 85 grams. The *Zakât* due is 2.5%.

   b) Silver: 5 *Awâq* which equals 595 grams. The *Zakât* due is 2.5%.

   c) Paper Money: The value of 85 grams of gold or 595 grams of silver in that currency.

3. Merchandise for sale: The value is calculated, and if it reaches the *Nisâb* of gold or silver, *Zakât* is due on it at the rate of 2.5% of its value.

4. Livestock:

   a) Camels: the minimum *Nisâb* is five camels. The *Zakât* due is a sheep.

   b) Cattle: The minimum *Nisâb* is 30 cows. The *Zakât* due is a one year old.

   c) Sheep and goats: The minimum *Nisâb* is 40 head. The *Zakat* due is one sheep.

One in need of more details should refer to books of *Hadîth* or *Fiqh*.

Table of *Zakât* for free grazing livestock
SHEEP AND GOATS

Liable to pay		*Zakât due*
from	**to**	
40	120	One sheep
121	200	Two sheep
201	300	Three sheep

And so on, for every 100 extra sheep, one extra sheep is due.

Note: Billy goat and too old animal whose teeth are fallen should not be taken for *Zakât* nor the worst of wealth. Likewise a pregnant ewe or a female camel should not be taken for *Zakât* nor the best of wealth.

CAMELS

Liable to pay		*Zakât due*
from	**to**	
5	9	One ewe (female sheep)
10	14	Two ewes
15	19	Three ewes
20	24	Four ewes
25	35	One 1-year-old female camel
36	45	One 2-year-old female camel
46	60	One 3-year-old female camel
61	75	One 4-year-old female camel
76	90	Two 2-year-old female camels
91	120	Two 3-year-old female camels
121	160	Three 2-year-old female camels

After that, for every forty camels, one extra 2-year-old camel is due; and for every extra fifty camels, one extra 3-year-old camel is due.

CATTLE

Liable to pay		Zakât due
from	to	
30	39	One 1-year-old cow
40	59	One 2-year-old cow
60	89	Two 1-year-old cows

After that, for every thirty extra head, one extra 1-year-old cow is due and for every forty extra head, one extra 2-year-old cow is due.

(This table is taken from the book 'A Zakât Guide' by Adil Rashad Ghunaim).

HOW ZAKÂT SHOULD BE DISTRIBUTED

The basic text which describes how Zakât should be distributed is the Word of Allah عز وجل :

﴿ ۞ إِنَّمَا ٱلصَّدَقَٰتُ لِلۡفُقَرَآءِ وَٱلۡمَسَٰكِينِ وَٱلۡعَٰمِلِينَ عَلَيۡهَا وَٱلۡمُؤَلَّفَةِ قُلُوبُهُمۡ وَفِى ٱلرِّقَابِ وَٱلۡغَٰرِمِينَ وَفِى سَبِيلِ ٱللَّهِ وَٱبۡنِ ٱلسَّبِيلِ فَرِيضَةً مِّنَ ٱللَّهِ وَٱللَّهُ عَلِيمٌ حَكِيمٌ ﴾

"As-Sadaqat (here it means obligatory charity, i.e. Zakât) are only for the Fuqarâ (the poor who do not beg), and Al-Masâkin (the poor who beg) and those employed to collect the (funds); and for to attract the hearts of those who have been inclined (towards Islam); and to free the captives; and for those in debt; and for Allah's cause (i.e. for Mujahidûn — those fighting in a holy battle), and for the way-farer (a traveller who is cut off from everything); a

167

duty imposed by Allah. And Allah is All-Knower, All-Wise." (V. 9: 60)

Allah explained in this *Ayah* eight categories, all of them deserving to receive *Zakât*, they are :

1. The *Faqir* (destitute): He is the poor person who possesses half of his minimum needs or less. He is more needy than the *Miskîn*.

2. The *Miskîn*: He is poor, but he is better off than the *Faqîr*, like one who possesses 70% or 80% of his needs, for instance. The proof that the *Faqîr* is more in need than the *Miskîn* is the Statement of Allah عز وجل :

﴿ أَمَّا ٱلسَّفِينَةُ فَكَانَتْ لِمَسَٰكِينَ يَعْمَلُونَ فِى ٱلْبَحْرِ ﴾

"As for the boat, it belonged to poor people working in the sea..." (V. 18: 79)

They were described as being *Miskîn* although they owned a boat.

The *Miskîn* and *Faqîr* should be given of the *Zakât* what will suffice them for the coming year since *Zakât* is only due once a year, so it is only fitting that they get enough to last them until its next distribution.

The necessity should be based on what he and his family need of food, clothing, housing, and anything which one cannot do without, living on a moderate level, neither extravagantly nor very tight. (The family includes everyone whom the recipient has a responsibility to support). The level of necessity varies from era to era and place to place and to some extent between one individual and another. What is sufficient for a person in one society is not sufficient for a person in another. And what was enough ten years ago may not be enough today, and likewise what is enough for one person may not be enough for another, according to the different number of dependents and obligatory expenditures, etc.

The scholars have given the *Fatwa* (legal verdict) that necessity includes medical treatment of the ill, and helping single people to get married, and acquiring necessary books of religious knowledge.

For the *Faqîr* and *Miskîn* to be eligible for receiving *Zakât*, they must be Muslim and not from the lineage of Bani Hashim and their slaves.* Also, they should not be close relatives of the donor for whom he is sponsor as his parents, children, and wives. Finally, he should not be able-bodied who is able to earn a living, based on the statement of the Prophet صلى الله عليه وسلم :

«لا حظ فيها لغني ولا لقوي مكتسب». [رواه أحمد وأبوداود

والنسائي وصححه محقق جامع الأصول].

"There is no portion in it for the wealthy nor for the strong, who can earn his living." (*Ahmad, Abû Dâwûd* and *An-Nasa'î*).

3. The collectors of *Zakât*: They are those appointed by the ruler of the Muslim state or his deputy to perform one of the duties necessary for the establishment of *Zakât* in the society, such as collecting it, storing it, keeping its records and accounts, guarding it, transporting it and distributing it, etc.

The *Zakât* employee should be paid a wage comparable to that of a person doing a similar job in some other organization, and according to how much time he works for the *Zakât* purpose, even if he is rich, as long as he is a

---

* It is permissible to give *Zakât* to the descendants of the Prophet صلى الله عليه وسلم since they have been prevented from receiving a fifth of spoils of war, which used to suffice them.

rational, adult Muslim, trustworthy, and qualified for the job; however, if he is from Bani Hashim he cannot receive a wage from the *Zakât* money; based on the *Hadîth* of *Muslim*, on the authority of Al-Muttalib bin Rabi'ah that the Prophet صلى الله عليه وسلم said:

«إِنَّ الصَّدَقَةَ لَا تَنْبَغِي لِآلِ مُحَمَّدٍ».

"*Sadaqah* (charity) is not befitting for the family of Muhammad."

4. For the weakly faithful: Those whose hearts are to be drawn close. These are persons of authority and influence among their clans, tribes, nations, etc. who, it is hoped, will become Muslim; or if they are shaky new Muslims, to strengthen their attachment to Islâm so that their belief can take root firmly; or that his peers might become Muslim, or to protect the Muslims or to deflect the harm they are capable of inflicting.

And this category is still eligible for *Zakât*, it has not been abrogated, and they are to be given what it takes to reconcile their hearts to Islâm and supporting and defending it. This portion may even be given to a disbeliever, because the Prophet صلى الله عليه وسلم gave Safwan bin Umaiyah a portion of the spoils of Hunain. (*Muslim*).

It may also be given to a Muslim, for the Prophet صلى الله عليه وسلم gave to Abû Sufyan bin Harb, and also to Aqra' bin Habis, and to Uyainah bin Hisn, to each of them 100 camels. (*Muslim*)

5. To free slaves: This includes freeing a slave outright, or helping a slave, who has contracted with his owner to purchase his own freedom, to make his payments, or to ransom Muslim prisoners of war from the enemy. This is included in the category because the prisoner of war is in a state of bondage and his need is even more pressing as he is

in danger of being killed or forced to abandon Islâm.

6. Debtors : They are those who have incurred debts and they are specified as responsible for the discharge of those debts.

Debts are of two kinds :

A) Debts incurred by a person on his own behalf for something which is permissible in Islâm, for instance, for clothing, or his family's living expenses, or to get married, or for medical treatment, or to build a house, or necessary furnishing, or to pay for accidental damages to another person's property. In such cases he should be given what it takes to discharge the debt if he is too poor to do so himself, and if the debt was incurred in obedience to Allah or in a lawful matter.

And it is required that the recipient be a Muslim, and that he, not be well-off, able to discharge the debt on his own, and that the debt was not incurred in disobedience to Allah, and that payment is already due, or will be due in the coming year, and, finally, the debt must be owed to a human being, which excludes financial debts to Allah such as expiation for broken oaths or other sins or *Zakât* payments.

B) Debts incurred by a person who incurs a debt for someone else's benefit, for instance to make peace between two parties. He is eligible for *Zakât*, based on the *Hadîth* of Qabisah Hilali رضي الله عنه who said:

«تَحَمَّلْتُ حَمَالَةً فَأَتَيْتُ رَسُولَ الله ـ ﷺ ـ أَسْأَلُهُ فِيهَا فَقَالَ : أَقِمْ حَتَّى تَأْتِيَنَا الصَّدَقَةُ فَنَأْمُرَ لَكَ بِهَا، ثُمَّ قَالَ : يَاقَبِيصَةُ إِنَّ الْمَسْأَلَةَ لَا تَحِلُّ إِلَّا لِأَحَدِ ثَلَاثَةٍ : رَجُلٍ تَحَمَّلَ حَمَالَةً فَحَلَّتْ لَهُ الْـمَسْأَلَةُ حَتَّى يُصِيبَهَا ثُمَّ يُمْسِكُ، وَرَجُلٍ أَصَابَتْهُ جَائِحَةٌ اجْتَاحَتْ مَالَهُ فَحَلَّتْ لَهُ الْمَسْأَلَةُ حَتَّى يُصِيبَ قِوَاماً مِنْ عَيْشٍ أَوْ قَالَ : (سِدَاداً

مِنْ عَيْشٍ) وَرَجُلٍ أَصَابَتْهُ فَاقَةٌ حَتَّى يَقُومَ ثَلَاثَةٌ مِنْ ذَوِي
الحِجَى : لَقَدْ أَصَابَتْ فُلَاناً فَاقَةٌ، فَحَلَّتْ لَهُ الْـمَسْأَلَةُ حَتَّى
يُصِيبَ قِوَاماً مِنْ عَيْشٍ ، أَوْ قَالَ سَدَاداً مِنْ عَيْشٍ ، فَمَا سِوَاهُنَّ
مِنَ الْمَسْأَلَةِ يَاقَبِيصَةُ سُحْتاً يَأْكُلُهَا صَاحِبُهَا سُحْتاً» . [رواه أحمد
ومسلم].

I took upon myself responsibility for someone else's debt, so
I came to the Prophet صلى الله عليه وسلم to ask his help. He صلى الله عليه
وسلم said, "Wait until some *Zakât* payment comes in and I will
order some of it to be given to you." Then he said, "O
Qabisah, asking for money is only permissible in three cases:
A man who took responsibility for another's debt, so it is
permissible for him to ask until he gets what covers the debt,
then he stops asking; or a man who was beset by a disaster
which destroyed his property and wealth, in which case it is
permissible for him to ask until he gets what it takes to put
him back on his feet (or he صلى الله عليه وسلم said: what it takes to
fill his need); or a person beset by poverty, and three men of
discernment from his people say: so-and-so is poverty
stricken, so asking is permissible for him until he gets what
is takes to put him back on his feet, (or he صلى الله عليه وسلم said:
what it takes to fill his need); anything besides that is
corruption, O Qabisah, the one who gets it is consuming
corruption." (*Ahmad* and *Muslim*)

It is also permissible to pay the debt of a dead person from
Zakât funds, because it is not necessary for the money to pass
through the debtor's hands. (This is a fine point of the
Qur'ânic text, because for some categories it is stated that the
Zakât is for them but as for the debtor, a different preposition
is used which would be translated as "in the debtor", that is:
in his case or in his interest.)

7. In the way of Allah: This goes to volunteers who are not on the government payroll, both the poor and the rich are eligible, and those who guard the Muslim frontiers militarily, and it doesn't include general charitable spending, otherwise there would have been no point in mentioning the other seven categories in the Qur'ânic verse, since they would all be included in general charitable spending.

The broad meaning of *Jihâd* is appropriate for inclusion in this category. That is, comprehensive Islâmic education repelling the idiological onslaught of anti-Islâmic forces, answering the doubts and suspicions they raise, distribution of useful Islâmic books, and funding reliable sincere Islâmic workers to devote their energies full-time to the propagation of Islâm and the countering of anti-Islamic missionary and atheist activities; etc. the basis for this is the *Hadîth* of the Prophet صلى الله عليه وسلم :

«جَـاهِـدُوا الـمُشْرِكِينَ بِأموالِكُم وأنْفُسِكُم وألْـسِنَتِكُم» . [رواه أبوداود بإسناد صحيح].

"Strive against the idolaters with your wealth and your lives and your tongues." (*Abû Dâwûd*)

8. The wayfarer: This is a person travelling from one land to another. If he doesn't have the means to complete his journey, he may be given from the *Zakât* what it takes him to complete his journey, as long as the reason for his travel is not disobedience to Allah, that is, for a purpose which is mandatory or recommended in Islam, or at least permissible. Another condition is that he can not find anyone to loan him the money. It is also permissible to give the *Zakât* to the wayfarer even if he has stayed a long time in some place in the course of his journey, if the reason for his delay is to

secure some need within the range of possibility.

It is not mandatory to distribute the *Zakât* on all eight categories every year. But it is preferable bearing in mind the overall needs and benefits, as perceived by the Muslim ruler or his deputy, or the individual who is paying the *Zakât* (in the absence of an organized collection and distribution system).

SOME BENEFITS OF PAYING *ZAKÂT*

1. Complying with the Order of Allah and His Messenger and giving precedence to what Allah and His Messenger love over the selfish love for wealth.

2. Multiplying the reward of one's good deeds. Allah عز وجل said:

﴿ مَّثَلُ ٱلَّذِينَ يُنفِقُونَ أَمْوَٰلَهُمْ فِى سَبِيلِ ٱللَّهِ كَمَثَلِ حَبَّةٍ أَنۢبَتَتْ سَبْعَ سَنَابِلَ فِى كُلِّ سُنۢبُلَةٍ مِّاْئَةُ حَبَّةٍ وَٱللَّهُ يُضَٰعِفُ لِمَن يَشَآءُ ﴾

"The likeness of those who spend their wealth in the way of Allah, is as the likeness of a grain (of corn); it grows seven ears, and each ear has a hundred grains. Allah gives manifold increase to whom He pleases." (V. 2: 261)

3. Giving in charity and paying *Zakât* is a proof for one's belief, and a marker indicating its presence. As mentioned in the *Hadîth*:

«الصَّدَقَةُ بُرْهَانٌ». [رواه مسلم].

"Charity is a proof." (*Muslim*).

4. Purification from the pollution of sins and degraded character. Allah عز وجل said:

﴿ خُذْ مِنْ أَمْوَٰلِهِمْ صَدَقَةً تُطَهِّرُهُمْ وَتُزَكِّيهِم بِهَا ﴾

"Take *Sadaqah* (alms) from their wealth in order to purify them and sanctify them with it..." (V. 9: 103)

174

5. The increase of wealth and the presence of blessing in it and its protection from its evil, as per the *Hadîth*:

«﴿مَانَقَصَ مَالٌ مِنْ صَدَقَةٍ﴾» . [رواه مسلم].

"Wealth never decreases due to charity." (*Muslim*)

And the Statement of Allah عز وجل :

﴿ وَمَآ أَنفَقْتُم مِّن شَىْءٍ فَهُوَ يُخْلِفُهُۥ وَهُوَ خَيْرُ ٱلرَّٰزِقِينَ ﴾

"...and whatsoever you spend of anything (in Allah's cause), He will replace it. And He is the Best of providers." (V. 34: 39)

6. The giver of charity will be in the shade of his charity on the Day of Judgement, as in the *Hadîth* about the seven categories of the people that Allah will shade in His Shade on the day when there will be no shade except His Shade:

«ورجلٌ تَصَـدَّقَ بِصَدَقَةٍ فَأخفَاهَا حَتى لا تَعلمَ شِمالُهُ مَاتُنفِقُ يَمينُهُ» . [متفق عليه].

"And a man who gives charity, secretly, until his left hand doesn't know what his right hand spent." (Agreed upon)

7. It is a cause for the Mercy of Allah:

﴿ وَرَحْمَتِى وَسِعَتْ كُلَّ شَىْءٍ فَسَأَكْتُبُهَا لِلَّذِينَ يَتَّقُونَ وَيُؤْتُونَ ٱلزَّكَوٰةَ ﴾

"...and My Mercy embraces all things. That (Mercy) I shall ordain for those who are *Muttaqûn* and give *Zakât*..." (V. 7:156)

WARNINGS TO THOSE WHO DON'T PAY *ZAKAT*

1. Allah عز وجل said:

$$\text{﴿وَٱلَّذِينَ يَكْنِزُونَ ٱلذَّهَبَ وَٱلْفِضَّةَ وَلَا يُنفِقُونَهَا فِى سَبِيلِ ٱللَّهِ}$$
$$\text{فَبَشِّرْهُم بِعَذَابٍ أَلِيمٍ ٠ يَوْمَ يُحْمَىٰ عَلَيْهَا فِى نَارِ جَهَنَّمَ}$$
$$\text{فَتُكْوَىٰ بِهَا جِبَاهُهُمْ وَجُنُوبُهُمْ وَظُهُورُهُمْ هَٰذَا مَا كَنَزْتُمْ}$$
$$\text{لِأَنفُسِكُمْ فَذُوقُوا مَا كُنتُمْ تَكْنِزُونَ﴾}$$

"...And those who hoard up gold and silver (*Al-Kanz*: the money, gold and silver etc., the *Zakât* of which has not been paid), and spend it not in the way of Allah, — announce unto them a painful torment. On the Day when that will be heated in the fire of Hell and with it will be branded their foreheads, their flanks, and their backs (and it will be said unto them): 'This is the treasure which you hoarded for yourselves. Now taste of what you used to hoard'." (V. 9: 34 35)

2. Ahmad and Muslim reported from Abû Hurairah رضي الله عنه that the Prophet صلى الله عليه وسلم said:

$$\text{«مَامِنْ صَاحِبِ كَنْزٍ لَا يُؤَدِّي زَكَاتَهُ إِلَّا أُحْمِيَ عَلَيْهِ فِي نَارِ جَهَنَّم}$$
$$\text{فَيُجْعَلُ صَفَائِحَ فَيُكْوَى بِهَا جَنْبَاهُ وَجَبِينَهُ حتى يَحْكُمَ الله بَيْنَ}$$
$$\text{عِبَادِهِ فِي يَوْمٍ كَانَ مِقْدَارُهُ خَمْسِينَ أَلْفَ سَنَةٍ ثُمَّ يُرَى سَبِيلُهُ إِمَّا}$$
$$\text{إلى الجَنَّةِ وإمَّا إلى النَّارِ».}$$

"There is none who possessed and stored wealth without paying its *Zakât* except that it (the wealth) will be heated in the fire of Hell, then shaped into sheets with which his flanks and his forehead will be branded until Allah judges between His slaves on a day whose length will be 50,000 years. Then he will be shown his path, either to Paradise or to the Hell-fire."

3. Bukhari reported that the Prophet صلى الله عليه وسلم said:

«مَنْ أتاهُ اللهُ مَالاً فلم يُؤدِّ زَكَاتَهُ مُثِّل لَه يومَ القِيامةِ شُجاعاً أقرع لَه زَبِيبَتَانِ يُطوَّقُهُ يَوْمَ القِيَامةِ ثمَّ يَأخُذُ بِلهزمتيه (يعني شدْقيه) ثُمَّ يَقـولُ أنـا مَالُـكَ، أنـا كَنْـزُكَ ثُـمّ تَـلا

﴿ وَلَا يَحْسَبَنَّ ٱلَّذِينَ يَبْخَلُونَ بِمَآ ءَاتَىٰهُمُ ٱللَّهُ مِن فَضْلِهِۦ هُوَ خَيْرًا لَّهُم بَلْ هُوَ شَرٌّ لَّهُمْ سَيُطَوَّقُونَ مَا بَخِلُواْ بِهِۦ يَوْمَ ٱلْقِيَٰمَةِ ﴾

"Whoever is made wealthy by Allah, and does not pay the *Zakât* of his wealth, then on the Day of Judgement his wealth will be made to appear in the form of a poisonous snake with two (black) spots (over the eyes). It will coil around his neck, then it will seize him by the corners of his mouth, saying, 'I am your wealth, I am your treasure.'" Then he (صلى الله عليه وسلم) recited this verse:

"And let not those, who covetously withhold of that which Allah has bestowed on them of His Bounty (wealth), think that it is good for them [and so they do not pay the obligatory charity (*Zakât*)]. Nay, it will be worse for them; the things which they covetously withheld shall be tied to their necks like a collar on the Day of Resurrection..." (V. 3: 180)

4. Muslim reported the Prophet's صلى الله عليه وسلم statement:

«وَمَـا مِنْ صَاحِب إبـلٍ وَلَا بَقـرٍ وَلَا غَنمٍ لَا يُؤدِّي زَكَاتَهَا إلَّا جَاءَتْ يَوْمَ القِيَامَةِ أعظَمَ مَاكَانَتْ وَأسْمَنَهُ تَنْطحهُ بِقُرونِها وَتطأُهُ بِأظْلافِهَـا كُلَّمَا نَفَـدَتْ عَلَيْهِ أُخراهَا عَادتْ عَلَيهِ أُولاهَا حَتَّى يَقْضِي بَينَ النَّاسِ ».

"There is no owner of camels or cows or goats or sheep who does not pay their *Zakât* except that they (the animals) will come on the Day of Judgement as big and fat as they ever got, goring him with their horns, and trampling him with their hooves. As soon as the last of them has finished, the first of them is back again, and so on until Judgement between the people is completed."

SOME IMPORTANT INFORMATION REGARDING *ZAKÂT*

First: It is right to distribute all *Zakât* to one of the eight categories, and it is not mandatory to distribute it on every category even if they are present.

Second: It is permissible to pay all of a debtor's debt or just part of it.

Third: *Zakât* should not be paid to a disbeliever nor to an apostate (except for those whose hearts are to be drawn close) nor to one who has abandoned *Salât*, if one accepts the view that such a person has become a disbeliever (which may be the weightier view) except if it is given to him on the condition that he performs *Salât*, as an incentive for him.

Fourth: It is not permissible to give *Zakât* to a wealthy person, since the Prophet صلى الله عليه وسلم said:

«لَا حَظَّ فِيهَا لِغَنِيٍّ أَوَ لِقَوِيٍّ مُكْتَسِبٍ». . [رواه أبوداود وإسناده صحيح].

"There is no portion in it for the wealthy nor the strong person who can earn (his living)." (*Abû Dâwûd*)

Fifth: It is not permitted for an individual to give *Zakât* to those he is obligated to support them as parents, children and wives.

Sixth: It is permitted for a woman to pay her *Zakât* to her husband, if he is poor, since it is established that the wife of Abdullah bin Masûd رضي الله عنه wanted to pay *Zakât* to her husband and the Prophet صلى الله عليه وسلم affirmed her wish.

Seventh: *Zakat* may not be transferred from one country to another except in case of pressing need such as famine, or poor people are not to be found in the country transfering the *Zakât*, or to support *Mujahidîn*, or the righteous authority transfers it for general benefit, etc.

Eighth: A person from one country who gains wealth in another land, on which he is required to pay *Zakât*, must pay it where the wealth was acquired, and should not transfer it to his country of origin except in case of pressing need, as explained above.

Ninth: It is permissible to give a poor person from the *Zakât* what will suffice him for several months or for the full year.

Tenth: *Zakât* is mandatory on silver and gold, whether in the form of coins, or bars, or jewellery which is owned or lent out, or other forms, because the evidence mandating *Zakât* on gold and silver are general, without detailed distinctions. There are scholars who make an exception for jewellery which is worn or lent, that no *Zakât* is due on that, but the first point of view is stronger from the aspect of its supporting evidence and is safer in discharging ones responsibility.

Eleventh: There is no *Zakât* on the property that the person needs to use: for instance, food, drink, furnishing, a house, animals, a car, clothing etc. The proof for all of that is the statement of the Prophet صلى الله عليه وسلم:

«لَيْسَ عَلَى الْـمُسْلِمِ فِي عَبْدِهِ ولاَ فَرَسِهِ صَدَقَةٌ». [متفق عليه].

"There is no (obligatory) charity on a Muslim with regard to his horse and his slave." (Agreed upon)

The exception to this general rule is gold and silver jewellery, as mentioned earlier.

Twelfth: Property which is set aside for rental purposes, such as real estate and cars etc., the *Zakât* due on it is levied on the rent earned from it. After the lapse of a year, if it reaches the minimum *Nisâb* by itself or in conjunction with other property in the same category, *Zakât* is due on it.

179

THE BOOK OF *SIYÂM* (FASTINGS)

- *Siyâm* and its benefits
- What you are required to do in Ramadân
- *Âhadîth* on the virtues of fasting
- Voluntary fasting
- Things which break the fast
- *I'tikâf* (seclusion in the *Masjid*) is part of the religion.

SIYÂM (FASTINGS) AND ITS BENEFITS

Allah عز وجل said:

﴿ يَٰٓأَيُّهَا ٱلَّذِينَ ءَامَنُوا۟ كُتِبَ عَلَيْكُمُ ٱلصِّيَامُ كَمَا كُتِبَ عَلَى ٱلَّذِينَ مِن قَبْلِكُمْ لَعَلَّكُمْ تَتَّقُونَ ﴾

"O you who believe, fasting is prescribed for you as it was prescribed for those before you that you may achieve *Taqwa*." (V. 2:183)

(*Taqwa* is translated sometimes as piety, sometimes as consciousness of Allah, sometimes as fear of Allah. It is derived from the word *Wiqayah* for "Shield" and the connection is explained by scholars: To shield yourself from Allah's wrath by hurrying to do what He ordered you and by strictly avoiding what He has prohibited).

And the Prophet صلى الله عليه وسلم said:

«الصِّيَامُ جُنَّةٌ». [متفق عليه].

"*Saum* (fasting) is a shield (or a screen or a shelter) from Hell-fire." (Agreed upon)

1. He صلى الله عليه وسلم also said:

«مَنْ صَامَ رَمَضَانَ إِيمَاناً وَاحْتِسَاباً غُفِرَ لَهُ مَاتَقَدَّم مِن ذَنْبِهِ».

[متفق عليه]. .

"Whoever observed fasting in Ramadan with perfect faith and seeking reward, he will have his previous sins forgiven." (Agreed upon)

«مَنْ قَامَ رَمَضَانَ إِيمَاناً وَاحْتِسَاباً غُفِرَ لَهُ مَاتَقَدَّمَ مِنْ ذَنْبِهِ». . .

[متفق عليه].

181

2. "Whoever stood to pray (*Tarawîh*) in Ramadan with perfect faith and seeking reward, he will have his previous sins forgiven." (Agreed upon)

You should know, my fellow Muslims, that Allah has made fasting obligatory, and it is an act of worship, and it has many benefits, among them:

1. Fasting gives the digestive organs a rest, causes the body to get rid of accumulated wastes which are detrimental to health. It strengthens the body and is beneficial for the treatment of many diseases. It also presents an opportunity for smokers to break their addiction since they cannot smoke during the day.

2. Fasting is a training for the self, getting it used to good deeds, discipline, obedience, patience and sincerity.

3. The fasting person feels his equality with all his fasting brethren; he fasts with them and breaks fast with them, and he experiences the general Islamic unity, and he experiences hunger which should make him sympathize with his brethren who are hungry and needy.

WHAT YOU ARE REQUIRED TO DO IN *RAMADÂN*

We should realize that Allah made *Saum* (fasting) obligatory on us as a way for us to worship Him: and for the fasting to be acceptable and beneficial, we should observe the following conditions:

1. Guard the *Salât*; unfortunately many fasting persons neglect *Salât* which is a pillar of the religion and abandoning it is an act of disbelief.

2. Be well-mannered: beware of disbelief and cursing the

religion, and treating people badly, using the fast as an excuse; fasting is to train the self not to ruin the manners, and disbelief puts a Muslim outside of the religion.

3. Do not use foul or harsh language, even while joking, as it will spoil (the reward of) the fast. Listen to the statement of the Prophet صلى الله عليه وسلم:

«إِذَا كَانَ يَوْمُ صَوْمِ أَحَدِكُم فَلَا يَرْفُثْ يَوْمَئِذٍ وَلاَ يَصْخَبْ : فَإِنْ شَاتَمَهَ أَحَدٌ أَو قَاتَلَهُ فَلْيَقُلْ إِنِّي صَائِمٌ إِنِّي صَائِمٌ» . [متفق عليه].

"If one of you is fasting, he should not use obscenity that day nor shout; and if someone speaks abusively or wants to fight with him, he should say: 'Verily I'm fasting, verily I'm fasting'".(Agreed upon)

4. Take advantage of fasting to give up smoking, which causes cancer, high blood pressure and other diseases; try to make a firm conviction to leave it by night as you left it by day. Save your health and your money.

5. Do not overeat at the time of breaking the fast, as the benefit of fasting is cancelled and it is not healthy.

6. Do not waste your time by going to movies or watching television.

7. Do not stay up so late at night that you are not able to wake up for *Sahûr* (the predawn meal) or *Salât-ul-Fajr*, and take your duty on early morning. The Prophet صلى الله عليه وسلم said:

«اللَّهُمَّ بَارِك لأمتي فِي بُكُورِهَا» . [صحيح رواه أحمد الترمذي].

"O Allah, bless my *Ummah* in their early mornings (acts)." (*Ahmad* and *Tirmidhi*)

[*Ummah* is sometimes translated as nation, or community of believers, or followers. Each Prophet had an *Ummah* that he

183

was sent to. The word *Ummah* is usually used for the people who believed in the Prophet].

8. Increase spending in charity, on relatives and the needy, visit your relatives, and make peace with those with whom you have had disputes.

9. Increase your remembrance of Allah, and recitation of Qur'ân and listening to it, and contemplation of its meanings. Act on it and attend the beneficial discussions in the mosques, and practise *I'tikâf* in the *Masjid* at the end of Ramadan (this is *Sunnah*).

10. Read the pamphlets on fasting to learn its rules, for instance, if you ate or drank, forgetting that you were fasting, it doesn't break the fast (but you have to stop immediately as soon as you realize what you're doing); another example: A person who became *Junub* at night (because of intercourse, for example), and he doesn't get a chance to perform a *Ghusl* (bath) before the appearance of dawn, that doesn't prevent him from fasting; he just has to perform the *Ghusl* and offer *Salât* and go ahead and observe *Saum* (fast).

11. Be mindful of the fast of Ramadan, and get your children used to it when they are able to endure it, and beware of breaking the fast without a valid excuse. Whoever does so must repent for that and make up for that day, and whoever has intercourse with his wife during the daytime of Ramadan he has to expiate the sin. He must free a slave if he's able to do so. If not, he should fast two months continuously (60 days without missing a day); and if he can't do that, he should feed 60 poor persons one meal.

12. Beware, my Muslim brothers, from breaking the fast of Ramadan without excuse. And beware of doing so openly in front of people. Because breaking the fast is audacity with Allah, and disrespect for Islam, and shamelessness among

people. And you should realize that the one who doesn't fast, doesn't really have an *'Eid* (festival) because the *'Eid* is the occasion of great happiness for those who completed the fasts and hope their worship to be accepted.

AHADITH ON THE VIRTUES OF FASTING

Virtues of Ramadan:

1. The Prophet ﷺ said:

«إِذَا دَخَلَ رَمَضَانُ فُتِّحَتْ أَبْوابُ السَّماءِ، وأُغْلِقَتْ أَبوابُ جهنَّم، وَسُلْسِلَتِ الشَّياطينُ» .

وفي رواية : «إِذَا جَاءَ رَمَضَانُ فُتحتْ أَبوابُ الجَنةِ» . [متفق عليه].

وفـي روايـة أخـرى «فُتحـتْ أَبْـوابُ الـرَّحَمَـةِ» [أخرجـه البخاري ومسلم].

"When Ramadan starts, the doors of heaven are opened, and the doors of Hell are closed and the devils are chained up." And in another version: "When Ramadan starts, the doors of Paradise are opened." And in another version: "The doors of mercy are opened." (Agreed upon)

2. In a version reported by Tirmidhi:

«ويُنَـادِي مُنَـادِي يَابَاغِي الخَيْرِ هَلُمَّ وأُقْبِلْ ويابَاغِي الشَّرِّ أَقْصِر، ولله عُتَقَاءُ مِنَ النَّارِ، وذَلِكَ في كُل ليلَةٍ حتى يَنقَضِي رَمَضَانُ» . [حسنه الألباني، في المشكاة].

"And a caller calls out: O you who crave the good, come on! And O you who crave evil, abstain! And Allah has certain people whom he frees from the (Hell) Fire every night until Ramadan ends." (Declared *Hasan* by Albâni in the *Mishkât*)

3. Allah عزوجل says:

«كُلُّ عَمَلِ ابنِ آدَمَ يُضَاعَفُ الحَسَنَةُ بعشرِ أمثالِهَا إلى سبعمائة ضِعْفٍ قَالَ اللهُ عَزَّ وُجَلَّ : إلَّا الصَّومُ فَإِنَّهُ لي وَأَنَا أجزي بهِ ، يَدعُ شَهْوَتَهُ وطَعَامَهُ مِنَ أجْلي ، للصَّائِمِ فَرْحَتَانِ : فَرْحَةٌ عِندَ فِطْرِهِ ، وَفَرَحَةٌ عِندَ لِقاءِ رَبِّهِ ، وَلَخلوفُ فمِ الصَّائِمِ أطْيَبُ عِندَ اللهِ مِنْ رِيحِ الـمِسْكِ». [متفق عليه].

"Every good deed of the son of Adam is multiplied in reward 10 to 700 times except for fasting, for it is for Me and I will grant the reward for it, he leaves his passion and his food for My sake. The fasting person has two moments of happiness: One moment when he ends his fasting for the day (*Iftâr*) and the other when he meets his Lord. And the smell which issues from the mouth of the fasting person is more pleasant to Allah than the smell of musk (fragrance)." (Agreed upon)

Guarding the tongue:

Allah's Messenger صلى الله عليه وسلم said:

«مَنْ لَـمْ يَدعْ قَـولَ الـزُّورِ والعَمَـلَ بهِ ، فَليسَ لله حاجَـةٌ في أنْ يَـدَعَ طَعَامَـهُ وشَرَابَهُ». [رواه البخاري].

"Whoever do not abstain from deceitful speech and actions, Allah is not in need of him leaving his food and drink." (*Bukhari*)

Ending the fast (*Iftâr*), supplication, and the predawn meal (*Sahûr*):

1. The Prophet صلى الله عليه وسلم said:

«إِذَا أَفْطَرَ أَحَدُكُم فَـلْيُفْطِر عَلى تَمر فَإِنَّهُ بَرَكَةٌ فإن لَم يَجِدْ تَـمْرَاً فَالـمَاءِ فَإِنَّهُ طَهُورٌ» . [أخرجه الترمذي وقال محقق جامع الأصول إسناد صحيح].

"When one of you breaks the fast, he should do so with dates, because it is blessed. If he couldn't get dates, then (break your fast with) water, because it purifies." (*Tirmidhi*).

2. The Prophet صلى الله عليه وسلم used to say at the time of *Iftâr*:

«اللَّهُمَّ لَكَ صُمْتُ وعَلى رزقِكَ أفطَرتُ، ذَهَبَ الظَّمأ وَابْتَلَّتِ العُروقُ، وَثَبَتَ الأجرُ إنْ شَاء اللهُ» . [رواه أبوداود وحسنه محقق الأصول والألباني في المشكاة رقم ١٩٩٤].

"O Allah I kept the fast for You, and with Your sustenance I am breaking (my fast). The thirst is gone, and the veins replenished, and the reward is confirmed, if Allah wills," (*Abû Dâwûd*)

3. And the Prophet صلى الله عليه وسلم said:

«لَا يَزَالُ النَّاسُ بِخَيْرٍ مَاعَجَّلُوا الفِطَرَ» . [متفق عليه].

"The people will continue to be in welfare as long as they hurry to *Iftâr* (break fast after the sun sets)." (Agreed upon)

4. And the Prophet صلى الله عليه وسلم said:

«تَسَحَّرُوا فَإن في السُّحُورِ بَرَكَةٌ» . [متفق عليه].

187

"Take *Sahûr* before dawn, for verily in the *Sahûr* there is blessing". (Agreed upon)

VOLUNTARY FASTING

The Prophet صلى الله عليـه وسـلم used to encourage fasting in the following days:

1. Six days in Shawwal (the month after Ramadan); the Prophet صلى الله عليه وسلم said:

$$«مِنْ صَامَ رَمَضَانَ ثُمَّ اتْبَعَهُ سِتًّا مِنْ شَوَّالِ فَكَأَنَّما صَامَ الدَّهرَ» .$$

[رواه مسلم وغيره].

"Whoever fasts Ramadan, then follows it up with six days in Shawwâl, it is as if he fasted the whole (year)." (*Muslim*)

The scholars said that the reward of the good deeds are multiplied by ten. 30 x 10 = 300 + [6 days x 10] = 360 which is slightly longer than a lunar year, and next Ramadan he will fast again so it is as if he fasted his whole life.

2. Fasting the first ten days of Dhul-Hijjah and the day of 'Arafah (the 9th day of Dhul-Hijjah) (for those who are not performing *Hajj*); the Prophet صلى الله عليه وسلم said:

$$«صَوْمُ يَوْم عَرَفَةَ يُكَفِّرُ سَنَتَيْنِ مَاضِيَةً وَمُسْتَقبِلَةً وَصَوْمُ يَوْم$$
$$عَاشُورَاءَ يُكَفِّرُ سَنَةً مَاضِيَةً» . [رواه مسلم وغيره].$$

"Fasting on the day of 'Arafah expiates two years of sins, last year's and next year's and fasting on the tenth of Muharram ('Aashura) expiates the previous year's (of sins)." (*Muslim* and others)

$$«وَقَـدْ أُرسِـلَ لَبَنٌ إلَى رَسُولِ اللهِ ـ ﷺ ـ فَشَرِبَ وَهُوَ يُخْطُبُ$$
$$النَّاسَ بعرفةَ» . [متفق عليه].$$

"Milk was sent to the Prophet صلى الله عليه وسلم while he was giving his sermon on the day of *Arafah* and he drank from it." (Agreed upon)

3. Fasting on the day of '*Aashûra*, along with one day before it, or one day after it. The Prophet صلى الله عليه وسلم said:

«هَذَا يُومُ عَاشُورَاء، وَلَمْ يُكتَبْ عَلَيْكُمْ صِيَامُهُ، وَأنا صَائِمٌ فَمَنْ شَاءَ صَامَ، وَمِنْ شَاء فَلْيُفْطِرِ». [متفق عليه].

"Today is the day of '*Aashûra*, and its fasting is not mandatory on you, and I am fasting, so whoever wants should fast, and whoever wants should break his fast." (Agreed upon)

And he (صلى الله عليه وسلم) said:

«لَئِنْ بَقِيتُ إلـى قَابِلٍ لأصُومَنَّ التَّاسِـعَ». [رواه مسلم].

"If I live till the next year, I will fast definitely on the 9th (the day before '*Aashûrâ*)." (*Muslim*)

(This shows that it is preferable to fast an extra day along with the tenth, preferably the ninth, but, if not possible, then the 11th).

4. Fasting most of the month of Sha'bân.

«كَان رَسولُ الله ـ ﷺ ـ يَصُومُ أكْثَرَ شَعبْانَ». [متفق عليه].

"Allah's Messenger صلى الله عليه وسلم used to fast most of Sha'ban." (Agreed upon)

5. Fasting Monday and Thursday. The Prophet صلى الله عليه وسلم mentioned that:

«صَـوْمُ يَومِ الاثنَيْنِ وَالـخَميس تعرض الاعـمال كل اثنين وخميس، فأحِبُّ أن يُعـرَضَ عَمـلي وأنَـا صَائِمٌ». [رواه النسائي].

189

"The deeds of the worshippers are presented before Allah on Monday and Thursday, I like my deeds to be presented while I am fasting." (*Nasa'i*)

«سُئل ـ ﷺ ـ عَن صَوْمِ يَوْمِ الاثْنَيْنِ فَقَالَ : ذَاكَ يَوْمٌ وُلدتُ فيه وَأُنزِلَ عَليَّ فيه». [رواه مسلم].

He صلى الله عليه وسلم was asked about fasting on Monday, he said: "That is the day I was born and the day (the first Revelation) was sent down on me." (*Muslim*)

6. Fasting the 13th, 14th and 15th of every lunar month. One of the *Sahâb'ah* رضي الله عنهم said:

«أَمَرَنَا رَسُولُ الله ـ ﷺ ـ أَنْ نَصُومَ مِنَ الشَّهرِ ثَلاَثَةَ أَيَّامِ البيضِ : ثَلاَثَةَ عَشَرَ، وَأَربَعَةَ عَشَرَ، وَخَمسة عَشَرَ» [رواه النسائي وغيره].

"The Prophet صلى الله عليه وسلم instructed us to fast three days of every month: the 13th, 14th, and 15th." (*Nasa'i* and others)

THINGS WHICH BREAK THE FAST

The things which break the fast are of two categories:

A) What breaks the fast and requires only to make up for it (*Qadâ*).

B) What breaks it and requires to make up for it (*Qadâ*), and also to perform an act of expiation (*Kaffârah*).

A) What requires *Qadâ* only:

1. To eat and drink, knowingly and intentionally.

2. To induce vomiting intentionally, the Prophet صلى الله عليه وسلم said:

«وَمَن استَقَاءَ فَعَليْهِ القَضَاءَ». [صحيح رواه الحاكم وغيره].

"Whoever induced vomiting must make up for (the fast)." (*Hâkim* and others)

190

3. Menstruation and post-partum bleeding. Even if the bleeding starts just before the sun sets, that day's fasting must be repeated.

4. Ejaculation, either by masturbation or any other method of ejaculating short of intercourse, whether the cause was kissing the wife, or hugging her, or by use of the hand, etc. This nullifies the fast but requires *Qadâ* only.

B) What requires *Qadá* and *Kaffarah* both:

As for that which requires both *Qadâ* (repeating) and *Kaffârah* (expiation), it is only sexual intercourse and nothing else, in the opinion of a great number of scholars. The expiation is to free a slave, or to fast two lunar months in succession without missing a day, or to feed sixty poor people. Some scholars say the obligation is in that order, i.e. first one should free a slave; then, if that's not possible, to observe fast; then, if that's not possible, to feed the poor. (The man and the woman are both equal for their act and both must make expiation).

THINGS WHICH DO NOT SPOIL THE FAST

1. To eat or drink forgetfullly or mistakenly, or due to another person's threats and compulsion. There is no necessity for *Qadâ* or *Kaffârah*. The Prophet صلى الله عليه وسلم said:

«مَنْ نَسِيَ وَهُوَ صَائِمٌ فَأَكَلَ أوْ شَرِبَ فَلْيُتِمَّ صَوْمَهُ فَإِنَّمَا أَطْعَمَهُ اللهُ وَسَقَاهُ». [متفق عليه].

"Whoever forgot while he was fasting and ate or drank he should complete his fast, for it was Allah Who fed him and gave him to drink". (Agreed upon)

And he (صلى الله عليه وسلم) said:

«إِنَّ اللهَ وَضَعَ عَنْ أُمَّتِي الْخَطَأَ وَالنِّسْيَانَ وَمَا اسْتُكْرِهُوا عَلَيْهِ».

[صحيح رواه الطبراني].

191

"Allah has laid off for my *Ummah* (the burden of) mistakes and forgetfulness and what they are forced to do against their wills". (*Tabarani*).

2. Unintentional vomiting. The Prophet صلى الله عليه وسلم said:

«مَنْ ذَرَعَهُ الْقَيْءُ وَهُوَ صَائِمٌ فَلَيْسَ عَلَيْهِ قَضَاءٌ». [صحيح رواه الحاكم].

"One who happened to vomit while fasting, there is no *Qadâ* on him." (*Hâkim*).

I'TIKAF (SECLUSION IN THE *MASJID*) IS PART OF THE RELIGION

1. According to *Shari'ah*, *I'tikâf* means staying in the *Masjid* (mosque) with the intention of drawing himself closer to Allah.

2. All the scholars agree that it is *Mashrû'* (a legitimate part of Islâm) because:

«لأَنَّ النَّبِيَّ ـ ﷺ ـ كَانَ يَعْتَكِفُ فِي الْعَشْرِ الأَوَاخِرِ مِنْ رَمَضَانَ حَتَى تَوَفَّاهُ اللهُ عَزَّ وَجَل، ثُمَّ اعْتَكَف أَزْوَاجُهُ مِنْ بَعْدِهِ». [متفق عليه].

"The Prophet صلى الله عليه وسلم used to stay in the *Masjid,* the last ten days of Ramadân until he died, then his wives used to do the same after him." (Agreed upon)

3. *I'tikâf* is of two kinds: Supererogatory (*Masnûn*) and Compulsory (*Wâjib*).

The *Masnûn* kind is what a Muslim does voluntarily, in order to get closer to Allah and to follow the Messenger صلى الله عليه وسلم and it is especially recommended during the last ten days of Ramadân.

192

The *Wajib I'tikâf* is what a person makes compulsory upon himself by a vow (*Nadhr*).

4. The time to begin *I'tikâf*:

«كَانَ النَّبِيُّ ـ ﷺ ـ إِذَا أَرَادَ أَنْ يَعْتَكِفَ صَلَّى الفَجْرَ ثُمَّ دَخَلَ مُعْتَكَفَهُ» . [متفق عليه].

"The Prophet صلى الله عليه وسلم , if he intended to perform *I'tikâf*, used to pray *Fajr*, then enter the area he set aside for *I'tikâf* in the *Masjid*." (Agreed upon)

5. Necessary conditions for practising *I'tikâf*: The person should be Muslim, having reached the age of discernment, purified from *Janaba* and menses and post-partum bleeding.

6. The basic element of *I'tikâf*: Staying in the *Masjid* with the intention of getting closer to Allah.

7. What is permitted to do while in *I'tikâf*:

   a) Going out from the place of *I'tikâf* to bid farewell to his family.

   b) Combing his hair, shaving his head, clipping his nails, cleaning his body, perfuming, and wearing the best of clothing.

   c) To go out of the *Masjid* for pressing necessities like using the toilet, or to eat and drink, if no one brings him food.

   d) It is permitted to eat and drink and sleep in the *Masjid* with the proper care taken to maintain its cleanliness.

8. Etiquettes of *I'tikâf*: 'Aisha رضي الله عنها said:

«السُّنَّةُ على الـمُعْتَكِفِ أَنْ لاَ يَعُودَ مَرِيضاً، وَلاَ يَشْهَدَ جَنَازَةً، وَلاَ يَمَسَّ امْرَأَةً وَلاَ يُبَاشِرُهَا، ولاَ يَخْرُجَ إلاَّ لِلْحَاجَةِ الَّتِي لاَبُدَّ مِنْهَا

193

وَلاَ اعْتِكَافَ إِلاَّ بِصَوْمٍ وَلاَ اعْتِكَافَ إِلاَّ فِي مَسْجِدٍ جَامِعٍ.»

[صحيح رواه البيهقي وأبوداود].

The *Sunnah* for one in *I'tikâf* is not to leave the *Masjid* to
visit the sick, nor to attend a burial, nor to touch a woman
nor to have sex with her, and not to leave the *Masjid*
except for unavoidable need; and there is no *I'tikâf*
without fasting; and there is no *I'tikâf* except in a *Masjid*
where *Jumu'ah* (Friday prayer) is established." (*Baihaqi*
and *Abû Dâwûd*)

9. Things which nullify *I'tikâf*:

a) Leaving the *Masjid* without need, intentionally.

b) Losing one's rationality through insanity or drunkenness.

c) Menstruation and post-partum bleeding.

THE BOOK OF *HAJJ* (PILGRIMAGE)

* The virtues of *Hajj* and *'Umrah*
* The actions of *'Umrah* (the lesser pilgrimage)
* The actions of *Hajj* (the pilgrimage to Makkah)
* Some etiquettes of *Hajj* and *Umrah*
* Some etiquettes of the Prophet's Mosque
* Upon whom is *Hajj* obligatory ?
* Fundamental constituents (*Arkân*) of *Hajj*
* Compulsory acts (*Wajibât*) of *Hajj*
* Things forbidden to a person in the state of *Ihrâm*
* The rule if one does something forbidden for those in the state of *Ihrâm*
* How the Prophet صلى الله عليه وسلم performed *Hajj*
* The sacrificial animals, their types and conditions

195

THE VIRTUES OF *HAJJ* AND *UMRAH*

1. Allâh عز و جل said:

$$
\text{﴿ وَلِلَّهِ عَلَى ٱلنَّاسِ حِجُّ ٱلْبَيْتِ مَنِ ٱسْتَطَاعَ إِلَيْهِ سَبِيلًا وَمَن كَفَرَ فَإِنَّ ٱللَّهَ غَنِيٌّ عَنِ ٱلْعَالَمِينَ ﴾}
$$

"... And *Hajj* (pilgrimage to Makkah) to the House (Ka'bah) is a duty that mankind owes to Allah, those who can afford the expenses (for conveyance, provision and residence); and whoever disbelieves (i.e. denies *Hajj*, then he is a disbeliever of Allah), then Allah stands not in need of any of the *'Alâmin* (mankind and jinns)." (V.3:97)

2. The Prophet صلى الله عليه وسلم said:

«العُمْرَةُ إلى العُمْرةِ كَفَّارَةٌ لِما بَيْنَهُما، وَالحَجُّ الـمَبْرُورُ لَيسَ لَهُ جَزَاءٌ إلَّا الجَـنَّةُ». [متفق عليه].

"From one *'Umrah* to another is expiation for what is between them and *Hajj Mabrûr* has no reward except Paradise". (Agreed upon)

[*Hajj Mabrûr* is the *Hajj* accepted by Allah for being performed perfectly according to the Prophet's *Sunnah* with legally earned money avoiding the sin and evils during *Hajj*].

3. And he (صلى الله عليه وسلم) said:

«مَنْ حَجَّ فَلَمْ يَرْفُثْ وَلم يَفْسُقْ رجَعَ مِنْ ذُنُوبِهِ كَيَوْمٍ وَلَدَتْهُ أمُّهُ».

[متفق عليه].

"One who performed *Hajj* and did not speak obscenely, nor act corruptly, will return without his sins, like the day his mother gave birth to him." (Agreed upon)

4. And he (صلى الله عليه وسلم) said:

«خُذُوا عَنِّي مَنَاسِكَكُم». [رواه مسلم].

"Take from me your rites (the rituals of the *Hajj*)". (*Muslim*)

5. My Muslim brethren, hurry to fulfill the obligation of *Hajj* when you have enough money to cover the expenses of the round trip journey. Do not wait until you have enough money to buy presents and sweets etc., for friends and relatives after the *Hajj*, as these are not valid excuses for delay. You don't know, perhaps you will get too sick to travel, or get poor, or die; and in that case you will die in a state of disobedience, because you didn't do it when you were able, and *Hajj* is one of the pillars of Islâm.

6. The wealth you spend to perform *Hajj* and *'Umrah* must be *Halâl* (earned lawfully) so that Allah may accept it.

7. It is forbidden for a woman to travel for *Hajj* or anywhere else without a *Mahram* to accompany her [a *Mahram* is either her husband or close male relatives who are not permitted to marry her, like her father, brother, uncle, son etc. The *Mahram* has to be old enough to be able to protect her]. The Prophet صلى الله عليه وسلم said:

«لَا تُسَافِرِ الْـمَرْأَةُ إِلَّا وَمَعَهَا ذُوْ مَحْرَمٍ». [متفق عليه].

"A woman may not travel except if a *Mahram* is with her". (Agreed upon)

8. Make peace with those with whom you have a dispute, and pay your debts, and advise your family not to be extravagant in their ornament and cars and sweets and slaughtered animals, etc. Allâh عز وجل said:

﴿وَكُلُواْ وَٱشۡرَبُواْ وَلَا تُسۡرِفُوٓاْ﴾

"... and eat and drink but waste not by extravagance..." (V. 7:31)

9. *Hajj* is a great meeting of Muslims; it provides a unique

opportunity to get to know each other, and love each other, and to help each other and solve their problems, and to witness that which is of benefit to them in their religion and their worldly affairs.

10. And it is very important for you to rely upon Allah Alone in seeking the help needed to solve your problems, calling upon Him in *Du'â*, not on anyone else. As Allâh عز و جل said:

﴿ قُلۡ إِنَّمَآ أَدۡعُواْ رَبِّى وَلَآ أُشۡرِكُ بِهِۦٓ أَحَدًا ﴾

"Say (O Muhammad صلى الله عليه وسلم): I invoke only my Lord (Allah Alone) and I associate none as partners along with Him." (V. 72: 20)

11. *'Umrah* (the lesser pilgrimage) is permitted at anytime, but it has most reward in Ramadân, as the Prophet صلى الله عليه وسلم said:

«عُمۡرَةٌ فِي رَمَضَانَ تَعۡدِلُ حَجَّةً». [متفق عليه].

"*'Umrah* in Ramadân is equal to a *Hajj* (in reward)." (Agreed upon)

12. One *Salât* in *Al-Masjid Al-Harâm* (the Sacred Mosque in Makkah) has more reward than 100,000 *Salât* in other mosques; based on the statement of the Prophet صلى الله عليه وسلم :

«صَلَاةٌ فِي مَسۡجِدِي هَذَا أَفۡضَلُ مِنۡ أَلۡفِ صَلَاةٍ فِيمَا سِوَاهُ مِنَ الۡمَسَاجِدِ إِلَّا الۡمَسۡجِدِ الۡحَرَامِ». [متفق عليه].

"A *Salât* in my *Masjid* is better than 1000 *Salât* anywhere else except in *Al-Masjid Al-Harâm*." (Agreed upon)

And his statement:

«وَصَلَاةٌ فِي المَسۡجِدِ الحَرَامِ أَفۡضَلُ مِنۡ صَلَاةٍ فِي مَسۡجِدِي هَذَا بِمِائَةِ صَلَاةٍ». [صحيح رواه أحمد].

198

"And *Salât* in *Al-Masjid Al-Harâm* is better than 100 *Salât* in my *Masjid*." (*Ahmad*).

[1000 x 100 = 100,000 (one hundred thousand *Salât*)]

13. The best way to perform the *Hajj* and '*Umrah* is called *Tamattu'*, which means you perform '*Umrah* first, then come out of *Ihrâm* until *Hajj* starts, whereupon you put on *Ihrâm* again. The Prophet صلى الله عليه وسلم is reported to have said:

«يَا آلَ مُحَمَّدٍ، مَنْ حَجَّ مِنْكُمْ فَلْيُهِلَّ بِعُمْرَةٍ فِي حَجَّةٍ» . [رواه ابن حبان وصححه الألباني].

"O family of Muhammad! whoever performs *Hajj* amongst you, should enter *Ihram* for '*Umrah* along with *Hajj*." (Ibn Hibbân)

THE ACTIONS OF '*UMRAH*
(THE LESSER PILGRIMAGE)
Ihrâm, Tawâf, Sa'y, **shaving or cutting hair of the head,**
coming out of *Ihrâm*

1. *Ihrâm:* Put on the clothes of *Ihrâm* at the *Miqât* and recite [to make the intention for '*Umrah* at one of the *Mîqât** after putting on specific clothing (unstitched cloth, similar to a towel or sheet, one piece around the upper part and one piece wrapped around the lower part of the body). This clothing is for men only. The intention here should be made verbally, as that is *Sunnah*]:

Labbaik Allahumma bi'Umrah «لَبَّيْكَ اللهُمَّ بِعُمرةٍ»

---

* The *Mîqât* are the places specified by the Prophet صلى الله عليه وسلم for people to enter into the state of *Ihrâm*. The places differ depending on the direction from which the pilgrims come. When coming from Syria, Palestine etc., the *Mîqât* is Juhfah which is near Rabigh. From Najd it is Qarn-ul-Manazil, from Al-Madinah it is Dhul-Hulaifah, and for Yemen it is Yalamlam, and for Iraq the *Mîqât* is Dhât 'Irq.

"At Your service (literally: "In response to Your call"); O Allah for *'Umrah*",

then, in a loud voice keep repeating the *Talbiyah:*

Labbaik Allahumma Labbaik «لَبَّيْكَ اللهُمَّ لَبَّيْكَ»

"At Your service; O Allah, at Your service."

2. *Tawâf*: When you reach Makkah, go to the *Haram*, and walk around the K'abah seven times, counterclockwise, starting from the corner with the *Hajar Al-Aswad* (the Black Stone), saying:

Bismillah wa Allahu Akbar «بِسْمِ اللهِ وَاللهُ أَكْبَرُ» .

"In the Name of Allah, Allah is the Most Great."

Kiss the stone if you are able to do so without pushing and jostling, if you cannot, then point toward it with your right hand raised; (when you get 3/4 of the way around) touch the Yemâni Corner with your right hand if you can but don't kiss it; and don't point at it if you are moving round at a distance. Between it and the corner with the Black Stone say the following *Du'â:*

«رَبَّنَا آتِنَا فِي الدُّنْيَا حَسَنَةً وَفِي الآخِرَةِ حَسَنَةً، وَ قِنَا عَذَابَ النَّارِ» .

"O our Lord grant us good in this life and in the Hereafter and protect us from the torment of the Fire".

When you reach the Black Stone, repeat as before until you complete seven rounds. Then pray two *Rak'a* behind *Maqâm Ibrâhîm*, reciting *Surah Al-Kafirûn* in the first *Rak'â*, and *Surah Al-Ikhlâs* in the second. (After the prayer, it is *Sunnah* to drink Zamzam water and invoking for greater knowledge and what one may like. Then *Sa'y* is to be done).

3. *Sa'y*: Climb up the hill called As-Safa. Face the *Qiblah* and

raise your hand towards the sky, saying:

«إِنَّ الصَّفا وَالمروة من شعائرِ اللهِ، أَبْدأُ بِمَا بَدَأَ بِهِ، وَكَبِّر ثَلاثَةً بِلاَ إِشَارَةٍ وقُل : لَا إله إلاَّ اللهُ وَحْدَهُ لَا شَرِيكَ لَهُ، لَهُ المُلْكُ وَلهُ الحَمدُ، وَهُوَ عَلى كُلِّ شيءٍ قَدِيرٌ، لا إله إلاَّ اللهُ وحدَهُ، انجَزَ وَعدهُ وَصدَقَ عَبدُهُ، وَهَزمَ الأحزَابَ وحدُهُ»

"Verily! As-Safâ and Al-Marwah (two mountains in Makkah) are of the signs of Allah. I start with what Allah started with (As-Safa)."

Then say: *Allahu Akbar* three times without pointing; and say:

"None has the right to be worshipped except Allah, Who is Alone without partners. The dominion belong to Him and all praise belong to Him alone. And He has power over all things. None has the right to be worshipped except Allah Alone. He executed His promise, and confirmed the truthfulness of His slave, and defeated the opponents Himself."

Say that three times, and repeat the whole things each time you reach As-Safa and Al-Marwah. And make *Du'â* for anything you want. There is a certain part of the distance between the two hills, marked by green lines, where it is recommended for men to run. Make seven passages between the two hills (each one-way traversal is counted as one passage, so the whole *Sa'y* is 3.5 round trips).

4. Shave your whole head, or shorten your hair; women should cut a small portion of their hair.

5. With that you have completed your *'Umrah* and you should come out from the state of *Ihrâm*, (changing into your normal clothes, and being free to do everything forbidden in the state of *Ihrâm*).

201

THE ACTIONS OF *HAJJ*
(THE PILGRIMAGE TO MAKKAH)

Ihrâm, spending the night at Mina, staying at 'Arafat, spending the night at Muzdalifah, casting pebbles, sacrificing an animal, shaving of the head, *Tawâf, Sa'y,* coming out of *Ihram*

1. Put on the clothes of *Ihrâm* on the 8th day of Dhul-Hijjah in Makkah. Say:

   Labbaik Allahumma bi Hajjah «لَبَّيْكَ اللهُمَّ بِحَجَّةٍ»

   "At Your service, O Allah, to perform *Hajj.*"
   Go to Mina and spend the night there. The *Sunnah* is to offer five *Salât* there from *Zuhr* on the 8th until *Fajr* of the 9th, shortening *Zuhr, Asr,* and *'Isha* to two *Rak'a,* but not joining any *Salât* together.

2. After sunrise on the 9th, go to 'Arafah, pray *Zuhr* and *Asr* together at the time of *Zuhr,* with one *Adhân* and two *Iqâmah* and no *Sunnah Salât.* Make sure you are within the boundaries of 'Arafat. Do not observe fast, repeat the *Talbiyah* frequently and devote yourself to *Du'â* calling upon Allah only. Staying at 'Arafât is a fundamental constituent of *Hajj.* (Note: Most of *Masjid* Namirah is outside of 'Arafât).

3. Leave 'Arafât after sunset, calmly; head for Muzdalifah. When you get there, pray *Maghrib* and *'Isha* together at the time of *'Isha,* sleep there in order to pray *Fajr* there and remember Allah in the proximity of the sacred monument. It is permitted for the weak (women, children, the old, etc. and those who must accompany them) to leave Muzdalifah after midnight, without sleeping there.

4. After *Fajr* and before sunrise, leave Muzdalifah for Mina. This is the 10th of Dhul-Hijjah, the day of *'Eid.* Pray *'Eid Salât* if you can. Cast seven pebbles at the *Jamratul.Kubra*

(big pillar in Mina), saying *Takbîr* with each pebble, anytime from sunrise until the night.

5. Slaughter an animal and skin it, either at Mina or at Makkah, on any of the days of *'Eid*, eat from it and feed the poor. If you cannot afford the price of an animal (and are making *Tamatt'u*) you must fast 3 days during *Hajj*, and seven more when you return to your family. Men and women are exactly the same in this rule, they must sacrifice or fast.

6. Shave your head or get a haircut, shortening from all over the head; shaving is better [Note: It is better to shorten the hair in *'Umrah* so there will be something left to shorten or shave for *Hajj*]. Put on normal clothes, and everything is now permitted to you except sex and its precursors.

7. Return to Makkah and perform *Tawâf*, seven rounds then perform *Sa'y*, seven passages between As-Safa and Al-Marwah (3.5 round trips); it is permissible to postpone *Tawâf* until the last day of the *Eid*. After *Tawâf*, your wife becomes permissible for you again, after being forbidden to you while in the state of *Ihrâm*.

8. Return to Mina for the days of *'Eid*, spending the nights of *'Eid* there is mandatory. On the 11th and 12th, stone all the three *Jamarât* (pillars), starting with the smallest pillar first. The time for that starts after the sun passes the zenith of high noon, each day, and lasts until the night. Use seven pebbles for each pillar, saying *Allahu Akbar* for each one you throw. You should be certain that the pebbles hit the pillar or landed within the little wall surrounding each pillar. If it didn't, repeat until it does. It is *Sunnah* to step aside after stoning the small and middle pillars to make *Du'â* with your hands raised.

It is permitted to appoint someone to stone on your behalf if you are sick or too old or weak to withstand the crowding and jostling. [There is difference of opinion on this permission for a woman who is healthy. It is better for her to stone for herself at night when the crowds are thinner]. It is also permissible to delay the stoning to the second or third day if necessary.

9. The Farewell *Tawâf* is mandatory, one should travel straight away after it.

SOME ETIQUETTES OF *HAJJ* AND *'UMRAH*

1. Make your *Hajj* purely for the pleasure of Allah, saying:

«اَللّٰهُمَّ هٰذِهِ حَجَّةٌ لَا رِيَاءَ فِيهَا وَلَا سُمْعَةَ» .

"O Allah, this is a *Hajj* in which I have no desire for showing-off or reputation."

2. Keep the company of pious people, and serve them, be patient if your neighbour annoys you.

3. Beware of smoking or buying or selling cigarettes. It is *Haram* (unlawful), harmful to your body and your neighbours and to your wealth, and it is an act of disobedience to Allâh عزوجل.

4. Use *Miswak* (tooth stick) to clean the mouth for every *Salât* and take some back as gifts along with *Zam-zam* water and dates. There are many *Ahâdîth* testifying to the virtues of both of these.

5. Beware of touching women or looking at them, and screen your women from other men.

6. Do not climb over the people waiting for *Salât*, as it is annoying; occupy the closest available place without disturbing others.

7. Beware of passing in front of persons who are offering *Salât*, as this is an action from *Shaitan's* repertoire (see the beginning of the book for the proofs).

8. Take time to pray devotedly, and pray towards a *Sutrah*. (e.g. a wall or the back of a man or a bookcase, etc.) and, if you

are following an *Imâm* in *Salât*, his *Sutrah* is sufficient for
those who follow him.

9. Be gentle with your neighbours while performing *Tawâf*, and
Sa'y, and stoning the *Jamarah*, and in kissing the Black
Stone, gentleness is desirable in most actions.

10. Beware of making *Du'â* to the dead instead of Allah, as this
is *Shirk* which will ruin your *Hajj* and all your good deeds.
Allâh عز و جل said:

$$\text{﴿ لَئِنْ أَشْرَكْتَ لَيَحْبَطَنَّ عَمَلُكَ وَلَتَكُونَنَّ مِنَ ٱلْخَٰسِرِينَ ﴾}$$

"... If you join others in worship with Allah, (then) surely
(all) your deeds will be in vain, and you will certainly be
among the losers." (V.39:65).

SOME ETIQUETTES OF THE PROPHET'S MOSQUE

1. When you enter the *Masjid,* put your right foot inside first,
and say:

$$\text{«بسمِ الله والسَّلامُ على رسُول الله، اللهُمَّ افتَح لِي أبوابَ رَحْمَتِك» .}$$

"In the Name of Allah, peace be upon the Messenger of
Allah, O Allah! forgive me and open for me the doors of
Your Mercy."

2. Pray two *Rak'a* (*Tahiyatul Masjid*) to greet the *Masjid*, send
Salâm upon the Messenger صلى الله عليه وسلم saying:

$$\text{«السَّلامُ عَلَيكَ يَارَسُول الله، السَّلامُ عَلَيكَ يَاأَبَابكر، السَّلَامُ عَلَيك يَاعُمرَ» .}$$

"As-Salâmu alaika yâ Rasûlallah, As-Salâmu alaika yâ Aba Bakr, As-Salmu aliaka yâ 'Umar."

Then face the *Qiblah* and make *Du'a*, keeping in mind the statement of the Prophet صلى الله عليه وسلم :

«إِذَا سَأَلْتَ فَاسْـأَلِ اللهَ وَإِذَا اسْتَعَنْتَ فَاسْتَعِنْ بِاللهِ» . [رواه

الترمذي وقال حسن صحيح].

"When you ask, ask Allah, and when you seek help, seek it from Allah." (Reported by Tirmidhi, who classed it *Hasan-Sahih*).

3. Visiting the *Masjid* of the Messenger صلى الله عليه وسلم is recommended, but the validity of the *Hajj* is not dependent on it, and there is no particular time which is prescribed for it.

4. Beware of kissing or touching the grill or the walls around the tomb. This is a heresy.

5. Walking backwards away from the tomb to leave the *Masjid* is also a heresy, for which there is no supportive evidence.

6. Send salutations on the Messenger صلى الله عليه وسلم as much as possible. As he (صلى الله عليه وسلم) said:

«مَنْ صَلَّى عَلَيَّ صَلَاةً وَاحِدَةً صَلَّى اللهُ عَلَيْهَا بِهَا عَشْرًا» . [رواه

مسلم].

"Whoever asks Allah to bless me once, Allah will bless him for that ten times". (*Muslim*)

7. It is recommended to visit the *Al-Baqî'* cemetery and the martyrs of *Uhud*. But not the seven *Masjid*.

8. The journey to Al-Madinah should be with the intention of visiting the Prophet's Mosque only and nothing else. But on arriving there

say *Salam* on him also. Because *Salât* in his *Masjid* is better than 1000 *Salât* in any other *Masjid;* the Prophet صلى الله عليه وسلم said:

$$ \text{«لَا تُشَدُّ الرِّحَالُ إِلَّا إِلَى ثَلَاثَةِ مَسَاجِدَ: الْمَسْجِدِ الْحَرَامِ،} $$

$$ \text{وَالْمَسْجِدِ الْأَقْصَى، وَمَسْجِدِي هَذَا».} \quad \text{[متفق عليه].} $$

"Do not travel except to three *Masjid, Al-Masjid Al-Harâm, Al-Masjid Al-Aqsa* (in Jerusalem) and my *Masjid*". (Agreed upon)

UPON WHOM IS *HAJJ* OBLIGATORY ?

Hajj is a pillar of *Islâm*, it is obligatory on:

1. The Muslim; it is not obligatory on the *Kâfir* or the apostate from *Islâm*.

2. One in his right mind; it is not *Wâjib* on the insane.

3. The freeman; it is not obligatory on the slave, who is the property of his master.

4. One who has attained puberty; it is not obligatory on the child; if the child performs *Hajj*, it doesn't absolve him of the obligation to perform it when he attains puberty.

5. One who is healthy; it is not obligatory on the sick person until he gets well.

6. One who has the ability; it is not *Wâjib* on one too poor to make the journey.

7. It is obligatory only once in a lifetime; if a person performs more than once, he will get reward, and women and men are the same in this regard.

8. For a woman; she has to have a *Mahram* to accompany her, since the Prophet صلى الله عليه وسلم said:

$$ \text{«وَلَا تُسَافِرِ الْمَرْأَةُ إِلَّا وَمَعَهَا ذُو مَحْرَمٍ».} \quad \text{[متفق عليه].} $$

"A woman should not travel except if a *Mahram* is with her." (Agreed upon)

FUNDAMENTAL CONSTITUENTS (*ARKAN*) OF *HAJJ*

The *Hajj* has some fundamental constituents, if any one of these is missing, the *Hajj* will not be valid. They are :

1. Entering the state of *Ihrâm* for *Hajj*. It is the intention, plus the wearing of unstitched cloth, for men: one piece wrapped around the upper part and one piece wrapped around the lower part of the body. Women would remain in their normal clothing.

2. Staying at 'Arafât on the 9th of Dhul-Hijjah from the time the sun passes the zenith of high noon until sunset. (For latecomers, their *Hajj* is valid as long as they can get to 'Arafât before the start of *Fajr Salat* on the 10th).

3. *Tawâf-al-Ifâdah*: It can be performed anytime after *Fajr* on the 10th until the last day of Dhul-Hijjah. (the 12th month of the Islamic calendar).

4. *Sa'y* between As-Safa and Al-Marwah. Start from As-Safa and make 7 passages back and forth (3.5 round trips).

COMPULSORY ACTS (*WAJIBAT*) OF *HAJJ*

If any compulsory act is not performed, one must offer a sacrifice of an animal to compensate for the omission. These compulsory acts are as follows:

1. Assuming *Ihrâm* from the *Mîqat*.

2. Extending one's stay at 'Arafât from the afternoon until a part of the night.

3. Spending the night at Muzdalifah or Mina.

4. Stoning the *Jamarât* (pillars)

5. The Farewell *Tawâf* (except on a woman who is menstruating at the time she's about to travel).

THINGS FORBIDDEN TO A PERSON IN THE STATE OF *IHRAM*

1. Sex, and anything which might lead up to it such as kissing or touching with desire.

2. Doing bad deeds and sins which expel a person from the obedience of Allah.

3. Arguing with one's companions, servants, or anyone else.

The basis for the prohibition of these three things is the Statement of Allâh عزوجل:

﴿ فَمَن فَرَضَ فِيهِنَّ ٱلۡحَجَّ فَلَا رَفَثَ وَلَا فُسُوقَ وَلَا جِدَالَ فِي ٱلۡحَجِّ ﴾

"...So whosoever intends to perform *Hajj* (therein by assuming *Ihrâm*), then he should not have sexual relations (with his wife), nor commit sin, nor dispute unjustly during the *Hajj*..." (V.2:197)

4. Wearing of sewn clothes (for men) such as shirts, hooded robes, pants, and covering the head with a cap or turban or shawl, etc. Also, it is forbidden to wear clothing that is dyed with a fragrant dye; also it is forbidden to wear leather socks; but it is permissible to wear sandals. If one cannot find sandals, the leather socks should be cut so that they don't come up to the ankle.

5. All scholars agree that the prohibitions in item 4 are for men only.

6. As for women, they can wear all of that, except for a garment

that has perfume on it and the *Niqâb* (veil) which covers her face and gloves, as it is reported that the Prophet صلى الله عليه وسلم said:

«لَا تَنْتَقِب الْمَرْأَةُ الْـمُحْرِمَةُ وَلَا تَلْبَسِ الْـقُفَّازَيْنِ». [رواه البخاري].

"A woman in *Ihrâm* shouldn't wear a *Niqâb*, nor should she wear gloves." (*Bukhâri*)

It is permissible to cover her face from men by using an umbrella or to let a portion of her outer garment hang over it. 'Aisha رضي الله عنها said:

«كَانَ الرُّكْبَانُ يَمُرُّونَ بِنَا، وَنَحْنُ مَعَ رَسُولِ اللهِ ﷺ - مُحْرِمَاتٍ، فَإِذَا حَاذُوا بِنَا سَدَلَت إِحْدَانَا جِلْبَابَهَا عَلى وَجْهِها، فَإِذَا جَاوَزُوا بِنَا كَشَفْنَاهُ». [رواه أبوداود].

"Riders would pass us while we were with Allah's Messenger صلى الله عليه وسلم in *Ihrâm*, when they drew close, each of us would let part of her outer garment hang over her face, and when they would pass, we would uncover our faces." (*Abû Dawûd*).

7. If a man is unable to find or acquire the two sheets normally worn for *Ihrâm*, or sandals, he should wear what he has. The Prophet صلى الله عليه وسلم said:

«إِذَا لَمْ يَجِد الْـمُسْلِمُ إِزَاراً فَلْيَلْبَسِ السَّرَاوِيل، وَإِذَا لَمْ يَجِد النَّعْلينِ فَلْيَلْبَسِ الْخُفَّيْنِ». [متفق عليه].

When a Muslim can't find the *Izâr* and *Rida* (the two sheets), he should wear pants/trousers, and if he can't find sandals he should wear leather socks." (Agreed upon)

8. It is forbidden for a person in *Ihrâm* (for *Muhrim*) to arrange a marriage for someone else, or to get married himself, or to propose marriage; based on the statement of the Prophet صلى الله عليه وسلم :

«لاَ يَنْكِحِ الْـمُحْرِمُ وَلاَ يُنْكِح ، وَلاَ يَخْطُبْ». [رواه مسلم].

"The *Muhrim* should not marry, nor arrange for another marriage, nor propose." (*Muslim*).

9. It is prohibited for the *Muhrim* to trim his nails, or to remove any hair by shaving or clipping, or by any other method; based on Allah's Statement:

﴿ وَلَا تَحْلِقُوا۟ رُءُوسَكُمْ حَتَّىٰ بَلَغَ ٱلْهَدْىُ مَحِلَّهُۥ ﴾

"... and do not shave your heads until the *Hady* (sacrificial animal) reaches the place of sacrifice..." (V.2:196).

10. It is prohibited for the *Muhrim*; men and women to use perfumes on their bodies or garments.

11. It is prohibited for the *Muhrim* to hunt land animals, or slaughter it; he may not even point towards it or make it flee so another person could kill it, but it is permissible to catch fish or take any sea dwelling animal out of it, as well as eating it. Allâh عز وجل said:

﴿ أُحِلَّ لَكُمْ صَيْدُ ٱلْبَحْرِ وَطَعَامُهُ مَتَٰعًا لَّكُمْ وَلِلسَّيَّارَةِ وَحُرِّمَ عَلَيْكُمْ صَيْدُ ٱلْبَرِّ مَا دُمْتُمْ حُرُمًا ﴾

"Lawful to you is (the pursuit of) water- game and its use for food — for the benefit of yourselves and those who travel, but forbidden is (the pursuit of) land-game as long as you are in a state of *Ihrâm* (for *Hajj* or '*Umrah*)..." (V.5:96)

RULES FOR PERPETRATORS OF THE PROHIBITIONS OF THE STATE OF *IHRAM*

1. If one has an excuse and had a need to do a prohibited act of *Ihrâm*, other than sexual intercourse, like shaving the head, or wearing stitched clothing to protect oneself from heat or cold etc., he has to sacrifice a sheep; or feed six poor people, providing each poor person 1/2 *Sa'* * of food; or fast for three days; he can choose any one of these three alternatives.

Allâh عز و جل said:

﴿ فَمَن كَانَ مِنكُم مَّرِيضًا أَوْ بِهِۦٓ أَذًى مِّن رَّأْسِهِۦ فَفِدْيَةٌ مِّن صِيَامٍ أَوْ صَدَقَةٍ أَوْ نُسُكٍ ﴾

".... And whosoever of you is ill or has an ailment in his scalp (necessitating shaving), he must pay a *Fidyah* (ransom) of either fasting (three days) or giving *Sadaqah* (feeding six poor persons) or offering sacrifice (one sheep)... " (V.2:196).

2. There is no penalty for one who wore something or applied perfume forgetfully or out of ignorance. Ya'la bin Umaiyah reported:

فعن يعلي بن أمية قال: «أَتَى رَسُولَ اللهِ ـ ﷺ ـ رَجُلٌ بِالـجِعْرَانَةِ وَعَلَيْهِ جُبَّةٌ وَهُوَ مُصَفِّرٌ لِحيتَهُ وَرَأْسَهُ، فَقَالَ: يَارَسُولَ اللهِ أَحْرَمْتُ بِعُمْرَةٍ وَأَنَا كَمَا تَرى فَقَالَ: اغْسِلْ عَنْكَ الصُّفْرَةَ، وَانْزِعْ عَنْكَ الـجُبَّةَ وَمَاكُنْتَ صَانِعاً فِي حَجِّكَ فَاصْنَعْ فِي عُمْرَتِكَ». [متفق عليه].

---

* A measure of volume equal to 2.6 kilograms (the food can be any grain, rice, wheat etc.)

212

A man came to Allah's Messenger صلى الله عليه وسلم at (a place called) *Ji'rânah*, wearing a robe with saffron on his beard and head; he said; "O Messenger of Allah, I entered into the state of *Ihrâm* for *'Umrah* in the condition you see me in." He (صلى الله عليه وسلم) said to him; "Wash away the saffron and take off the robe, and what you used to do in *Hajj*, do in your *'Umrah*." (Agreed upon)

This allowance is not made for one who kills a game animal, forgetfully or in ignorance of the prohibition. He has to pay the penalty, because he is responsible for destroying property, for which there is no differentiation between knowledge and ignorance nor between forgetfulness and intent, similar to the responsibility for destroying property of humans.

3. If a *Muhrim* has intercourse with his wife, his *Hajj* is rendered invalid. He must continue with the rituals to their end, but he must also come back in a future year to make up for it, and he must sacrifice an animal.

HOW THE PROPHET صلى الله عليه وسلم PERFORMED *HAJJ*

Jabir رضي الله عنه narrated: The Prophet صلى الله عليه وسلم remained nine years without performing *Hajj*, then he made a public announcement in the tenth year that Allah's Messenger صلى الله عليه وسلم was about to perform *Hajj*. A large number of people came to Al-Madinah, all of them anxious to follow Allah's Messenger صلى الله عليه وسلم and to act according to his actions. We set out with him till we reached Dhul-Hulaifah. Asmâ, daughter of Umais, gave birth to Muhammad bin Abû Bakr. She sent a message to Allah's Messenger صلى الله عليه وسلم asking him: "What should I do?" He said: "Take a bath, bandage your private parts, and put on *Ihrâm*." Allah's Messenger صلى الله عليه وسلم then prayed in the mosque and then mounted *Al-Qaswa* (his she-camel) and it stood erect with him on its back at Al-Baidâ', and as far as I could see in front of me were riders and pedestrians, and the same on my right and left and behind me. Allah's Messenger صلى الله عليه وسلم was among us and the Revelation was descending on him, and he knows its (true) significance. And whatever he did, we also did the same. He pronounced the Oneness of Allâh:

«لَبَّيْك اللَّهُمَّ لَبَّيْكَ، لَبَّيْكَ لاَ شَرِيكَ لَكَ» .

"Labbaik (there I am! at Your service), O Allah, Labbaik (there I am! at Your service), Labbaik (there I am! at Your service), You have no partner, Labbaik. Verily, all praise and grace is Yours, and the sovereignty, too. You have no partner."

And the people pronounced Talbiyah as the people do today, and Allah's Messenger صلى الله عليه وسلم did not reject anything of it rather Allah's Messenger صلى الله عليه وسلم adhered to his own Talbiyah. Jabir said: We did not make intention for anything except Hajj. We did not recognize 'Umrah (along with Hajj) but, when we came with him to the House, he touched the corner (containing the Black Stone) and went round the Ka'bah (performed Tawâf) seven times, trotting during three of them, and walking normally during four and then while going to the station of Ibrâhim he recited:

﴿وَاتَّخِذُوا مِن مَّقَامِ إِبْرَاهِيمَ مُصَلًّى﴾

"... And take you (people) the Maqam (place) of Abraham (or the stone on which Abraham عليه السلام stood while he was building the Ka'bah) as a place of prayer (for some of your prayers, e.g. two Rak'at after the Tawâf of the Ka'bah at Makkah...)"

He stood with the station between him and the House. (Jabir bin Abdullah, who reported this Hadîth from his father, said: My father used to say, and I don't know from anyone beside the Prophet صلى الله عليه وسلم that) he recited in the two Rak'at Surah Al-

214

Ikhlâs (No. 112) and *Surah Al-Kafirun* (No. 109). He (صلى الله عليه وسلم) then returned to the corner (the Black Stone) and touched it, he then went out of the gate to As-Safa, and as he reached near it, he recited:

﴿إِنَّ الصَّفَا وَالْمَرْوَةَ مِنْ شَعَائِرِ اللهِ﴾ أَبْدَأُ بِمَا بَدَأَ اللهُ بِهِ،

"Verily! As-Safa and Al-Marwah (two mountains in Makkah) are some of the symbols of Allâh. (Adding) I begin with what Allah began with."

He started with As-Safa, mounting it until he saw the House, and facing the *Qiblah*, he declared the Oneness of Allah and glorified him and said:

لَا إِلَهَ إِلَّا اللهُ وَحْدَهُ لَا شَرِيكَ لَهُ، لَهُ الْمُلْكُ وَلَهُ الْحَمْدُ،
وَهُوَ عَلَى كُلِّ شَيْءٍ قَدِيرٌ، لَا إِلَهَ إِلَّا اللهُ وَحْدَهُ أَنْجَزَ وَعْدَهَ،
وَنَصَرَ عَبْدَهُ، وَهَزَمَ الْأَحْزَابَ وَحْدَهُ،

"None has the right to be worshipped except Allah, He is Alone with no partner. His is the Sovereignty, to Him praise is due, and He is Powerful over everything. Nothing deserves worship except Allah Alone, He fulfilled His Promise, helped His servant, and Alone routed the Confederates."

He (صلى الله عليه وسلم) then made supplication, in the course of which he repeated the same three times. He then descended and walked toward Al-Marwah and when his feet came down in the bottom of the valley, he ran; and when he began to ascend, he walked until he reached Al-Marwah. There he did as he had done at As-Safa. And when it was his last passage on Al-Marwah, he said:

لَوْ أَنِّي اسْتَقْبَلْتُ مِنْ أَمْرِي مَا اسْتَدْبَرْتُ لَمْ أَسُقِ الْهَدْيَ،
وَجَعَلْتُهَا عُمْرَةً، فَمَنْ كَانَ مِنْكُم لَيْسَ مَعَهُ هَدْيٌ

215

فَلِيَحِلَّ وَلْيَجْعَلْهَا عُمْرَةً،

"If I had known beforehand what I have come to know afterwards, I would not have brought sacrificial animals and would have performed (a separate) 'Umrah. So, he among you who doesn't have the sacrificial animals with him should put off *Ihrâm* and treat it as an *'Umrah*."

Surâqah bin Mâlik bin Ju'sham got up and said, "O Messenger of Allah! Does it apply to the present year, or for ever?" Thereupon Allah's Messenger صلى الله عليه وسلم intertwined his fingers, one into another, and said twice:

«دَخَلَتِ العُمرَةُ في الحَجِّ مَرَّتين، لاَ بَل لأَبَدِ أَبَدٍ»

"The *'Umrah* has been incorporated into the *Hajj*. (Adding:) No, but for ever and ever".

Ali رضي الله عنه came from Yemen with the (sacrificial) animals of the Prophet صلى الله عليه وسلم and found that Fatimah رضي الله عنها was one of those who had put off *Ihrâm* and put on dyed clothes, and has applied antimony (*Kuhl*) (to her eyes). He expressed his disapproval of that to her. Whereupon she said, "My father has ordered me to do this." The narrator said: Ali used to say in Iraq: "I went to Allah's Messenger, showed annoyance at Fâtimah for what she had done and asked Allah's Messenger صلى الله عليه وسلم the verdict regarding what she has narrated from him, and told him I had rebuked her for that. He (صلى الله عليه وسلم) said: "She told the truth, she told the truth (then he asked me). What did you say when you undertook to go to *Hajj*?" Ali said: "I said: O Allah, I am putting on *Ihrâm* of the same type as your Messenger has put on." He said, "I have with me sacrificial animals, so do not put off the *Ihrâm*." Jabir said: The total number of sacrificial animals which Ali brought from Yemen and which the Prophet صلى الله عليه وسلم brought was 100. Then all the people except the Prophet صلى الله عليه وسلم and those who had with them sacrificial animals, put off *Ihrâm* and got their hair shortened; when it was the day of *Tarwiyah* (the 8th of Dhul-Hijjah), they went to Mina (after) putting on *Ihrâm* for *Hajj*. The Prophet صلى الله عليه وسلم rode, and he led *Zuhr, Asr, Maghrib, Isha* and *Fajr Salât*. He then waited a little until the sun rose and commanded that a tent of hair should be pitched at Namirah (at the edge of Arafat). Allah's Messenger صلى الله عليه وسلم then set out and the Quraish didn't doubt that he would halt at *Al-Mash'âr Al-Harâm* (the sacred monument) as the Quraish used to do in the pre-Islamic period.

However, he passed on till he came to Arafât and he found that the tent had been pitched for him at Namirah. There he got down till the sun had passed the meridian; he commanded that *Al-Qaswâ* should be brought and saddled for him. Then he came to the bottom of the valley, and addressed the people saying:

«إِنَّ دِماءَكُمْ وأَمْوالَكُمْ حَرامٌ عَلِيكُم كَحُرمةِ يَومِكُم هَذا، في شَهرِكُم هَذا، في بَلَدِكُم هَذا، أَلاَ كُلُّ شيءٍ مِنْ أمرِ الجاهليَّةِ تَحتَ قَدَميَّ مَوضُوعٌ، وَدِماءُ الجَاهليةِ مَوضُوعَةٌ وإِنَّ أَوَّلَ دَم أَضَعُ مِنْ دِمائِنا دَمُ ابنِ رَبِيعَةَ بْنِ الحَارِثِ كانَ مُسترْضِعاً في بَني سَعْدٍ فَقَتلَتهُ هُذَيلٌ ـ وَرِبَا الجَاهِليَّةِ مَوضُوعٌ وَأَوَّلُ رِبًا أَضَعُ رِبانَا، رِبَا عَبَّاسِ بْنِ عَبدِالمُطَّلِبِ، فَإنهُ مَوضُوعٌ كُلُّهُ، فاتَّقُوا اللهَ في النِّساءِ فَإِنَّكُمْ أَخَذتُمُوهُنَّ بِأمانِ اللهِ ، وَاستْحْللتُم فُرُوجَهُنَّ بِكَلِمةِ اللهِ ، وَلَكم عَليهِنَّ أَنْ لا يُوطِئْنَ فُرُشكُم أَحَداً تَكرَهُونهُ، فَإن فَعلنَ ذَلِكَ فَاضرِبُوهُنَّ ضَرْباً غَيْرَ مُبرِّح وَلَهُنَّ عَلَيكُم رِزْقُهُنَّ وَكِسْوتُهُنَّ بِالمعرُوفِ، وَقَد تَركتُ فيكُم مَا لَنْ تَضلُّوا بَعدَهُ إِن اعْتَصمتُم

217

بِهِ: كِتَابَ اللهِ، وَأَنْتُمْ تُسْأَلُونَ عني فَمَا أَنْتُمْ قَائِلُونَ؟

قَالُوا: نَشْهَدُ أَنَّـكَ قَدْ بَلَّغْتَ وَأَدَّيْتَ وَنَصَحْتَ، فَقَالَ

بِإِصْبَعِهِ السَّبَّابَةِ يَرْفَعُهَا إِلَى السَّمَاءِ وَيَنْكُتُهَا إِلَى النَّاسِ: اللَّهُمَّ

اشْهَـدْ، اللَّهُمَّ اشْهَدْ ثَلاثَ مَرَّاتٍ،

"Verily your blood and your property are as sacred and inviolable as the sacredness of this day of yours, in this month of yours, in this town of yours. Behold! Everything pertaining to the Days of Ignorance is under my feet completely abolished. Abolished are also the blood-revenges of the Days of Ignorance. The first claim of ours on blood-revenge which I abolish is that of the son of Rabi'a bin Al-Harith, who was nursed among the tribe of Sa'd and killed by Hudhail. And the usury of the pre-Islamic period is abolished, and the first of our usury I abolish is that of 'Abbâs bin Abdul-Muttalib, for it is all abolished. Fear Allah concerning women! Verily you have taken them on the security of Allah, and intercourse with them has been made lawful unto you by the Words of Allah. You too have right over them, and that they should not allow anyone to sit on your bed whom you do not like. But if they do that, you can chastise them but not severely. Their rights upon you are that you should provide them with food and clothing in a fitting manner. I have left among you the Book of Allah, and if you hold fast to it, you would never go astray. And you would be asked about me (on the Day of Resurrection), (now tell me) what would you say?" They (the audience) said: "We will bear witness that you have conveyed (the Message), discharged (the duties of Prophethood) and given wise (sincere) counsel." He (the narrator) said: He (the Prophet صلى الله عليه وسلم) then raised his forefinger toward the sky and pointing it at the people (said): "O Allah, be witness. O Allah, be witness," said it thrice.

(Bilal then) pronounced *Adhân* and later on *Iqâmah* and he (the Prophet صلى الله عليه وسلم) led the Noon Prayer. He (Bilal) then uttered *Iqâmah* and he (the Prophet صلى الله عليه وسلم) led the Afternoon Prayer and he observed no other prayer in between the two. Allah's Messenger صلى الله عليه وسلم then mounted his camel and came to the place of stay, making his she-camel *Al-Qaswâ* turn towards the side where there were rocks, having the path taken by those who went on foot in front of him, and faced the *Qiblah*. He kept standing there till the sunset, and the yellow light had somewhat gone, and the disc of the sun had disappeared. He made Usamah sit behind him, and he pulled the nosestring of *Qaswâ* so forcefully that its head touched the saddle (in order to keep her under perfect control), and he pointed out to the people with his right hand to be moderate (in speed), and whenever he happened to pass over an elevated tract of sand, he slightly loosened it (the nosestring of his camel) till she climbed up and this is how he reached Al-Muzdalifah. There he led the *Maghrib* (Evening) and *'Ishâ* (Night) prayers with one *Adhân* and two *Iqâmah* and did not glorify (Allah) in between them (i.e. he did not observe supererogatory *Raka'h* between *Maghrib* and *'Ishâ* prayers). Allah's Messenger صلى الله عليه وسلم then lay down till dawn and offered the *Fajr* (Dawn) prayer with an *Adhân* and *Iqâmah* when the morning light was clear. He again mounted *Al-Qaswâ,* and when he came to Al-Mash'ar Al-Harâm, he faced towards *Qiblah*, supplicated Him, glorified Him, and pronounced His Uniqueness (*La illaha illa-Allah*) and Oneness, and kept standing till the daylight was very clear. He then went quickly before the sun rose, and seated behind him was Al-Fadl bin Abbas; and he was a man having beautiful hair and fair complexion and handsome face. As Allah's Messenger صلى الله عليه وسلم was moving on, there was also going a group of women (side by side with them). Al-Fadl began to look at them. Allah's Messenger صلى الله عليه وسلم placed his hand on

219

the face of Fadl, who then turned his face to the other side and began to see, and Allah's Messenger صلى الله عليه وسلم turned his hand to the other side and placed it on the face of Al-Fadl. He again turned his face to the other side till he came to the bottom of Muhassir. He urged her (Al-Qaswâ) a little, and, following the middle road, which comes out at the greatest *Jamrah*, he came to the *Jamrah* which is near the tree. At this he threw seven small pebbles saying *Allahu Akbar* while throwing every one of them in a manner in which the small pebbles are thrown (with the help of fingers) and this he did in the bottom of the valley. He then went to the place of sacrifice, and sacrificed sixty-three (camels) with his own hand. Then he gave the remaining number to 'Ali who sacrificed them, and he shared him in his sacrifice. He then commanded that a piece of flesh from each sacrificed animal should be put in a pot, and when it was cooked, both of them (the Prophet صلى الله عليه وسلم and 'Ali (رضي الله عنه) took some meat out of it and drank its soup. Allah's Messenger صلى الله عليه وسلم again rode and came to the House, and offered the *Zuhr* prayer at Makkah. He came to the tribe of 'Abdul-Muttalib, who were supplying water at Zam-zam, and said:

«انْزِعُوا بَنِي عَبْدِالـمُطَلِبِ فَلَوْلاَ أَنْ يَغْلِبَكُمُ النَّاسُ عَلى سِقَايَتِكُم لَنَزَعْتُ مَعَكُم» [رواه مسلم ٤/٣٩ـ٤٣].

"Draw water, O Bani 'Abdul-Muttalib, were it not that people would usurp this right of supplying water from you, I would have drawn it along with you."

So they handed him a bucket and he drank from it. (*Muslim*)

THE SACRIFICIAL ANIMALS, THEIR TYPES AND CONDITIONS

The sacrificial animals (*Hady*) of the *Hajj* are those camels, cattle, sheep, or goats which are sacrificed in the vicinity of the

Haram to be distributed among its poor. The *Hady* can either be *Mustahab* (desirable) or *Wâjib* (compulsory).

A. The *Mustahab Hady* is that which is sacrificed by a person performing *Hajj Ifrâd* (i.e. *Hajj* by itself without an *'Umrah* performed along with it) or by one making an *'Umrah* only.

B. The *Wâjib Hady* is for the following situations:

1. *Wâjib* on someone performing *Hajj Qiran* (i.e. to perform *'Umrah* before *Hajj* and stay in the state of *Ihrâm*, then to perform *Hajj* with the same *Ihrâm*) and on the person performing *Hajj Tamattu'* (which is to perform *'Umrah* then to come out of *Ihrâm*, then to enter *Ihrâm* a second time for *Hajj*); in these situations, the person offering the sacrifice may eat from the meat of the *Hady*.

2. *Wâjib* on someone who failed to perform a *Wâjib* act of *Hajj*, such as stoning the *Jamarât*, or putting on *Ihrâm* at the *Mîqât*, or staying into a part of the night after the afternoon spent at 'Arafât, or spending the night at Muzdalifah, or Mina, or the Farewell *Tawâf*.

3. *Wâjib* on someone who did something prohibited to a person in the state of *Ihrâm*. Such as using perfume or shaving the hair.

4. *Wâjib* due to a transgression on the sanctity of the *Haram* area, such as hunting an animal or cutting a tree within its boundaries.

Conditions for the acceptability of the *Hady* (sacrificial animals):

1. The animal must be old enough: a camel should be at least five years old; or a cow should be two years old; a goat should be one year old (12 months); a sheep can be six months old, if it is fat.

2. The animal must be free of defects, it will not be accepted by

Allah if it is one eyed, or lame, or mangy, or thin.

The proper time and place for slaughtering the *Hady:*

The 10th of Dhul-Hijjah and the three days after that which are called the days of *Tashrîq* (which means: to cut meat into strips for drying, which was the traditional way of preserving meat which couldn't be eaten right away).

It is permissible to slaughter in Mina or Makkah.

THE BOOK OF *MU'AMALAT*
(Transactions and Mutual Relations)

* The importance of marriage in Islam; and the laws of marriage
* *Hijâb* (the veil) is a means of honouring and protecting women
* Rules regarding *Riba* (usury) and its different forms
* The prohibition of means of usury
* Doing business with banks
* The prohibition of usury for consumers and producers
* The prohibition on *Riba* (usury) in buying a house
* Means for getting rid of usury
* Rules regarding the *Luqtah* (lost and found articles)
* Special rules regarding *Luqtah* in the *Haram* (sanctuary) of Makkah

THE IMPORTANCE OF MARRIAGE IN ISLAM; AND THE LAWS OF MARRIAGE

Islâm encourages marriage;

1) Allâh عز و جل said:

﴿ وَٱللَّهُ جَعَلَ لَكُم مِّنْ أَنفُسِكُمْ أَزْوَٰجًا وَجَعَلَ لَكُم مِّنْ أَزْوَٰجِكُم بَنِينَ وَحَفَدَةً ﴾

"And Allah has given you wives of your own kind, and has given you, from your wives, sons and grandsons,... " (V.16:72)

2) And He عز و جل said:

﴿ وَأَنكِحُوا ٱلْأَيَٰمَىٰ مِنكُمْ وَٱلصَّٰلِحِينَ مِنْ عِبَادِكُمْ وَإِمَآئِكُمْ إِن يَكُونُوا فُقَرَآءَ يُغْنِهِمُ ٱللَّهُ مِن فَضْلِهِۦ وَٱللَّهُ وَٰسِعٌ عَلِيمٌ ﴾

"And marry those among you who are single (i.e. a man who has no wife and the woman who has no husband) and (also marry) the *Salihûn* (pious, fit and capable ones) of your (male) slaves and maid-servants (female slaves). If they be poor, Allah will enrich them out of His Bounty. And Allah is All-Suffcent for His creatures' needs, All-Knowing (about the state of the people)". (V.24:32)

3) The Prophet صلى الله عليه وسلم said:

«الدُّنْيَا مَتَاعٌ، وَخَيْرُ مَتَاعِهَا الـمَرْأَةُ الصَّالِحَةُ». [رواه مسلم].

"This worldly life is *Mata'* (a provision of temporary comfort) and the best *Mata'* in it is a pious woman." (*Muslim*)

4) And he (صلى الله عليه وسلم) said:

«أَمَا وَاللهِ إِنِّي لَأَخْشَاكُم لله وَأَتْقَاكُمْ لَهُ، لَكِنِّي أَصُومُ وَأُفْطِرُ، وَأُصَلِّي وَأَرْقُدُ، وَأَتَزَوَّجُ النِّسَاءَ، فَمَنْ رَغِبَ عَنْ سُنَّتِي فَلَيْسَ مِنِّي»

224

"By Allah, I am the most in awe of Allah amongst you and the one having most *Taqwa* for Allah, but I fast and I (also) eat, and I offer *Salât* and I (also) sleep and I marry women, and whoever has a distaste for my *Sunnah*, he is not of me." (Agreed upon)

The wisdom in the institution of marriage:

Marriage benefits the individual and the society, as well as all the humanity;

1. Marriage is the best format for slaking one's innate sexual drive and satisfying it in a way which will allow it to subside so that one is not drawn to prohibited means (which harm the self and the society).

   Allâh عز و جل said:

   ﴿ وَمِنْ ءَايَٰتِهِۦ أَنْ خَلَقَ لَكُم مِّنْ أَنفُسِكُمْ أَزْوَٰجًا لِّتَسْكُنُوٓا۟ إِلَيْهَا وَجَعَلَ بَيْنَكُم مَّوَدَّةً وَرَحْمَةً إِنَّ فِى ذَٰلِكَ لَءَايَٰتٍ لِّقَوْمٍ يَتَفَكَّرُونَ ﴾

   "And among His signs is this, that He created for you wives from among yourselves, that you may find repose in them, and He has put between you affection and mercy. Verily, in that are indeed signs for a people who reflect." (V.30:21)

2. Marriage is the best format for having children and raising them, and increasing one's progeny, and receiving reward. The Prophet صلى الله عليه وسلم said:

   «تَزَوَّجُوا فَإِنِّي مُكَاثِرٌ بِكُمُ الأُمَمَ ولاَ تَكُونُوا كَرُهبانِيّة النصَّارَى» .

   [صحيح رواه البيهقي انظر الجامع الصحيح ٢٩٣٨] .

   "Get married, for I would like you to be the largest of all the *Ummah*, and don't be like the monks (and priests) of the Christians." (*Baihaqi*)

225

3. The sense of responsibility in being married and caring for the children spurs one towards activity and work and taking care of his obligations.

4. Marriage induces a certain order in life, the woman takes care of the home and the man works outside.

5. Marriage promotes relationships between distant families, which promote cohesion and harmony in the society as a whole.

The rule about getting married:

Marriage is obligatory on one who has the ability to do so and has the craving for it and fears that he might commit fornication (if he doesn't marry). However, if one hankers after marriage, but doesn't have the material means, he should act according to Allâh's Statement:

﴿ وَلْيَسْتَعْفِفِ ٱلَّذِينَ لَا يَجِدُونَ نِكَاحًا حَتَّىٰ يُغْنِيَهُمُ ٱللَّهُ مِن فَضْلِهِۦ ﴾

"And let those who find not the financial means for marriage keep themselves chaste, until Allah enriches them of His Bounty...." (V.24:33)

And the statement of the Prophet صلى الله عليه وسلم:

«يَامَعْشَرَ الشَّبَابَ مَنِ اسْتَطَاعَ مِنْكُمُ الْبَاءَةَ فَلْيَتزوج فِإنَّهُ أَغَضُّ لِلبصَرِ وَاحْصَنُ لِلْفَرْجِ ، وَمَنْ لَمْ يَسْتَطِعَ فَعَلَيْهِ بِالصَّوْمِ ، فَإنَّهُ لَهُ وِجَاءٌ». [متفق عليه] .

"O you assemblage of young men! Whoever among you is capable of marriage (financially and physically), he should marry, for it is more helpful in lowering ones gaze and guarding one's private parts (from prohibited sex); and whoever is not able, he should fast, for it will be a shield for him." (Agreed upon)

226

As for one who desires it and has the ability to marry, yet he doesn't fear committing fornication, it is recommended for him to marry, and it is better than his single minded concentration on devotionary worship because monasticism is not part of Islâm.

Precedence of marriage over *Hajj:*

If a Muslim fears committing fornication, he should give precedence to marriage over *Hajj;* and if he doesn't fear, he should give precedence to *Hajj.*

Turning away from marriage:

Many Muslims have made marriage a difficult process, and placed many obstacles in its path; they ask for expensive dowries and lavish weddings resulting in huge expenses, until many young men give up on trying to marry and have had to suffer the pains of bachelorhood, along with the young women whom they are unable to marry. And the responsibility for that lies on the parents' shoulders, the fathers and the mothers.

Picking a pious wife:

A wife should be a source of tranquillity and repose for her husband, so it is imperative to choose one who is religious. The Prophet صلى الله عليه وسلم said:

«تُنْكَحُ الْـمَرْأَةُ لأَرْبَعٍ : لِمَالِـهَا وَلِـحَسَبِهَا، وَلِجَمَالِهَا، وَلِدِينِهَا، فَاظْفَرْ بِذَاتِ الْـدِّينِ تَرِبَتْ يَدَاكَ» . [متفق عليه].

"A woman is married for four (reasons); for her wealth, for her lineage, for her beauty and for her religion, so triumph (by choosing) a religious woman; may your hands be coated with dust." (Agreed upon)

(The last part of the *Hadîth* is a *Du'â* for poverty of one, who does not make the religion one of his goals).

227

Choosing a right husband:

The guardian of the girl should choose for her a husband, who is religious and of good character. The Prophet صلى الله عليه وسلم said:

«إِذَا أَتَاكُمْ مَنْ تَرْضَوْنَ خُلُقَهُ وَدِينَهُ فَزَوِّجُوهُ إِن لَا تَفْعَلُوا تَكُنْ فِتْنَةٌ فِي الأَرْضِ وَفَسَادٌ عَرِيضٌ». [حسن رواه الترمذي انظر الجامع الصحيح ٢٦٧].

"When one comes to you (asking for your daughter) and you are pleased with his religion and his character, marry her to him. If you don't, there will be a trial on the earth, and widespread corruption (will prevail)." (*Tirmidhi*)

HIJAB (THE VEIL) IS A MEANS OF HONOUR AND PROTECTION FOR WOMEN

Islâm honoured the woman by appointing her as the educator and developer of the generations, and bound the goodness of the society to her goodness, and made the *Hijâb* mandatory upon her to protect her from evil men, and to protect the society from her exposure. *Hijâb* is a means of maintaining love and mercy between husband and wife, because when a man sees other women more beautiful than his own wife, it affects his relationship with his own wife negatively, perhaps even leading to divorce.

Hijâb is mentioned in the Qur'ân in the following passages, Allâh عز و جل said:

﴿ يَٰٓأَيُّهَا ٱلنَّبِيُّ قُل لِّأَزْوَٰجِكَ وَبَنَاتِكَ وَنِسَآءِ ٱلْمُؤْمِنِينَ يُدْنِينَ عَلَيْهِنَّ مِن جَلَٰبِيبِهِنَّ ذَٰلِكَ أَدْنَىٰ أَن يُعْرَفْنَ فَلَا يُؤْذَيْنَ ﴾

"O Prophet! Tell your wives and your daughters and the

228

women of the believers to draw their cloaks (veils) all over their bodies (i.e. screen themselves completely except the eyes or one eye to see the way). That will be better, that they should be known (as free respectable women) so as not to be annoyed..." (V.33:59)

And the Qur'ân speaks about the covering of a woman's head using the command form:

$$ \text{﴿ وَلْيَضْرِبْنَ بِخُمُرِهِنَّ عَلَىٰ جُيُوبِهِنَّ وَلَا يُبْدِينَ زِينَتَهُنَّ ﴾} $$

"...and to draw their veils all over *Juyubihinna* (i.e. their bodies, faces, necks and bosoms, etc.) and not to reveal their adornment ..." (V.24:31)

And Allah forbid women from displaying their charms in the various ways that occur, stating:

$$ \text{﴿ وَلَا تَبَرَّجْنَ تَبَرُّجَ الْجَاهِلِيَّةِ الْأُولَىٰ ﴾} $$

"... and do not display yourselves like that of the times of ignorance,... " (V.33:33)

Women in pre-Islâmic period used to cover their heads and drape their scarves onto their backs, leaving their necks and the upper portion of their chests exposed, as well as their ears, and jewellery such as ear-rings etc. This verse prohibited that, and ordered the believing women to cover these parts also.

From these verses and others, the proper covering (*Hijâb*) for a Muslim woman becomes clear. The following points must be observed for the proper implementation of *Hijâb*:

1. The woman's clothing should cover her entire body including the hands and the feet.

2. The outer covering should not be tight; revealing the shape of her body especially the breasts.

3. The material should not be thin or transparent so that one can make out what is underneath.

4. A woman's clothing should not resemble a man's clothing.

5. It shouldn't be flashy or brightly coloured, or having eye catching designs which attract attention or stir desire.

6. It should not resemble the dress of disbelieving women, because who ever imitates a people, is one of them.

7. The clothing should not be perfumed. The Prophet صلى الله عليه وسلم said:

«أيُّما امْرَأةٍ اسْتَعْطَرَتْ ثُمَّ خَرَجَت فَمَرَّتْ عَلى قَوْمٍ لِيَجِدُوا رِيحَهَا فَهِيَ زَانِيَةٌ وَكُلُّ عَيْنٍ زَانِيَةٌ». [حسن رواه أحمد وغيره وانظر الجامع الصحيح رقم ٢٦٩٨].

"Any woman who applies perfume, then goes out and passes by people so that they can smell her scent is an adulteress, and every eye (that looks at her) is adulterous." (*Ahmad* and others).

RULES REGARDING *RIBA* (USURY) AND ITS DIFFERENT FORMS

Definition:

Riba is an additional amount received on capital, whether the amount is small or large.

Allâh عزوجل said:

﴿ وَإِن تُبۡتُمۡ فَلَكُمۡ رُءُوسُ أَمۡوَٰلِكُمۡ لَا تَظۡلِمُونَ وَلَا تُظۡلَمُونَ ﴾

"...and if you repent, you shall have your capital sums. Deal not unjustly (by asking more than your capital sums), and you shall not be dealt with unjustly (by receiving less than your capital sums)." (V.2:279)

The ruling on *Riba*:

It is *Harâm* in all the revealed religions—Judaism, Christianity and Islam, except that the Jews do not see the prohibition as preventing them from taking *Riba* from non-Jews. As Allah عزوجل mentioned about them (in the course of describing their blameworthy qualities):

﴿ وَأَخۡذِهِمُ ٱلرِّبَوٰاْ وَقَدۡ نُهُواْ عَنۡهُ ﴾

"And their taking of *Riba* (usury) though they were forbidden from taking it..." (V.4:161)

The Qur'ân discusses *Riba* in a number of different places, and in periodic order. In the Makkan period, the following verse was revealed:

﴿ وَمَآ ءَاتَيۡتُم مِّن رِّبَا لِّيَرۡبُوَاْ فِيٓ أَمۡوَٰلِ ٱلنَّاسِ فَلَا يَرۡبُواْ عِندَ ٱللَّهِ ﴾

"And that which you give in gift (to others), in order that it may increase (your wealth by expecting to get a better one in return) from other people's property, has no increase with Allâh..." (V.30:39)

In the Madnian period, the following verses were releaved:

﴿ يَٰٓأَيُّهَا ٱلَّذِينَ ءَامَنُواْ لَا تَأْكُلُواْ ٱلرِّبَوٰٓاْ أَضْعَٰفًا مُّضَٰعَفَةً ﴾

"O you who believe! Eat not *Riba* (usury) doubled and multiplied... " (V.3:130)

The final legislation in this issue was the Statement of Allâh عز وجل :

﴿ يَٰٓأَيُّهَا ٱلَّذِينَ ءَامَنُواْ ٱتَّقُواْ ٱللَّهَ وَذَرُواْ مَا بَقِىَ مِنَ ٱلرِّبَوٰٓاْ إِن كُنتُم مُّؤْمِنِينَ ۝ فَإِن لَّمْ تَفْعَلُواْ فَأْذَنُواْ بِحَرْبٍ مِّنَ ٱللَّهِ وَرَسُولِهِۦ ۖ وَإِن تُبْتُمْ فَلَكُمْ رُءُوسُ أَمْوَٰلِكُمْ لَا تَظْلِمُونَ وَلَا تُظْلَمُونَ ﴾

"O you who believe! Be afraid of Allah and give up what remains (due to you) from *Riba* (usury) (from now onward), if you are (really) believers. And if you do not do it, then take a notice of war from Allah and His Messenger, but if you repent, you shall have your capital sums. Deal not unjustly (by asking more than your capital sums), and you shall not be dealt with unjustly (by receiving less than your capital sums)." (V.2:278,279)

In this verse is a decisive refutation of those who say usury is prohibited only if the sum paid back is doubled and multiplied, because Allah made lawful only the retrieval of the capital (i.e. the sum which was loaned) without any addition.

Ribâ is a major sin, as proved by the statement of the Prophet صلى الله عليه وسلم :

«اجْتَنِبُوا السَّبْعَ الـمُوبِقَاتِ، قَالُوا، وَمَاهُنَّ يَارَسُولَ اللهِ؟ قَالَ : الشِّرْكَ بِاللهِ، وَالسِّحْرَ، وَقَتْلَ النَّفْسِ الَّتِي حَرَّمَ اللهُ إِلاَّ بِالْحَقّ وأكْلِ الرِّبَا، وأكْلَ مَالِ الْيَتِيمِ، وَالتَّوَلِّي يَوْمَ الزَّحْفِ، وَقَذْفَ الـمُحْصَنَاتِ الْغَافِلَاتِ الـمُؤْمِنَاتِ» . . [متفق عليه] .

232

"Stay away from the seven destroyers". They asked, "What are they, O Messenger of Allah"? He said "Ascribing partners with Allah; witchcraft; killing the soul which Allah has prohibited except for just reasons; consuming *Ribâ*; consuming the property of an orphan; running away from the battle; and slandering chaste, believing women who are unaware of the possible misinterpretation of their innocent but indiscreet acts."(Agreed upon)

«لَعَنَ رَسُولَ اللهِ ﷺ ـ آكِلَ الرِّبَا، ومؤكلَهُ، وَكَاتِبَهُ، وشَاهِدَيْهِ وَقَالَ : «هُمْ سَوَاءٌ» . [رواه مسلم] .

The Prophet صلى الله عليه وسلم cursed the one who consumes *Ribâ* and the one who pays it, and the scribe who writes the contract, and the witnesses to it; and said, "They are equal (in sin)". (*Muslim*)

The wisdom behind the prohibition of *Riba*:

The reason for its prohibition is its harm incurred by the society economically, socially and morally:

1. It sows the seed of enmity between individuals, and destroys the spirit of mutual help and aid between them.

2. It leads to the formation of a leisure class, which does no work at all, yet money piles up and concentrates in their hands with no effort on their part, so that they become the economic equivalent of parasites which grow and relish at the expense of others.

3. *Riba* has been and remains a major instrument of colonialism and imperialism (in fact of neocolonialism), it is said that imperialism follows in the wake of traders and priests. (We

233

have known the damage of usury in some countries' colonialism).

4. *Riba* is the appropriation of people's wealth without compensation which is prohibited, as the Prophet صلى الله عليه وسلم said:

«إِنَّ دِمَاءَكُمْ وأَمْوَالَكُمْ عَلَيْكُمْ حَرَامٌ . . . » . [رواه مسلم].

"Verily, your blood and your wealth are inviolable (amongst yourselves)" (*Muslim*)

The types of *Ribâ:*

A. *Riba An-Nasi'ah* : This is the stipulated interest which the lender takes from the borrower in consideration of the time given to the borrower to pay back the capital. It is *Harâm* based on the Qur'ân and the *Sunnah* and the consensus of Muslim scholars.

B. *Riba Al-Fadl:* This applies to barter, where commodities of the same type are exchanged in unequal amounts, especially the exchange of precious metals and foodstuffs, it is *Harâm*, by the *Sunnah* and the consensus of scholars; as it paves the way for *Riba Nasî'ah.*"

1. The Prophet صلى الله عليه وسلم said:

«لَا تَبِيعُوا الدَّرَهَمَ بِالدَّرْهَمَيْنِ، فَإِنِّي أَخَافَ عَلَيْكُمْ الرَّمَاءَ» . [رواه

أحمد وصححه أحمد شاكر في المسند رقم ١١٠١٩].

"Do not sell one *Dirham* for two *Dirhams*, for I fear for you regarding *Riba*." (*Ahmad*)

2. Numerous *Ahâdîth* have demonstrated the prohibition with regard to gold, silver, wheat, barley, dates, and salt.

The Prophet صلى الله عليه وسلم said:

234

«الـذَّهَبُ بِالـذَّهَبِ، وَالفِضَّةُ بِالفِضَّةِ، وَالبُرُّ بِالبُرِّ، وَالشَّعِيرُ بِالشَّعِيرِ، وَالتَّمْرُ بِالتَّمْرِ، وَالـمِلْحُ بِالـمِلْحِ، مِثْلاً بِمِثْلٍ، سَوَاءً بِسَوَاءٍ، يَداً بِيَدٍ، فَإذا اخْتَلَفَتْ هَذِهِ الأَصْنَافُ فَبِيعُوا كَيْفَ شِئْتُمْ إذَا كَانَتْ يَداً بِيَدٍ».

"Gold for gold, and silver for silver, and wheat for wheat, and barley for barley, and dates for dates, and salt for salt, like for like, equal for equal, from hand to hand (i.e. the transaction must be completed before the two sides leave each other). But if the types are different then sell as you wish, as long as it is hand to hand". (*Muslim*)

The Prophet صلى الله عليه وسلم also said:

«فَمَنْ زَادَ أو اسْتَزَادَ، فَقَدْ أَرْبَى الآخِذُ والـمُعْطِي فِيهِ سَوَاءٌ».

[رواه مسلم].

"Whoever gives more or asks for more (than what he gave) comits an act of *Ribâ,* the given and the taken are equivalent (in this sin)." (*Muslim*)

The reason for its prohibition :

The commodities mentioned in the above *Hadîth* are fundamental necessities of life:

1. Gold and silver have been, throughout most of the history, the mediums of exchange which make precise commercial transactions possible.

2. Wheat, barley, dates and salt are essentials foodstuffs (specially in Al-Madinah at the time the Prophet صلى الله عليه وسلم was giving these instructions, so they were tailored to the particular audience, but the general can be inferred from the specific).

3. If *Riba* is present in the exchange of these essential

235

commodities, it harms the people in general and leads to iniquity in their business transactions. So the Prophet صلى الله عليه وسلم prohibited it affectionately on them. And when the same reason is found in another medium of exchange besides gold and silver, it is subjected to the same ruling. Likewise, when the same reason is present in another foodstuff besides those mentioned, then it may not be sold except like for like, hand to hand, because:

«لِأَنَّ النَّبِيَّ ـ ﷺ ـ نَهَى عَنْ بَيْعِ الطَّعَامِ ، إِلاَّ مِثْلاً بِمِثْلٍ».

[رواه مسلم] .

"The Prophet صلى الله عليه وسلم prohibited selling food (of the same variety) except equivalent in weight and hand to hand." (*Muslim*)

Conditions for the valid transaction of currency (mediums of exchange) and food:

There are two conditions for the validity of these transactions:

1. The quantities of the two items exchanged must be the same, without any consideration of quality; based on the following evidence:

Abû Sa'îd Al-Khudri رضي الله عنه narrated:

«جَاءَ بِلاَلٌ إِلَى رَسُولِ اللهِ ـ ﷺ ـ بِتَمْرٍ بَرْنِيٍّ فَقَالَ لَهُ النَّبِيُّ ـ ﷺ ـ: مِنْ أَيْنَ هَذَا؟ قَالَ : كَانَ عِنْدَنَا تَمْرٌ رَدِيءٌ فَبِعْتُ مِنْهُ صَاعَيْنِ بِصَاعٍ ، فَقَالَ : «أَوَّهْ، عَيْنُ الرِّبَا، عَيْنُ الرِّبَا، لاَ تَفْعَلْ وَلَكِنْ إِذَا أَرَدْتَ أَنْ تَشْتَرِيَ فَبِعِ التَّمْرَ بِبَيْعٍ آخَرَ، ثُمَّ اشْتَرِ بِهِ».

Bilal رضي الله عنه came to the Allah's Messenger صلى الله عليه وسلم with some *Burni* dates (a high quality variety), the Prophet

236

صلى الله عليه وسلم asked, "Where did these come from?" He said, "We had some low quality dates so I sold two *Sâ'* of those for one *Sâ'* of these". The Prophet صلى الله عليه وسلم said, "Oh! (that is) exactly *Ribâ*, (that is) exactly *Ribâ*. Don't do that; if you want to buy, sell your dates in separate transaction (i.e. for cash or for some other commodity) then buy (the dates you want) with it (what you received form the first transaction)." (Agreed upon)

And the Prophet صلى الله عليه وسلم said:

$$\text{«الذَّهَبُ بالذَّهب وَزْنَاً بِوَزْنٍ» . [رواه مسلم]}.$$

"Gold for gold, equal in weight" (*Muslim*).

2. It is not permissible to delay the delivery of one of the two items exchanged, instead the transaction must be completed immediately as per the saying of Prophet صلى الله عليه وسلم : "hand to hand", and his صلى الله عليه وسلم statement:

$$\text{«لا تَبِيعُوا الذَّهَبَ بالذَّهَبِ إلاَّ مِثْلاً بِمِثْلٍ ، وَلاَ تُشْفُّوا بَعْضَهَا}$$
$$\text{عَلَى بَعْضٍ ، وَلاَ تَبِيعُوا الوَرَقَ بالورق إلاَّ مِثْلاً بِمِثْلٍ ، وَلاَ تُشْفُّوا}$$
$$\text{بَعْضَهَا عَلَى بَعْضٍ ، ولا تَبِيعُوا مِنْها غَائِباً بِحَاضِرٍ» . [متفق عليه]}.$$

"Do not sell gold for gold unless equivalent in weight (and from hand to hand), and do not sell less amount for greater amount or vice versa; and do not sell silver for silver unless equivalent in weight (and from hand to hand), and do not sell less amount for greater amount or vice versa and do not sell gold or silver that is not present at the moment of exchange for gold or silver that is present".(Agreed upon)

THE PROHIBITION OF MEANS OF USURY

Islâm did not prohibit anything except for a clear underlying reason, or a benefit which will be realized by the people. And pursuant to its prohibition, it prohibited the means which pave the way for it, in order to close the road that leads to it.

For instance, the sale known as *'Al-'Inah,* in Arabic, is prohibited in Islâm. Its format is as follows:

A commodity is sold for a specific price, with the payment delayed until a fixed date. Then the original owner buys back the commodity for a reduced price. Now he has cash in his hand and he owes the buyer an additional sum of money. This transaction has the appearance of a sale of a commodity, but it is in reality a loan on interest.

The indication that this transaction is *Harâm* is the *Hadîth* of the Prophet صلى الله عليه وسلم :

«إِذَا تَبَايَعْتُمْ بِالْعِينَةِ، وَأَخَذْتُمْ أَذْنَابَ البَقَرِ، وَرَضِيتُمْ الزَّرْعَ وَتَرَكْتُمُ الجِهَادَ فِي سَبِيلِ اللهِ سَلَّطَ اللهُ عَلَيْكُمْ ذَلاًّ، لَا يَنْزِعُهُ عَنْكُمْ حَتَّى تَرْجِعُوا إِلَى دِينِكُمْ». [صحيح رواه أحمد وغيره].

"When you buy and sell using the *Al-'Inah* format, and took hold of the tails of cattle, and become content with agriculture and abandon *Jihâd* in the way of Allah, Allah will impose disgrace upon you and He will not remove it from you until you return to your religion". (*Ahmad* and others)

DOING BUSINESS WITH BANKS

To lend a bank money or borrow from it on the condition of a payment of a fixed annual or monthly percentage rate of interest, say 2%, or more or less, is a form of prohibited *Riba.*

Hasan Abdullah Amin has quoted in his book "Bank Deposits and Investments in Islâm": The interest, then, is nothing else but a stipulated excess on a loan to the benefit of the depositor in the

238

case of savings accounts or interest bearing checking accounts, although it is not considered a valid loan in Islâm (because the borrower (the bank) is not given a fixed date to repay the loan, it must be ready to pay up upon the depositor's demand at anytime) likewise when someone borrows money from the bank, they must pay a stipulated percentage of interest on the loan. All of this is, without the slightest doubt, *Riba*. In fact it is one of the two forms of *Riba* which was practised by the pre-Islâmic period, which the Qur'ân prohibited decisively in the Statement of Allâh:

"...whereas Allah has permitted trading and forbidden *Riba* (usury)..." (V.2: 275)

THE PROHIBITION OF USURY FOR CONSUMERS AND PRODUCERS

Some western economists make a distinction between usury on consumer loans and usury on loans for commercial enterprise, claiming that it was necessary to prohibit usury in the past, but now it is necessary to permit it, because loans were used to be taken in the past for purposes of consumption, whereas now they are taken for purposes of production. This is a deceptive distinction, because if the usury was extracted on a consumer loan, the loan was taken by the consumer to spend on some of his necessities, so it is not permissible for him to pay back an extra percent on his debt, rather it is enough for him to repay the original debt when he is able.

And if the loan was taken for investment in a commercial enterprise, the profit of that enterprise is due to the effort expended by the borrower and not the capital of the loan, because capital by itself will never produce an increase without accompanying human effort.

THE PROHIBITION ON *RIBA* (USURY) IN BUYING A HOUSE

Some Muslims have become entangled in *Ribâ* as a result of interest loan taken from banks to buy a home. They got a *Fatwa* (religious verdict) from some people who said paying *Riba* in this situation is permissible for people who don't own houses already, because they are forced into it by necessity. In order to support their position, they made *Qiyâs* (analogy) on the permissibility of eating dead flesh (of an animal which was not slaughtered properly) when a person is starving to death.

The two situations are totally different. The person who is permitted to eat dead flesh is starving; if he doesn't eat, he may die. Whereas the person who doesn't own a home can rent one, or buy an apartment, or perhaps he could buy a very simple home without resorting to a loan, rather than buying a more luxurious home on interest.

That is far better for him than to enter into an interest loan, exposing himself to war with Allah and His Messenger صلى الله عليه و سلم. Also, the borrower may get behind on his payments which will result in increasing interest, and one day he might lose the house, either selling at a loss or having the bank foreclose the mortgage and take back the house.

The *Sahâbah* رضي الله عنهم also faced problems of poverty and housing shortages, but they didn't resort to *Riba*, so those who issue these "Modernistic" *Fatwa* and those seeking loans, should fear Allah and steer clear of *Riba*.

MEANS FOR GETTING RID OF USURY

One of the special features of Islâm is that it doesn't prohibit something without providing a lawful alternative which will make the unlawful things unnecessary. For instance, liquor is prohibited to drink, but it is permitted for a Muslim to drink any kind of juice (orange juice, grape juice, lemonade, etc.).

And when *Riba* was prohibited, business and trade in lawful commodities was made permissible. One form of permitted business is *Mudâraba,* which is a form of partnership where one person invests money and the other invests his skill and effort, and they share the profit or loss of the enterprise, so Islâm did not impose any hardship on the people (by prohibiting *Riba*) but rather it provided them with viable alternatives to it, among them are the following:

1. *Qard Hasan* (a beautiful loan): Instead of a Muslim loaning his money on interest which causes pollution and blight on all his property and oppresses the borrower, Islâm encourages him to make the loan *Qard Hasan,* and promised him a gracious reward for it; Allâh عز و جل said:

$$﴿ مَّن ذَا ٱلَّذِى يُقۡرِضُ ٱللَّهَ قَرۡضًا حَسَنًا فَيُضَٰعِفَهُۥ لَهُۥٓ أَضۡعَافًا كَثِيرَةً ﴾$$

"Who is he that will lend to Allah a goodly loan so that He may multiply it to him many times?..." (V. 2: 245)

2. Giving an extension to a person who cannot repay the loan on time because of financial difficulty, until he gets back on his feet. And Islâm encourages the lender to forgive the loan altogether in this circumstance; Allâh عز و جل said:

$$﴿ وَإِن كَانَ ذُو عُسۡرَةٍ فَنَظِرَةٌ إِلَىٰ مَيۡسَرَةٍ وَأَن تَصَدَّقُواْ خَيۡرٌ لَّكُمۡ إِن كُنتُمۡ تَعۡلَمُونَ ﴾$$

"And if the debtor is in a hard time (has no money), then grant him time till it is easy for him to repay, but if you remit it by way of charity, that is better for you if you did but know." (V. 2: 280)

3. Mutual aid by all means: This encompasses mutual aid on a social level, in industry and in agriculture, and social security

by financing farmers and industrialists and craftsmen in order to enable them to produce effectively. This returns a benefit to the whole *Ummah*. Also, opening schools and building hospitals and homes for the elderly and the incapacitated and all other items alike fall under the mutual aid mentioned in the verse:

$$ \text{﴿ وَتَعَاوَنُوا عَلَى ٱلْبِرِّ وَٱلتَّقْوَىٰ ﴾} $$

"... Help you one another in *Al-Birr* and *At-Taqwa* (virtue, righteousness and piety);..." (V. 5: 2)

The society which realizes these means will proceed, in the shade of this comprehensive mutual aid, happily and far removed from the distress of *Riba*.

4. We should not forget the payment of *Zakât* to those who deserve it. This will have a major impact on getting rid of *Riba*.

In conclusion: Beware, my Muslim brother, from putting your money in a (non-Islâmic) bank. Even if you don't take interest on it, the bank takes your money and loans it out to gain interest. So you are helping the *Riba* system, and are indirectly responsible. And beware, my brother who is poor, from taking loans from those banks.

RULES REGARDING THE *LUQTAH* (LOST AND FOUND ARTICLES)

Luqtah is any form of guarded property exposed to dissipation, whose owner is unknown.

The rule concerning it:

If the finder believes it to be safe if he left it where he found it, it is preferable for him to take it. If he believes it will not be safe if he leaves it in its place, it is *Wâjib* for him to take it. But if he knows he will covet it, then it is *Harâm* for him to take it.

1. The basis for this is the statement of the Prophet صلى الله عليه وسلم :

«أنَّ رسُولَ الله ﷺ سُئِلَ عَن اللقطة : الذهب أو الورقُ، فَقال : اعـرف وكـاءَهـا، وعفـاصَهَا، ثُم عَرفها سَنة، فإن لم تَعرف فَاستنفقهَا، وَلتكُن وديعة عندكَ عندك، فإن جَاء طَالبُها يوماً من الدَّهر فأدّها إليه، وَسَأله عَن ضَالَّة الإبل، فَقالَ : مَالكَ وَمَالُها؟ دَعهَا فإنَّ مَعَهَا غِذاؤهَا وسَقَاؤهَا، تَردُ الماءَ وتأكُلُ الشَّجر، حَتى يَجِدَهَا رَبُّها وَسَأله عن الشَّاةِ؟ فَقال : فإنها هِي لَك، أو لأخيكَ، أو للذنب». [متفق عليه].

When he was asked about finding gold or silver whose owner is unknown, he said, "Note the sack that holds it (the wealth) and the cord that draws the sack closed, then announce its recovery for a year. If no one (claims it), you can spend it, but it is a trust on deposit with you, so if its owner comes to you at anytime (without a deadline) give it to him." They asked him about the (lost) camel, he said, "What do you have to do with? Leave it alone because its food and drink are with it. It can find water and eat from trees until its owner finds it". And he was asked about a sheep, he said, "Take it, it's either for you or your brother or a wolf". (Agreed upon)

2. And he (صلى الله عليه وسلم) said:

«مَن وَجَدَ لُقطةً فَليشهد ذَا عَدل ـ أو ذوي عَدل ـ وَلا يَكتُم وَلا يُغيِّبُ، فإن وَجَدَ صَاحبَهَا فَليردَّهَا عَلَيه، وَإلاَّ فَهُوَ مَالُ الله يُؤتيه مَن يشَاءُ». [أخرجه أبوداود وصحح إسناده محقق جامع الأصول].

"Whoever finds a lost article, should have an honest person or two honest people bear witness to it; and he should not conceal it or go away then. If he finds its owner, he should return it to him, and if not, it is the wealth of Allah, which He gives to whom He wills". (*Abû Dawûd*)

«وَقَد اشْتَرَى ابن مسعود جَارِيَة، فَفَقَدَ صَاحِبَها، فَالتمسَ سَنةَ فَلم يُوجد فَقَدَ، فَأخذَ يُعطي الدّرهمَ والدّرهمَين، ويَقُولُ : اللّهُم عَن فُلان، فَإِن أبى فَلِي وَعَلَيَّ وَقَالَ هَكَذا فَافعَلوا بِالُّلقطة إذا لَم تَجِدُوا صَاحِبَها».

3. Ibn Mas'ûd رضي الله عنه bought a slave-girl. (Before he could pay the owner) the man went missing. He kept trying to find him, but at the end of a year he was still missing. So he distributed the price of the slave-girl as charity, a Dirham here, two Dirhams there, saying: "O Allah, this is on behalf of so-and-so, but if he doesn't agree, then on my own behalf and I owe him the payment", and he said, "This is the way to handle the *Luqtah* if the owner cannot be found." (*Bukhâri*)

4. It is recommended for a rich person who finds a lost article to give it in charity after a year of advertising its discovery, but if he's poor it's all right for him to make use of it.

SPECIAL RULES REGARDING *LUQTAH* IN THE *HARAM* (SANCTUARY) OF MAKKAH

It is (especially) prohibited to pick up a *Luqtah* in Makkah except to announce about it; based on the statements of Allah's Messenger صلى الله عليه وسلم :

1. «لاَ يُلَتَقطُ لُقْطَتُها إلاَّ مَنْ عَرَّفَها». [رواه البخاري].

"No one may pick up a *Laqtah* in Makkah, except the one who makes the announcement about it". (*Bukhâri*)

2. ‏«لَا يَلْتَقِطُهَا إِلَّا مُعَرِّفٌ»‏ . ‏[رواه البخاري]‏.

"No one may pick it up (in Makkah) except the one who announces about it". (*Bukhari*)

3. ‏«وَلَا تَحِلُّ سَاقِطَتُهَا إِلَّا لِمُنْشِدٍ»‏ . ‏[رواه البخاري]‏.

"Dropped articles are not permissible to be used except for the one who advertises it". (*Bukhari*)

Public announcement:

The one who finds it, should first note its special characteristics which distinguish it from others. And protect it as he protects his own wealth, and it remains as a trust with him. Then he should spread the news of its discovery among the people, in the market and other places. And if its owner comes and is able to describe the article by its distinguishing features, it is permissible for the finder to hand it over to him.

And it is permissible to announce the discovery of a lost article in *Al-Masjid Al-Harâm* in contrast to all other mosques. (See *Fath-al-Bari*: 5:88). It is preferable, however, to turn it in the government lost and found office which is reliable and well-known among the people. That is better for its protection and easier for people to refer to. The lost and found office is just inside the King Abdul Aziz door of *Al-Masjid Al-Harâm*. Lost articles are registered and held there to be returned to their owners. If no one claims them, they are distributed among the poor people of Makkah.

Exception is made for food and for articles of insignificant value:

It is not necessary to advertise found food items, and it is permissible to eat them. Anas رضي الله عنه reported that the Prophet صلى

245

صلى الله عليه وسلم passed by a date lying on the road. He (صلى الله عليه وسلم) said:

«لَوْلاَ أَنِي أَخَافُ أَنْ تَكُونَ مِنَ الصَّدَقَةِ لَأَكَلْتُهَا». [متفق عليه].

"If I were not afraid of it being from the Sadaqah, I would have eaten it." (Agreed upon).

Likewise, in case of paltry items like a whip or a rope, etc., the person can pick them up to make use of them.

THE BOOK OF MORALS & MANNERS

* Some of the morals of the noble Prophet صلى الله عليه وسلم
* Good manners of the Messenger صلى الله عليه وسلم and his humbleness
* The Prophet's call to Islâm and *Jihad*
* Love of the Messenger صلى الله عليه وسلم and following him
* Some *Ahâdith* regarding the Messenger صلى الله عليه وسلم
* Some *Ahâdith* regarding the Muslim
* Act upon the *Ahâdith* of the Messenger صلى الله عليه وسلم
* "Whatever the Messenger (صلى الله عليه وسلم) gave you, take it"
* Be slaves of Allâh, brothers (to each other)

SOME OF THE MORALS OF THE NOBLE PROPHET صلى الله عليه وسلم

His morals and character was the Qur'ân: he would get angry in accord with it, and he would be pleased in accord with it. And he never took revenge on his own behalf, nor used to get angry for his own sake, but if the sacred limits of Allah were violated, he would become angry for Allah's sake.

And he (صلى الله عليه وسلم) was the truest of people in speech, and the most careful in fulfilling his obligations, and the more soft in all of them in temperament, and the most generous in his relations with people, and more modest than a secluded virgin; he would lower his gaze, his expression was mostly thoughtful. He was not vulgar nor did he curse; he would forgive and pardon. Whoever asked him for something, he would not turn him away except after giving him what he requested for or with a gentle word. He was not harsh or tough mannered. He would never interrupt the speech of another unless they transgressed the truth, in which case he would prohibit him or correct him.

And he (صلى الله عليه وسلم) used to take care of his neighbours and extend hospitality to his guests. And he didn't pass time in activities other than those which draw one close to Allah, or actions which are unavoidable (parts of human life). He was always hopeful of Mercy of Allah and was an optimist and disliked pessimism. If he had a choice between two alternatives, he always chose the easier one as long as it was not a sin. He loved providing relief to the troubled, and aiding the oppressed ones.

And he (صلى الله عليه وسلم) used to love his Companions and he would consult them and kept himself informed about their conditions and needs. If one of them fell ill, he would visit him. And if one of them was absent (for a time) he would send for him; and whoever died, he would make Du'â for him. He used to accept the excuses of those who apologized. The powerful and the weak had the same rights before him. When he spoke and if someone cared to count his words, he would have been able to do it (due to his eloquence i.e. deep meanings in brief statements and the measured way in which he spoke).

And he (صلى الله عليه وسلم) used to joke, but he would never say anything except the truth.

GOOD MANNERS OF THE MESSENGER
AND HIS HUMBLENESS صلى الله عليه وسلم

He was the most merciful of people and the most generous to his Companions, making room for them if space was tight, being the first to offer salutation to whoever he met, and when he shook hands with a man, he would not withdraw his hand first.

He was the most humble of the people if he came to a gathering where people were sitting already, he would sit wherever he found space, and he instructed others to do the same. He would give those sitting with him a full chance to participate till everyone of them thought that he is most honourable one before the Prophet صلى الله عليه وسلم. And he would not stand to disengage himself from someone who sat down with him, unless he had some urgent business, in which case he would take permission of the person. And he (صلى الله عليه وسلم) used to dislike people standing up for him[*]. Anas bin Mâlik رضى الله عنه narrated:

«لَم يَكُن شَخْصٌ أَحَبَّ إِلَيهم مِنْ رَسُولِ اللهِ ـ ﷺ ـ وَكَانُوا إِذَا رَأَوْهُ لَم يَقُومُوا لَهُ لِمَا يَعْلَمُونَ مِن كَرَاهِيَّتِهِ لِذَلِكَ» . [صحيح رواه أحمد والترمذي] .

"No one was more beloved to (the Companions) than

---
[*] It is permissible for a host to stand to receive a guest since the Prophet صلى الله عليه وسلم did it, and it is permissible to stand to embrace someone arriving from a long journey.

Allah's Messenger صلى الله عليه وسلم and they did not used to stand up for him knowing how much he disliked that". (*Ahmad* and *Tirmidhi*)

He would not speak with anyone in a way that the person may dislike. He would visit the sick and loved the poor sitting in their company and attending their funerals. He never disdained a poor person because of his poverty nor was he awed by kings due to their sovereignty. He treated the smallest blessing as something great. He never criticized food; if he found it good, he ate, and if not, he left it; he used to eat and drink with his right hand saying *Bismillah* before, and praising Allah afterwards.

He loved the good and disliked what was noxious, such as onions and garlic because of their strong pungent smell.

When the Prophet صلى الله عليه وسلم performed *Hajj*, he said:

$$\text{«اللَّهُمَّ هَذِهِ حَجَّةٌ لا رِياءَ فِيهَا وَلاَ سُمْعَةً». [صحيح رواه المقدسي].}$$

"O Allah this is a *Hajj* without show-off and without the desire for fame." (*Maqdisi*)

And he (صلى الله عليه وسلم) could not be distinguished from his Companions in his clothing or sitting. A bedouin would enter the *Masjid* and ask, "Which one of you is Muhammad?" His favourite type of clothing was the *Qamîs* (a robe which stretched down to the middle of his calf). He did not waste food nor was he extravagant in his dress. He used to wear a cap and a turban, and a silver ring on the little finger of his right hand, and he had a full and long beard.

THE PROPHET'S CALL TO *ISLAM* AND *JIHÂD*

Allah sent His Messenger, Muhammad صلى الله عليه وسلم as a mercy for all the world. He invited the Arabs and all of humanity to that which will secure for them the well-being and the happiness of this world and the Hereafter.

The first thing he called toward was the dedication of all worship to Allah Alone, including supplication to Allah Alone, Allah عز و جل said:

﴿ قُلْ إِنَّمَآ أَدْعُواْ رَبِّى وَلَآ أُشْرِكُ بِهِۦٓ أَحَدًا ﴾

"Say (O Muhammad صلى الله عليه وسلم): I invoke only my Lord (Allah Alone), and I associate none as partners along with Him." (V. 72: 20)

The *Mushrikûn* opposed this call because it contradicted their belief in idol worship and because they were committed to a blind following of their forefathers. They accused the Messenger صلى الله عليه وسلم of sorcery and insanity despite they had previously nicknamed him "the truthful and honest."

The Prophet صلى الله عليه وسلم endured steadfastly all the insult and injury of his people, in obedience to the command of his Lord, Who said:

﴿ فَٱصْبِرْ لِحُكْمِ رَبِّكَ وَلَا تُطِعْ مِنْهُمْ ءَاثِمًا أَوْ كَفُورًا ﴾

"Therefore be patient (O Muhammad صلى الله عليه وسلم) and submit to the Command of your Lord (Allah, by doing your duty to Him and by conveying His Message to mankind), and obey neither a sinner nor a disbeliever among them." (V. 76: 24)

He remained in Makkah for 13 years, calling towards *Tauhîd* and bearing up tortures, along with his followers, under the persecution of his people. After some people in the city of Al-Madinah accepted Islâm, he and his Companions emigrated there to establish the new Islâmic society on the foundation of justice, love, and equality. And Allah aided him with miracles, the most important of which is the Qur'ân, which calls towards *Tauhîd*, and knowledge, and *Jihâd*, and the most noble morals.

He (صلى الله عليه وسلم) wrote to the rulers far and near, inviting them to Islâm, saying to the Qaiser (Caesar—the Roman emperor):

«أَسْلِمْ تَسْلَمْ يُؤْتِكَ اللهُ أَجْرَكَ مَرَّتَيْنِ» .

"Accept Islâm, you will be safe and Allah will reward you twice".

﴿ قُلْ يَٰٓأَهْلَ ٱلْكِتَٰبِ تَعَالَوْا۟ إِلَىٰ كَلِمَةٍ سَوَآءٍ بَيْنَنَا وَبَيْنَكُمْ أَلَّا نَعْبُدَ إِلَّا ٱللَّهَ وَلَا نُشْرِكَ بِهِۦ شَيْـًٔا وَلَا يَتَّخِذَ بَعْضُنَا بَعْضًا أَرْبَابًا مِّن دُونِ ٱللَّهِ ﴾

"Say (O Muhammad صلى الله عليه وسلم): O people of the Scripture (Jews and Christians): Come to a word that is just between us and you, that we worship none but Allah, and that we associate no partners with Him, and that none of us shall take others as lords besides Allâh." (V.3:64)

«لاَ نُطِيعُ الأَحْبَارَ فِيمَا أَحْدَثُوا مِنَ التَّحْرِيمِ وَالتَّحْلِيلِ» .

"We do not obey the priests in what they initiate of declaring things lawful and unlawful."

The Prophet صلى الله عليه وسلم fought the idolaters and the Jews and was victorious over them. He personally participated in about twenty campaigns as well as sent out tens of expeditions of his Companions for *Jihâd* and for invitation to Islâm and freeing nations from oppression and subjugation (to tyrannies) and he used to teach them to proceed by inviting to *Tauhîd*.

LOVE OF THE MESSENGER صلى الله عليه وسلم
AND FOLLOWING HIM

Allâh عز وجل said:

﴿ قُلْ إِن كُنتُمْ تُحِبُّونَ ٱللَّهَ فَٱتَّبِعُونِى يُحْبِبْكُمُ ٱللَّهُ وَيَغْفِرْ لَكُمْ ذُنُوبَكُمْ وَٱللَّهُ غَفُورٌ رَّحِيمٌ ﴾

"Say (O Muhammad صلى الله عليه وسلم to mankind): If you (really) love Allah then follow me (i.e. accept Islâmic Monotheism, follow the Qur'ân and the *Sunnah*), Allah will love you and forgive you your sins. And Allah is Oft-Forgiving, Most Merciful." (V. 3: 31)

And the Prophet صلى الله عليه وسلم said:

"None of you is a believer till I am dearer to him than his child, his father and the whole of mankind." (Agreed upon)

The Prophet صلى الله عليه وسلم was of noble character and courage and generosity. Those who saw him unexpectedly for the first time would be awe-struck by him. Those who were associated with him and got to know him, loved him. The Messenger (صلى الله عليه وسلم) conveyed the Message, and offered the *Ummah* sincere advice, wishing the best for them, and he united them, and he, along with his Companions, conquered the hearts of the people with their *Tauhîd*, as they conquered the lands with their *Jihâd*, released the humanity from the worship of slaves (other human beings) to the worship of the Lord.

And they conveyed this religion to us perfect and complete, free from all deviation and superstition, without any need of addition or deletion.

Allâh عز و جل said:

﴿ ٱلۡيَوۡمَ أَكۡمَلۡتُ لَكُمۡ دِينَكُمۡ وَأَتۡمَمۡتُ عَلَيۡكُمۡ نِعۡمَتِى وَرَضِيتُ لَكُمُ ٱلۡإِسۡلَٰمَ دِينًا ﴾

"...This day, I have perfected your religion for you, completed My Favour upon you, and have chosen for you Islâm as your religion..." (V. 5: 3)

And the Prophet صلى الله عليه وسلم said:

«إِنَّمَا بُعِثۡتُ لِأُتَمِّمَ مَكَارِمَ الأَخۡلَاقِ» .

"I was sent only to complete the noble moral qualities". (*Hâkim*).

These are the moral qualities of your Prophet صلى الله عليه وسلم , so hold fast to them to be his true lovers.

Allah عز و جل said:

﴿ لَّقَدۡ كَانَ لَكُمۡ فِى رَسُولِ ٱللَّهِ أُسۡوَةٌ ﴾

"Indeed in the Messenger of Allah (Muhammad صلى الله عليه وسلم) you have a good example to follow..." (V.33: 21)

Know that true love for Allah and His Messenger صلى الله عليه وسلم demands acting in accord with the Book of Allah and the authentic *Ahadîth* of His Messenger (صلى الله عليه وسلم), making them a judge in all matters and all disputes, loving *Tauhîd* that he (صلى الله عليه وسلم) called toward and practising it, and not giving precedence to the judgement or statement of anyone over the Qur'ân and *Sunnah*:

Allâh عز و جل said:

﴿ يَٰٓأَيُّهَا ٱلَّذِينَ ءَامَنُوا۟ لَا تُقَدِّمُوا۟ بَيۡنَ يَدَىِ ٱللَّهِ وَرَسُولِهِۦۖ وَٱتَّقُوا۟ ٱللَّهَ إِنَّ ٱللَّهَ سَمِيعٌ عَلِيمٌ ﴾

"O you who believe! Do not be forward in the presence of Allah and His Messenger (صلى الله عليه وسلم), and fear Allah. Verily! Allah is All-Hearing, All-Knowing".(V. 49: 1)

One of the signs of loving him (صلى الله عليه وسلم) is to love *Tauhîd* which was the core of his mission, and to practise it, and to love those who call towards it, and to refrain from tagging them with repulsive nicknames.

O Allah, grant us love for him and the ability to follow him and grant us his intercession and grant us moral qualities like his.

SOME *AHADITH* REGARDING THE
MESSENGER صلى الله عليه وسلم

«إِنِي قَدْ تَرَكْتُ فِيكُمْ مَا إِنِ اعْتَصَمْتُمْ بِهِ فَلَنْ تَضِلُّوا أَبَداً، كِتَابَ اللهِ وَسُنَّةَ نَبِيَّةٍ». ـ [رواه الحاكم وصححه الألباني].

1. "Verily I am leaving amongst you that which, if you hold fast to it, you will never go astray — the Book of Allâh (Qur'ân) and His Prophet's *Sunnah*." (*Hâkim*)

«عَلَيْكُمْ بِسُنَّتِي وَسُنَّةِ الْخُلَفَاءِ الرَّاشِدِينَ الْمَهْدِيِّينَ تَمَسَّكُوا بِهَا». [صحيح رواه أحمد].

2. "My *Sunnah* is obligatory upon you, and the *Sunnah* of my rightly guided successors, hold fast to it." (*Ahmad*)

«يَافَاطِمَةَ بِنْتَ مُحَمَّدٍ سَلِينِي مِنْ مَالِي مَاشِئْتِ لَا أُغْنِي عَنْكِ مِنَ اللهِ شَيْئاً». [رواه البخاري].

3. "O Fatimah, daughter of Muhammad, Ask me of my property what you wish. I will not be able to avail you with Allâh at all (if you disbelieve)." (*Bukhâri*)

«مَنْ أَطَاعَنِي فَقَدْ أَطَاعَ اللهَ، وَمَنْ عَصَانِي فَقَدْ عَصَى اللهَ».

4. "Whoever obeys me, obeys Allah, and whoever disobeys me, disobeys Allah." (*Bukhâri*)

«لَا تَطْرُونِي كَمَا أَطْرَتِ النَّصَارَى ابْنَ مَرْيَمَ، فَإِنَّمَا أَنَا عَبْدُاللهِ فَقُولُوا عَبْدُاللهِ وَرَسُولُهُ». [رواه البخاري].

5. "Do not exaggerate my position in praise of me as the Christians did with the son of Mary, for I am only the slave of Allah, so say: The slave of Allah and His Messenger." (*Bukhâri*)

«قَاتَلَ اللهُ الْـيَهُودَ اتَّخَذُوا قُبُورَ أَنْبِيَائِهِمْ مَسَاجِدَ» . [رواه البخاري] .

6. "May the curse of Allah be upon the Jews, they took the graves of their Prophets as mosques." (*Bukhâri*)

«مَـنْ تَقَـوَّلَ عَلَيَّ مَالَـمْ أَقُـلْ فَلْيَتَبَـوَّأْ مَقْعَدَهُ مِـنَ النَّارِ» .

[صحيح رواه أحمد] . .

7. "Whoever attributed something to me, which I didn't say, let him take his place in the Fire." (*Ahmad*)

«إِنِّي لَا أُصَافِحُ النِّسَاءَ» . [صحيح رواه الترمذي] .

8. "I do not shake hands with women". (*Tirmidhi*) (Meaning those not closely related to him, such that they would be permissible for him to marry).

«مَنْ رَغِبَ عَنْ سُنَّتِي فَلَيْسَ مِنِّي» . [متفق عليه] .

9. "Whoever has a distaste for my *Sunnah*, he is not of me". (Agreed upon)

«اللَّهُمَّ إِنِّي أَعُوذُ بِكَ مِنْ عِلْمٍ لَا يَنْفَعُ» . [رواه مسلم] .

10. "O Allah, I seek refuge with you from the knowledge which doesn't benefit." (*Muslim*) (That is: knowledge which I do not act upon, nor teach, nor does it change my character).

SOME *AHADITH* REGARDING THE MUSLIM

«الْـمُسْلِمُ مَن سَلِمَ الْـمُسلِمُونَ مِنْ لِسَانِهِ وِيَدِه» . [متفق عليه] .

1. "A (true) Muslim is one from whose tongue and hand the Muslims are safe." (Agreed upon)

256

«سِبَابُ الْـمُسْلِمِ فُسُوقٌ وَقِتَالُهُ كُفْرٌ» . [رواه البخاري].

2. "Verbal abuse of a Muslim is hateful disobedience (of Allah) and fighting him is *Kufr* (an act of disbelief)." (*Bukhâri*)

«غَطِّ فَخْذَكَ، فَإِنَّ فَخْذَ الرَّجلِ مِنْ عَوْرَتِهِ» . [صحيح رواه أحمد].

3. "Cover your thighs, because the thighs are part of a man's private area". (*Ahmad*)

«لَيْسَ الْـمُؤمِنُ بِالـطَّعَّانِ وَلاَ اللَّعَّانِ وَلاَ الفَـاحِشِ ولا البَذِي ءِ» . [رواه مسلم].

4. "A *Mu'min* is not given to character assassination nor to harsh, foul language." (*Muslim*)

«مَنْ حَمَلَ عَلَيْنَا السِّلاَح فَلَيْسَ مِنَّا» . [رواه مسلم].

5. "One who wields a weapon against us is not one of us". (*Muslim*)

«وَمَنْ غَشَّ فَلَيْسَ مِنَّا» . [صحيح رواه الترمذي].

"One who deceives is not one of us". (*Tirmidhi*)

«مَنْ يُحْرَم الرِّفْقَ يُحْرَم الخَيْرَ» . [رواه مسلم].

6. "One who is deprived of gentleness is deprived of all good." (*Muslim*)

«مَن الْـتَمَسَ رِضَا الله بِسَخَطِ النَّاس كَفَاهُ الله مَؤْنَةَ النَّاس وَمَنِ الْـتَمَسَ رِضَـا النَّـاس بِسَخَطِ الله، وَكَّلَهُ الله إلى النَّـاس » . [صحيح رواه الترمذي].

7. "Whoever seeks the pleasure of Allah in that which incurs

the anger of people, Allah will take care of him, so he doesn't depend on what the people have to bestow. And whoever seeks the pleasure of people in what incurs Allah's Anger, Allah leaves him to those people." (*Tirmidhi*)

«لَعَنَ رَسُولُ الله الرَّاشِي وَالْـمُرْتَشِي» . [حسن رواه الترمذي].

8. "May Allah curse the briber and the one who takes the bribe." (*Tirmidhi*)

«مَاأَسْفَلَ مِنَ الكَعْبَيْنِ مِنَ الإِزَارِ فَفِي النَّارِ» . [رواه البخاري].

9. "That which of the lower garment hangs (in pride) below the ankle, will be in the Fire." (*Bukhâri*)

«إِذَا قَالَ الرَّجُلُ لأَخِيهِ يَاكَافِرُ فَقَدْ بَاءَ بِهَا أَحَدُهُمَا» . [رواه البخاري].

10. "If a man says to his brother 'O *Kâfir*!' then it would return to one of them." (*Bukhâri*)

«لَا تَقُولُوا لِلْمُنَافِقِ سَيْدُنَا فَإِنَّهُ إِنْ يَكُنْ سَيِّدُكُم فَقَدْ أَسْخَطْتُمْ رَبَّكُم عَزَّ وَجَلَّ» . [صحيح رواه أحمد].

11. "Do not say to a hypocrite 'our master', because if you treat him (with deference) as if he is your master, you will anger Allâh عز وجل." (*Ahmad*)

«الْغُلَامُ مُرْتَهَنٌ بِعَقِيقَتِهِ، تُذبَحُ عَنْهُ يَوْمَ السَّابِعِ ، وَيُسَمَّىٰ وَيُحْلَقُ رَأْسُهُ» . [صحيح رواه أبوداود].

12. "The child is deposited as a security for his '*Aqîqah* (the animal slaughtered in gratitude to Allah for the blessing of the birth of the child). It should be slaughtered on his behalf the seventh day (after his birth) and he should be given a name and his head should be shaved." (*Abû Dawûd*)

ACT UPON THE *AHADITH* OF THE
MESSENGER صلى الله عليه وسلم

«لَا تَقُومُ السَّاعَةُ حَتَّى يُقَاتِلَ الْـمُسْلِمونَ الْـيَهُودَ، فَيَقْتُلُهُمُ الْـمُسْلِمُونَ». [رواه مسلم].

1. "The Day of Judgement will not come until the Muslims fight the Jews, then the Muslims will kill them (their fighters)." (*Muslim*)

«فَمَنْ قَاتَلَ لِتَكُونَ كَلِمَةُ الله هِيَ الْعُلْيَا فَهُوَ في سَبِيلِ الله». [رواه البخاري].

2. "Whoever fights so that the Word of Allah is held high (implemented), he is in the way of Allah." (*Bukhâri*)

«مَنْ أَرْضَى النَّاسَ بِسَخَطِ الله وَكَّلَهُ الله إلى النَّاسِ» ..

3. "Whoever pleases the people by angering Allah, Allah will leave him to the people. (*Tirmidhi*)

«مَنْ مَاتَ وَهُوَ يَدْعُو مِنْ دُونِ الله نِدًّا دَخَلَ النَّارَ». [رواه البخاري].

4. "Whoever dies and he was invoking someone as rival to Allah, will enter the Fire." (*Bukhâri*)

«مَنْ كَتَمَ عِلْمًا أَلْجَمَهُ الله بِلِجَامٍ مِنْ نَارٍ». [صحيح رواه أحمد].

5. "Whoever conceals knowledge, Allah will fit him with a bridle of fire." (*Ahmad*)

«مَنْ لَعِبَ بِالنَّرْدِ فَقَدْ عَصَى الله وَرَسُولَهُ». [صحيح رواه أحمد].

6. "Whoever plays backgammon definitely disobeyed Allah and His Messenger." (*Ahmad*)

«بَـدَأَ الإِسْلاَمُ غَرِيباً وَسَيَعُودُ غَرِيباً كَـمَا بَدَأَ فَطُوبَى لِلْغُرَبَاءِ» .

7. "Islâm started out in the state of strangeness, and it will return to being a strange, as it started. Then, *Tûba* (all kinds of happiness) is for the strangers." (*Muslim*)

And in one version:

«فَطُوبَى لِلْغُرَبَاءِ الَّذِينَ يُصْلِحُونَ إِذَا فَسَدَ النَّاسُ» . . [رواه أبو عمر الداني بسند صحيح] .

"So, *Tûba* will be for the strangers who strive to correct what the people corrupted." (Abu 'Amr Ad-Dani)

«طُوبَى لِلْغُرَبَاءِ: أُنَاسٌ صَالِحُونَ، فِي أُنَاسٍ سُوءٍ كَثِيرٍ، مَنْ يَعْصِيهِمْ أَكْثَرَ مِمَّنْ يُطِيعُهُمْ» صحيح رواه أحمد .

8. "*Tûba* will be for the strangers: Righteous people in the midst of a multitude of evil people, those who disobey them will be far more than those who obey them."

«لاَ طَاعَةَ فِي مَعْصِيَةِ الله، إِنَّـمَا الطَّاعَةُ فِي الْـمَعْرُوفِ» . [رواه البخاري] .

9. "There is no obedience (allowed to anyone) in the disobedience of Allah. Obedience is only (permitted) in what is known to be good." (*Bukhâri*)

"WHATEVER THE MESSENGER (صلى الله عليه وسلم) GAVE YOU, TAKE IT"

«لَعَنَ اللهُ النَّامِصَـاتِ وَالْـمُتَنَمِّصَاتِ الْـمُغَيِّرَاتِ لِخَلْقِ اللهِ» .

1. "Allah cursed women who pluck their eyebrows and women who do it (to show) for others; those who try to change the creation of Allah." (Agreed upon)

«وَنِسَاءٌ كَاسِيَاتٌ عَارِيَاتٌ مُمِيلَاتٌ مَائِلَاتٌ رُؤُوسُهُنَّ كَأَسْنِمَةِ الْبُخْتِ الْمَائِلَةِ لَا يَدْخُلْنَ الجَنَّةَ، وَلاَ يَجِدْنَ رِيحَهَا». [رواه مسلم].

2. "And the women who would be dressed but appear to be naked, who would be inclined (to evil) and make their husbands incline towards it. Their heads would be like the humps of *Bukht* camel inclined to one side. They will not enter Paradise and they would not smell its odour." (*Muslim*).

«اتَّقُوا الله وَأَجْمِلُوا فِي الطَّلَبِ». [صحيح رواه الحاكم].

3. "Fear Allah and seek your sustenance in what is lawful (and leave the *Harâm* alone)." (*Hâkim*)

«أَرْبِعُوا عَلَى أَنْفُسِكُمْ فَإِنَّكُمْ لَا تَدْعُونَ أَصَمَّ ولاَ غَائِباً». [رواه مسلم].

«اخفضوا اصواتكم في الذكر والدعاء».

4. "Lower your voices (in *Du'â* and in remembrance of Allah) for you are not calling upon One, Who is deaf or absent." (*Muslim*)

«أَشَدُّ النَّاسِ بَلاءً الأَنْبِيَاءُ ثُمَّ الصَّالِحُونَ». [صحيح رواه ابن ماجه].

5. "The people who are tested most severely are the Prophets, then those who are pious." (*Ibn Mâjah*)

261

«صِلْ مَنْ قَطَعَكَ، وَأَحْسِنْ إِلَى مَنْ أَسَاءَ إِلَيْكَ، وَقُلِ الْحَقَّ وَلَوْ عَلَى نَفْسِكَ». [صحيح رواه ابن النجار].

6. "Try to maintain relations (even) with those who want to cut relations, and treat well those who treat you badly, and speak the truth, even against yourself." (*Ibn Najjâr*)

«تَعِسَ عَبْدُ الدِّينَارِ وَالدِّرْهَمِ وَالْقَطِيفَةِ إِنْ أُعْطِيَ رَضِيَ وَإِن لَمْ يُعْطَ لَمْ يَرْضَ». [رواه البخاري].

7. "Perdition for the slave of the dollar and the cent and the robe, if he is given, he is pleased. And if he is not given, he is not pleased." (*Bukhâri*)

«أَوَ أَدُلُّكُمْ عَلى شَيْءٍ إِذَا فَعَلْتُمُوهُ تَحَابَبْتُمْ؟ أَفْشُوا السَّلَامَ بَيْنَكُمْ». [رواه مسلم].

8. "Should I not guide you to a thing, if you do it, you will love each other? Spread *Salâm* amongst yourselves." (*Muslim*)

(i.e. greet each other with *Salamu Alaikum* and respond with *Wa Alaikumus Salâm*, whether you know the other person or not).

«كُنْ فِي الدُّنْيَا كَأَنَّكَ غَرِيبٌ أَوْ عَابِرُ سَبِيلٍ». [رواه البخاري].

9. "Be in this world as if you are a stranger or a wayfarer". (*Bukhâri*)

«لَا يُقِيمُ الرَّجُلُ الرَّجُلَ مِنْ مَجْلِسِهِ ثُمَّ يَجْلِسُ فِيهِ، وَلَكِنْ تَفَسَّحُوا وَتَوَسَّعُوا». [رواه مسلم].

10. "(In a gathering) A man should not make another man

stand from where he was sitting, then take his place. Rather you should make room for each other and give each other space." (*Muslim*)

BE SLAVES OF ALLAH, BROTHERS (TO EACH OTHER)

Allah's Messenger صلى الله عليه وسلم said:

«لَا تَحَاسَدُوا وَلَا تَبَاغَضُوا، ولَا تَحَسَّسُوا ، وَلَا تَنَافَسُوا ، وَلَا تَجَسَّسُوا وَلَا تَنَاجَشُوا وَلَا تَهَاجَرُوا وَلَا تَدَابَرُوا وَلَا يَبِعْ بَعْضُكُمْ عَلَى بَيْعِ بَعْضٍ . وَكُونُوا عِبَادَ الله إِخْوَاناً كَمَا أَمَرَكُمْ أَلْمُسْلِمُ أَخُو الـمُسْلِمِ ، لَا يَظْلِمُهُ ولَا يَخْذُلُهُ وَلَا يَحْقِرُهُ» .

"Do not envy each other; and do not hate each other; and do not eavesdrop on each other; and do not compete with each other (each trying to get some worldly benefit and excluding others from it); and do not spy on each other (searching for each others faults); and do not bid for auctioned goods, which you don't intend to buy, in order to raise the price artificially; and do not avoid each other, and do not give each other the cold shoulder. And do not try to interfere in a business deal, where the buyer and seller have reached an agreement, in order to get one of them to abandon the deal and make the same deal with you. And be slaves of Allah, brothers (to each other) as he ordered you. A Muslim is the brother of Muslim, he doesn't oppress him nor abandon him to an oppressor nor does he look down upon him."

« التَّقْوَى هَاهُنَا، التَّقْوَى هَاهُنَا، وَيُشِيرُ إِلَى صَدْرِهِ» .

"*Taqwa* is right here. *Taqwa* is right here." (And he pointed to his chest)."

«بِحَسْبِ امْرِيءٍ مِنَ الشَّرِّ أَن يَحْقِرَ أَخَاهُ الْـمُسْلِمَ، كُلُّ الْـمُسْلِم عَلَى الْـمُسْلِم حَرَامٌ: دَمُهُ، وَعِرْضُهُ، وَمَالُهُ».

"It is sufficient sin for a man to look down upon his brother Muslim, every thing of a Muslim is sanctified for another Muslim: His blood and his honour and his property."

«إِيَّاكُمْ وَالظَّنَّ فَإِنَّ الظَّنَّ أَكْذَبُ الْـحَدِيثِ».

"Beware of suspicion, for verily suspicion is the most false (form) of speech."

«إِنَّ اللهَ لَا يَنْظُرُ إِلَى صُوَرِكُمْ وَأَمْوَالِكُمْ، وَلَكِنْ يَنْظُرُ إِلَىٰ قُلُوبِكُمْ وَأَعْمَالِكُمْ». [رواه مسلم وروى البخاري وأكثره].

"Verily Allah does not consider your appearances or your wealth in (appraising you) but He considers your hearts and your deeds." (*Bukhâri*)